Pavarotti
Hey Harry, mind if I tell you a story that's not about the movies?
Of course I'd mind!
Sometimes, Harry gets off a good one.
I was at the Kennedy Center Honors for Paul Simon. On the plane back to New York, Beverly Sills, the great coloratura soprano, was on the plane too.
So, what's it like to work with Pavarotti?
Oh, we loved each other. One minor disagreement.
After we finished a duet, Luciano stepped out of character to take a bow. I told him that was breaking reality. So, he agreed, no more bows.
One night, we finished a duet and the audience went crazy, applauding BRAVO! BRAVO!! Luciano looked to me and said,
"ONE LEETLE BOW."

NUMBER ONE IS WALKING

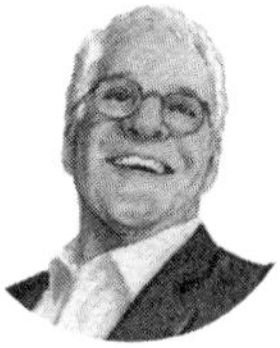

ALSO BY STEVE MARTIN AND HARRY BLISS

A Wealth of Pigeons

NUMBER ONE IS WALKING

My Life in the Movies and Other Diversions

Steve Martin

Drawings by

Harry Bliss

CELADON
BOOKS
NEW YORK

WWW.CELADONBOOKS.COM

DESIGNED BY JAMES SINCLAIR

THE LIBRARY OF CONGRESS CATALOGING-IN-PUBLICATION DATA IS AVAILABLE UPON REQUEST.

ISBN 978-1-250-81529-3 (PAPER OVER BOARD)
ISBN 978-1-250-86637-0 (SIGNED)

OUR BOOKS MAY BE PURCHASED IN BULK FOR PROMOTIONAL, EDUCATIONAL, OR BUSINESS USE. PLEASE CONTACT YOUR LOCAL BOOKSELLER OR THE MACMILLAN CORPORATE AND PREMIUM SALES DEPARTMENT AT 1-800-221-7945, EXTENSION 5442, OR BY EMAIL AT MACMILLANSPECIALMARKETS@MACMILLAN.COM.

THANKS TO VICTORIA DAILEY, FOR SUGGESTING "GOOD COCKTAIL, BAD COCKTAIL."

FIRST EDITION: 2022

10 9 8 7 6 5 4 3 2 1

NUMBER ONE IS WALKING

HOW I GOT INTO THE MOVIES

BY 1980, I VIEWED MY STAND-UP COMEDY ACT—WHICH I HAD BEEN DOING FOR ABOUT SEVENTEEN YEARS—AS A BALLERINA MIGHT VIEW HER EVENING'S PERFORMANCE: "I KNOW THE STEPS; THEY'RE THE SAME EVERY NIGHT. NOW I HAVE TO PERFORM THEM TO PERFECTION." HOWEVER, ON THE NIGHTS WHEN THAT PERFECTION WOULD HAPPEN, THE PERFORMANCE WENT UP IN SMOKE, HAZILY DISSIPATING IN MY AND THE AUDIENCE'S MIND.

I WAS LONELY, TOO, AND THE CONSTANT TRAVEL WAS CHIPPING AWAY AT MY PSYCHE.

IN MY YOUTH, MOVIE COMEDIANS BROUGHT ME JOY AND MADE ME WANT TO BE LIKE THEM. I STILL REMEMBER OLIVER HARDY SHOUTING FOR FIVE MINUTES AT HIS WIFE, "WHERE'S MY HAT? YOU'RE ALWAYS MISPLACING MY HAT!" HIS WIFE SAID NOTHING AND JUST STARED AT HIM WHILE HE SEARCHED HIGH AND LOW. IT WAS ON HIS HEAD.

PETER SELLERS'S SQUISHY TENNIS SHOES AFTER HE HAD FALLEN INTO A FOUNTAIN.

BOB HOPE BREAKING THE FOURTH WALL, STARING INTO CAMERA AND DIRECTING HIS WISECRACK RIGHT AT ME.

AND LET'S NOT FORGET LOU COSTELLO SCREAMING, "ABBOTTTT!"

JERRY LEWIS TRYING BUT FAILING TO PRONOUNCE HIS BOSS'S NAME: "MR. WAH-BAH-NAWT-LY."

I WONDERED IF I COULD BECOME A COMEDIAN IN MOVIES. "IF I COULD DO MOVIES," I THOUGHT, "I COULD PERFORM A SCENE AGAIN AND AGAIN UNTIL I GOT IT RIGHT." PLUS, I WOULD STAY HOME WHILE THE MOVIE WOULD DO THE LEGWORK, GOING FROM TOWN TO TOWN.

BY 1979, I FELT I WAS ON A SPEEDING TRAIN CALLED STAND-UP COMEDY. BUT COMING IN THE OTHER DIRECTION WAS A SPEEDING TRAIN CALLED MOVIES. MY JOB WAS TO GET OFF THE STAND-UP TRAIN AND THROW MY BAGS AND MYSELF ONTO THE MOVIE TRAIN, AND I KNEW I HAD TO DO IT WHILE I STILL HAD SOME CLOUT.

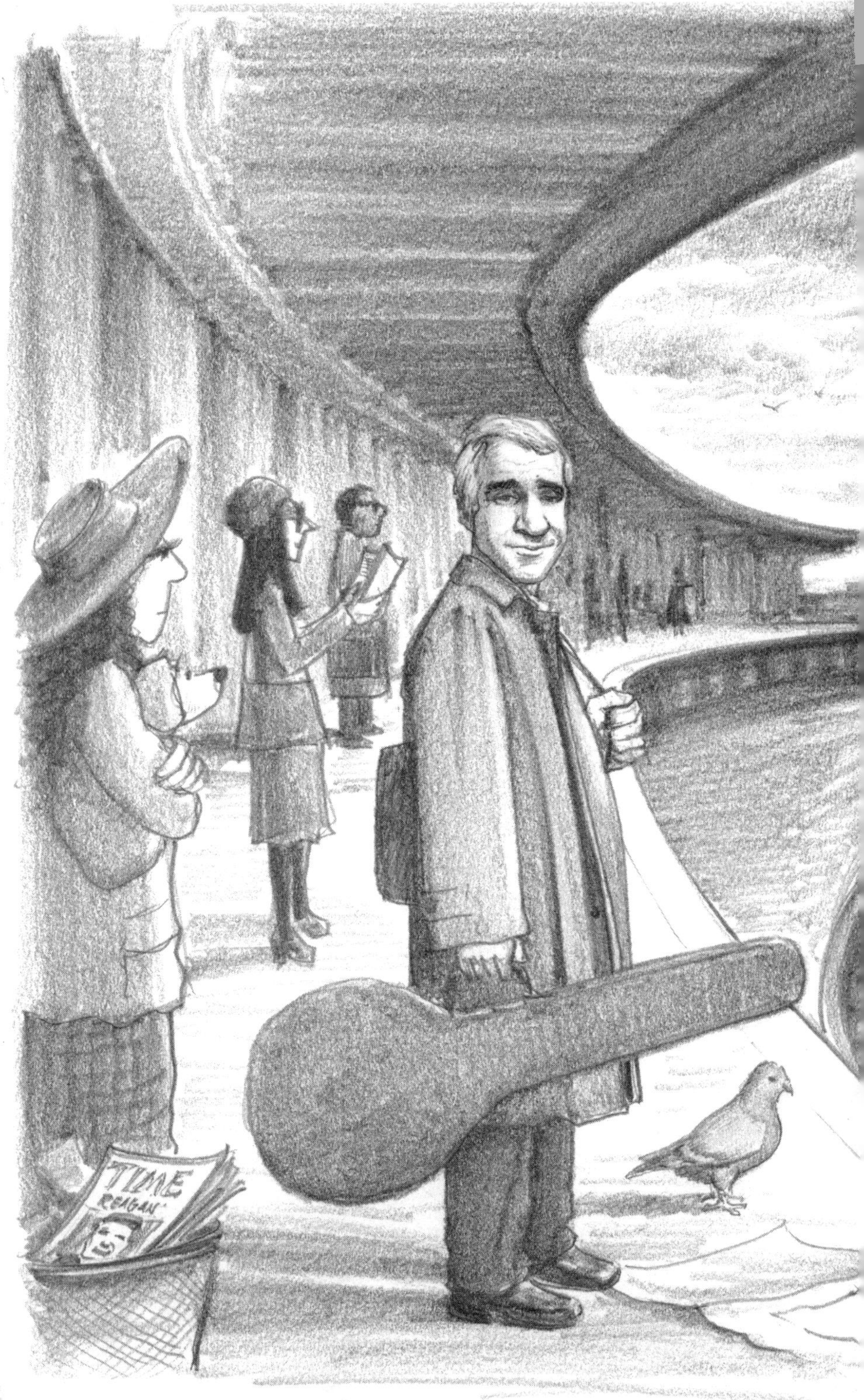
TIME
REAGAN

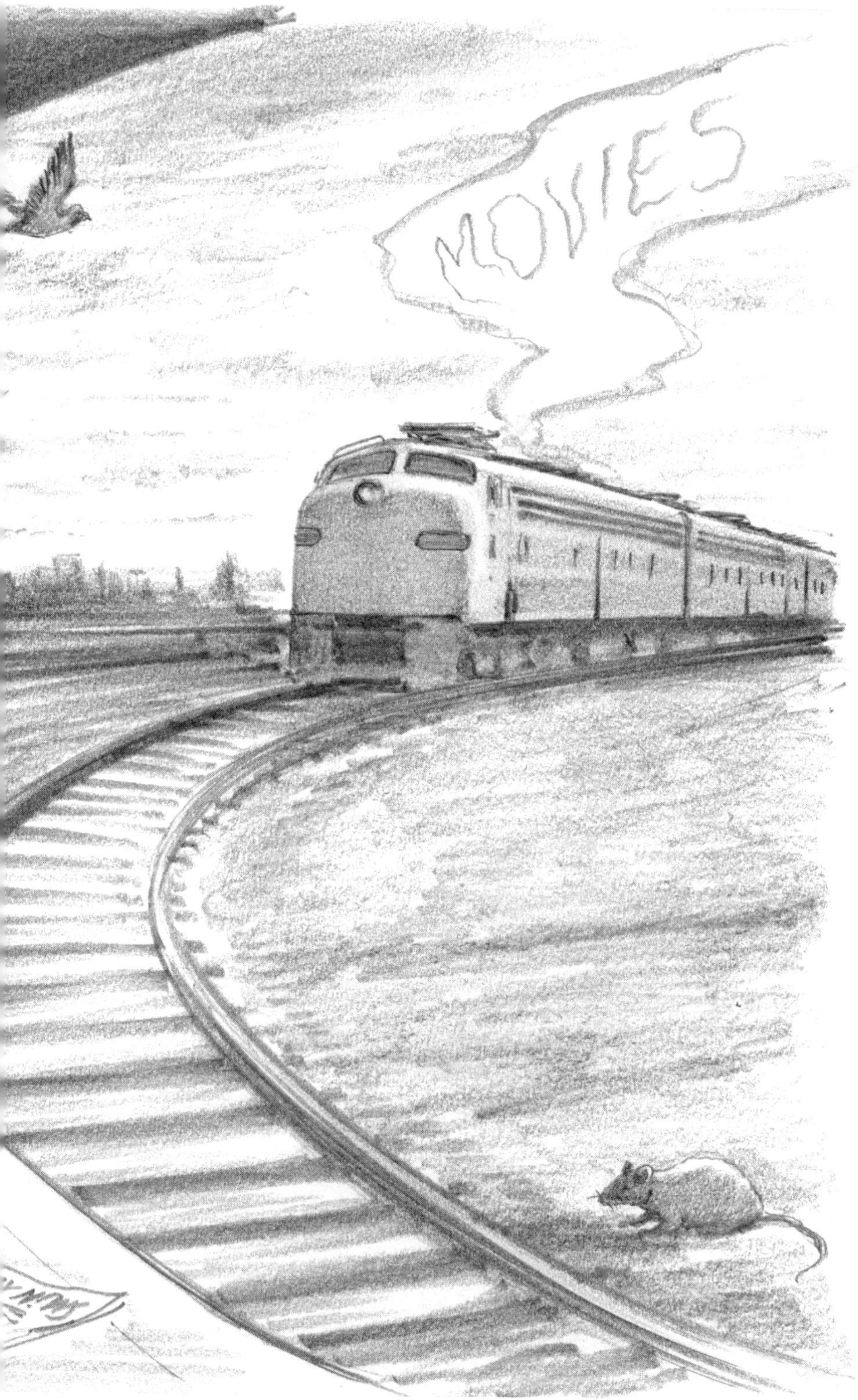
MOVIES

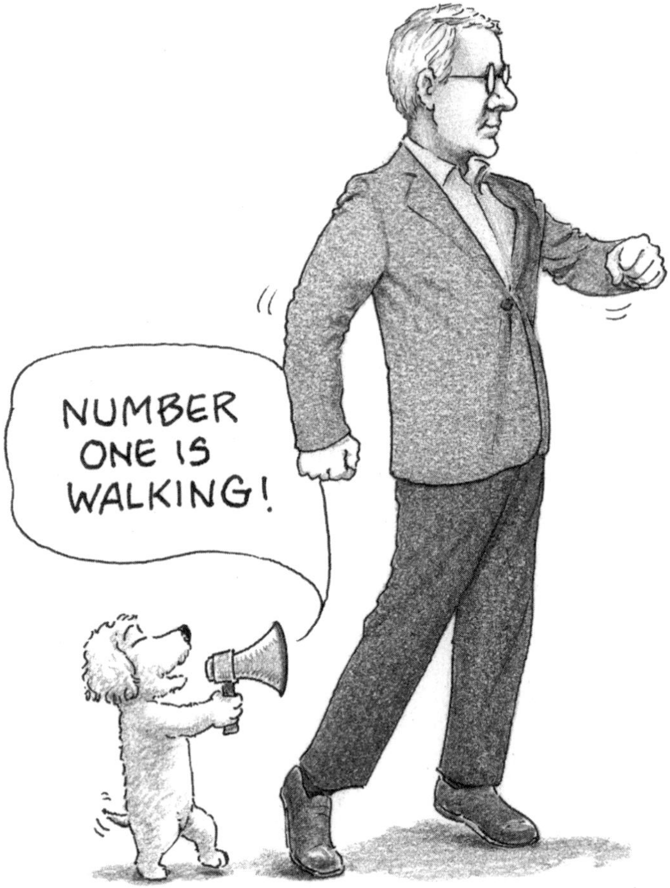
NUMBER ONE IS WALKING!

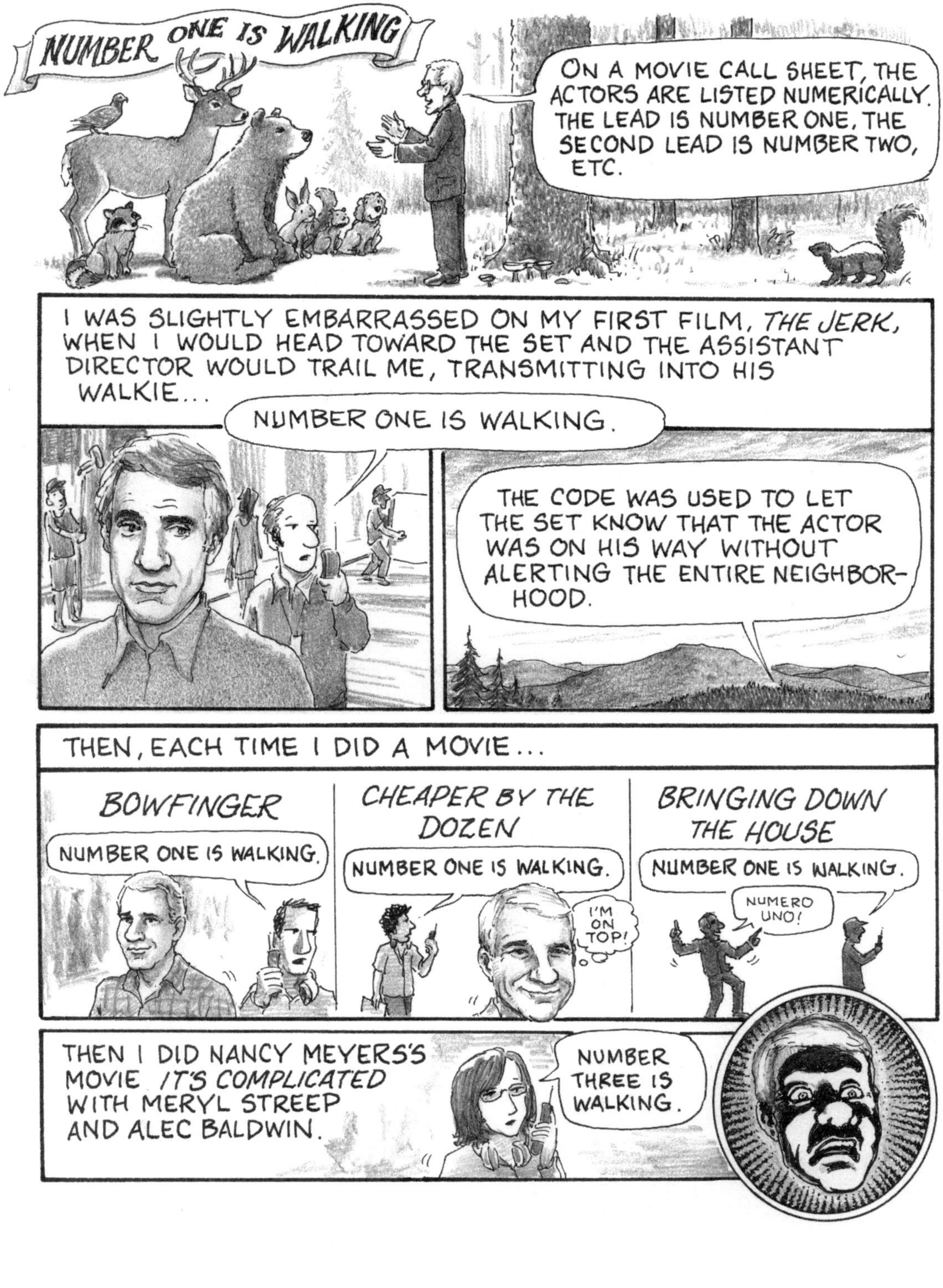
NUMBER ONE IS WALKING
ON A MOVIE CALL SHEET, THE ACTORS ARE LISTED NUMERICALLY. THE LEAD IS NUMBER ONE, THE SECOND LEAD IS NUMBER TWO, ETC.
I WAS SLIGHTLY EMBARRASSED ON MY FIRST FILM, *THE JERK*, WHEN I WOULD HEAD TOWARD THE SET AND THE ASSISTANT DIRECTOR WOULD TRAIL ME, TRANSMITTING INTO HIS WALKIE...
NUMBER ONE IS WALKING.
THE CODE WAS USED TO LET THE SET KNOW THAT THE ACTOR WAS ON HIS WAY WITHOUT ALERTING THE ENTIRE NEIGHBORHOOD.
THEN, EACH TIME I DID A MOVIE...
BOWFINGER
NUMBER ONE IS WALKING.
CHEAPER BY THE DOZEN
NUMBER ONE IS WALKING.
I'M ON TOP!
BRINGING DOWN THE HOUSE
NUMBER ONE IS WALKING.
NUMERO UNO!
THEN I DID NANCY MEYERS'S MOVIE *IT'S COMPLICATED* WITH MERYL STREEP AND ALEC BALDWIN.
NUMBER THREE IS WALKING.

The JERK

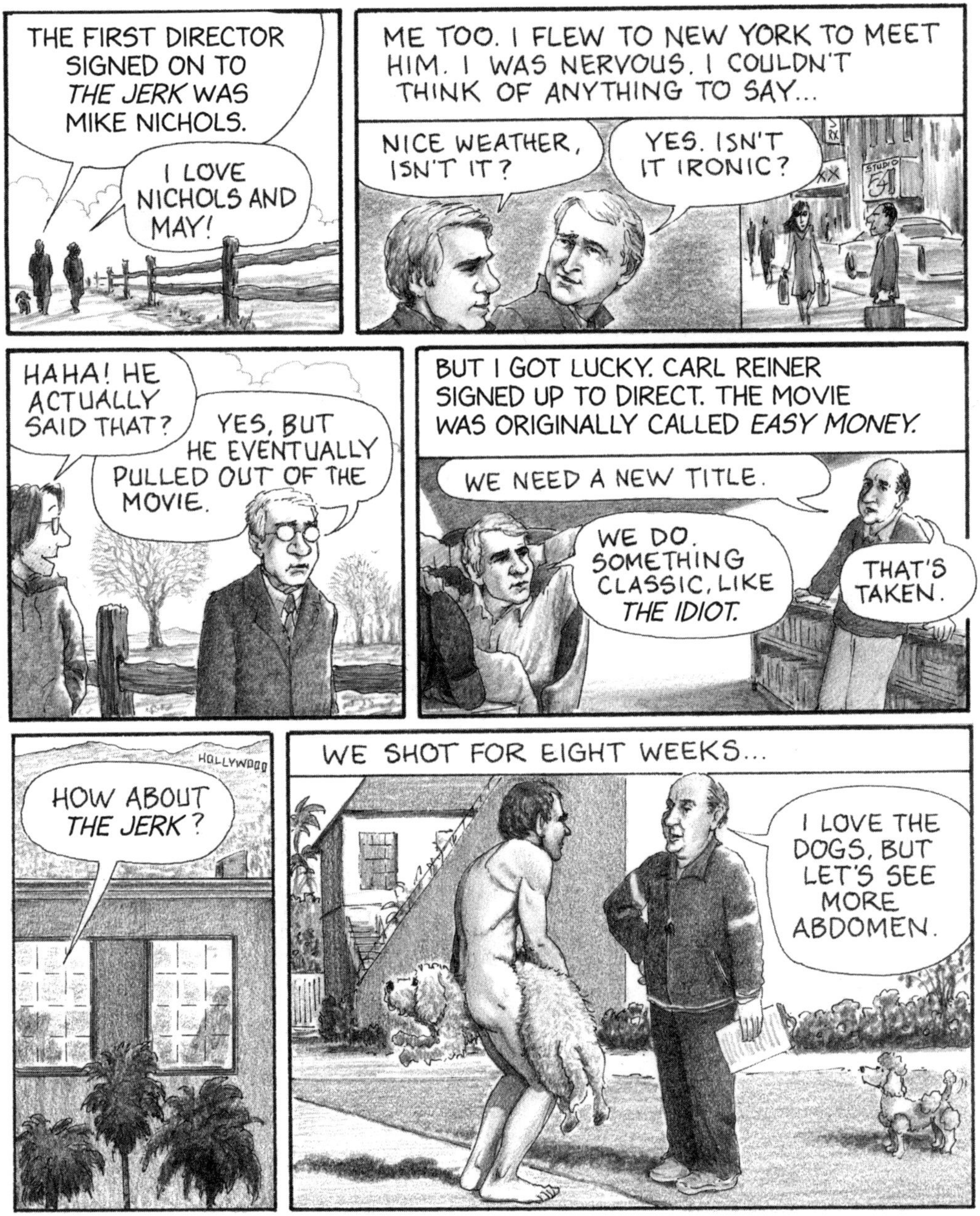
THE FIRST DIRECTOR SIGNED ON TO *THE JERK* WAS MIKE NICHOLS.
I LOVE NICHOLS AND MAY!
ME TOO. I FLEW TO NEW YORK TO MEET HIM. I WAS NERVOUS. I COULDN'T THINK OF ANYTHING TO SAY...
NICE WEATHER, ISN'T IT?
YES. ISN'T IT IRONIC?
HAHA! HE ACTUALLY SAID THAT?
YES, BUT HE EVENTUALLY PULLED OUT OF THE MOVIE.
BUT I GOT LUCKY. CARL REINER SIGNED UP TO DIRECT. THE MOVIE WAS ORIGINALLY CALLED *EASY MONEY.*
WE NEED A NEW TITLE.
WE DO. SOMETHING CLASSIC, LIKE *THE IDIOT.*
THAT'S TAKEN.
HOW ABOUT *THE JERK*?
WE SHOT FOR EIGHT WEEKS...
I LOVE THE DOGS, BUT LET'S SEE MORE ABDOMEN.

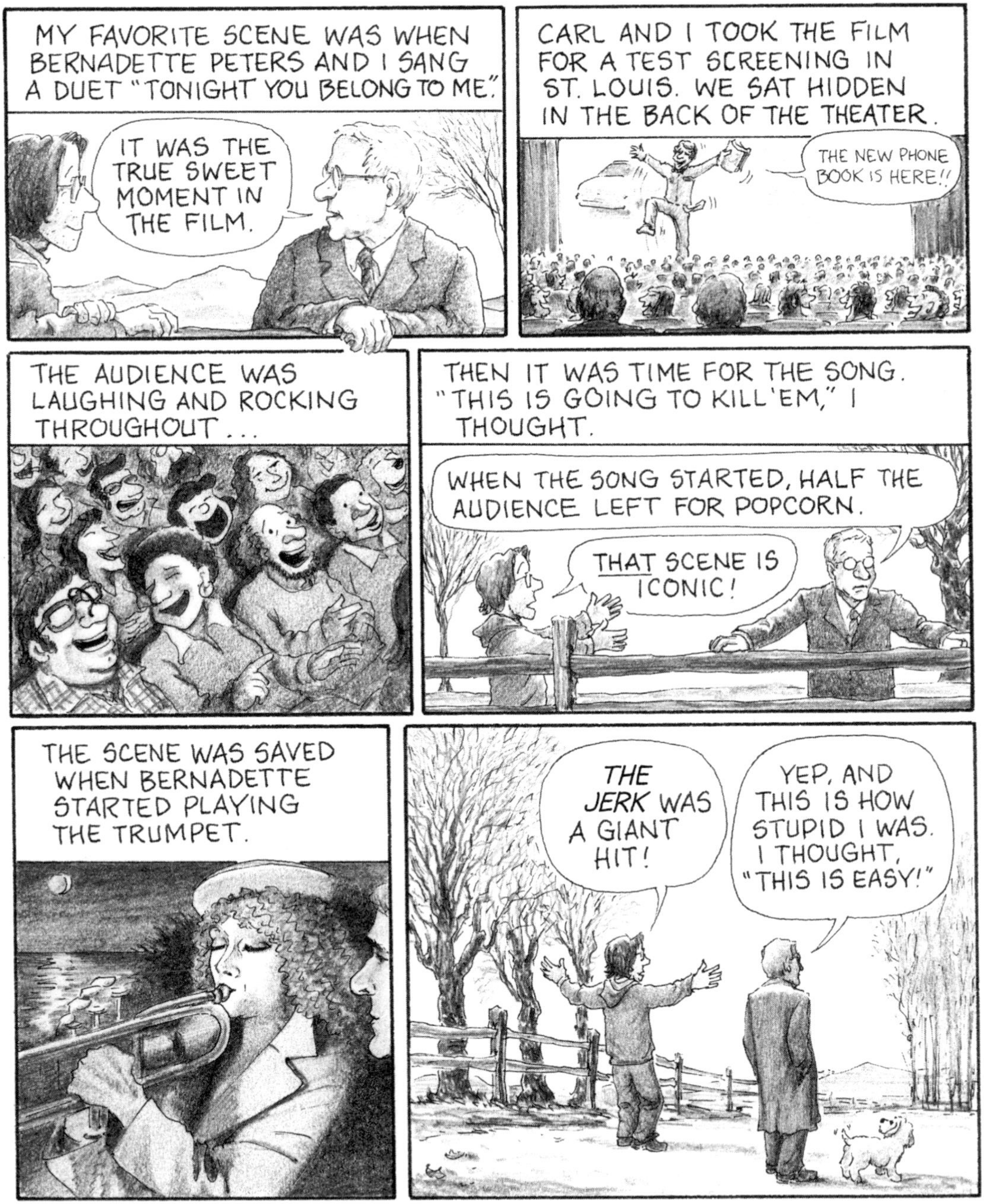
MY FAVORITE SCENE WAS WHEN BERNADETTE PETERS AND I SANG A DUET "TONIGHT YOU BELONG TO ME."
IT WAS THE TRUE SWEET MOMENT IN THE FILM.
CARL AND I TOOK THE FILM FOR A TEST SCREENING IN ST. LOUIS. WE SAT HIDDEN IN THE BACK OF THE THEATER.
THE NEW PHONE BOOK IS HERE!!
THE AUDIENCE WAS LAUGHING AND ROCKING THROUGHOUT . . .
THEN IT WAS TIME FOR THE SONG. "THIS IS GOING TO KILL'EM," I THOUGHT.
WHEN THE SONG STARTED, HALF THE AUDIENCE LEFT FOR POPCORN.
THAT SCENE IS ICONIC!
THE SCENE WAS SAVED WHEN BERNADETTE STARTED PLAYING THE TRUMPET.
THE JERK WAS A GIANT HIT!
YEP, AND THIS IS HOW STUPID I WAS. I THOUGHT, "THIS IS EASY!"

CARL REINER

I DID FOUR MOVIES WITH CARL REINER. HE WAS THE MOST EVEN-TEMPERED GENIUS I EVER WORKED WITH.

BUT ONCE, HE TOLD ME THIS STORY ABOUT THE MADDEST HE EVER GOT:

"I WANTED TO HIRE DEAN JONES FOR AN EPISODE OF *GOOD HEAVENS*, A TV SHOW I PRODUCED IN THE 1970S. DEAN, A BORN-AGAIN CHRISTIAN, WAS BOOKED TO DO SOME INTERMITTENT RELIGIOUS DUTIES EXACTLY WHEN THE SHOW NEEDED HIM. BUT DEAN WANTED TO DO THE SHOW, SO I WORKED OUT A SCHEDULE WHERE I WOULD SHOOT TWO DIFFERENT SHOWS SHUFFLED TOGETHER OVER TWO WEEKS. I COULD SHOOT DEAN ON MONDAY FOR SCRIPT ONE, THEN ON TUESDAY SHOOT PART OF SCRIPT TWO, THEN GET DEAN BACK ON THURSDAY TO SHOOT FOR TWO DAYS, AND THEN REPEAT THE PROCESS THE NEXT WEEK. I WAS MOVING ACTORS AROUND, MOVING SHOOTING DAYS AROUND, AND MOVING LOCATIONS AROUND. WHEN I CALLED DEAN TO TELL HIM THE PLAN, HE SAID, RELIEVED . . ."

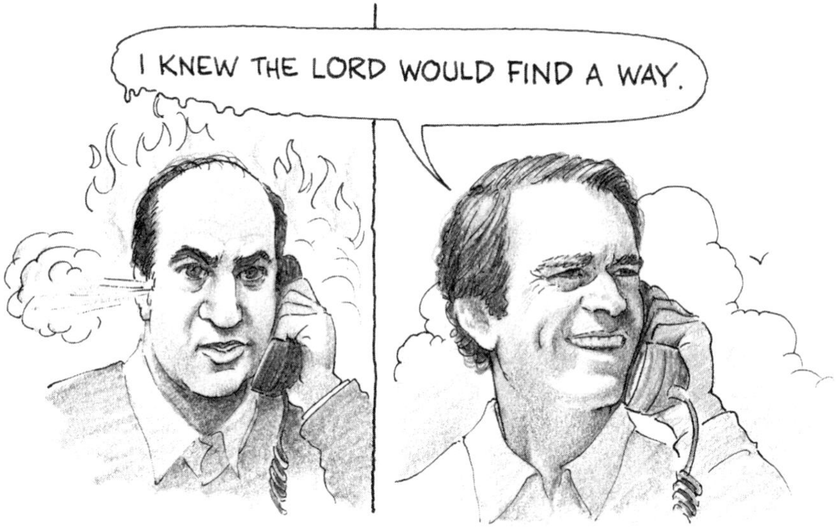
I KNEW THE LORD WOULD FIND A WAY.

CARL REINER *and* ME

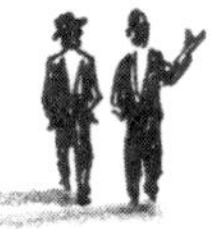

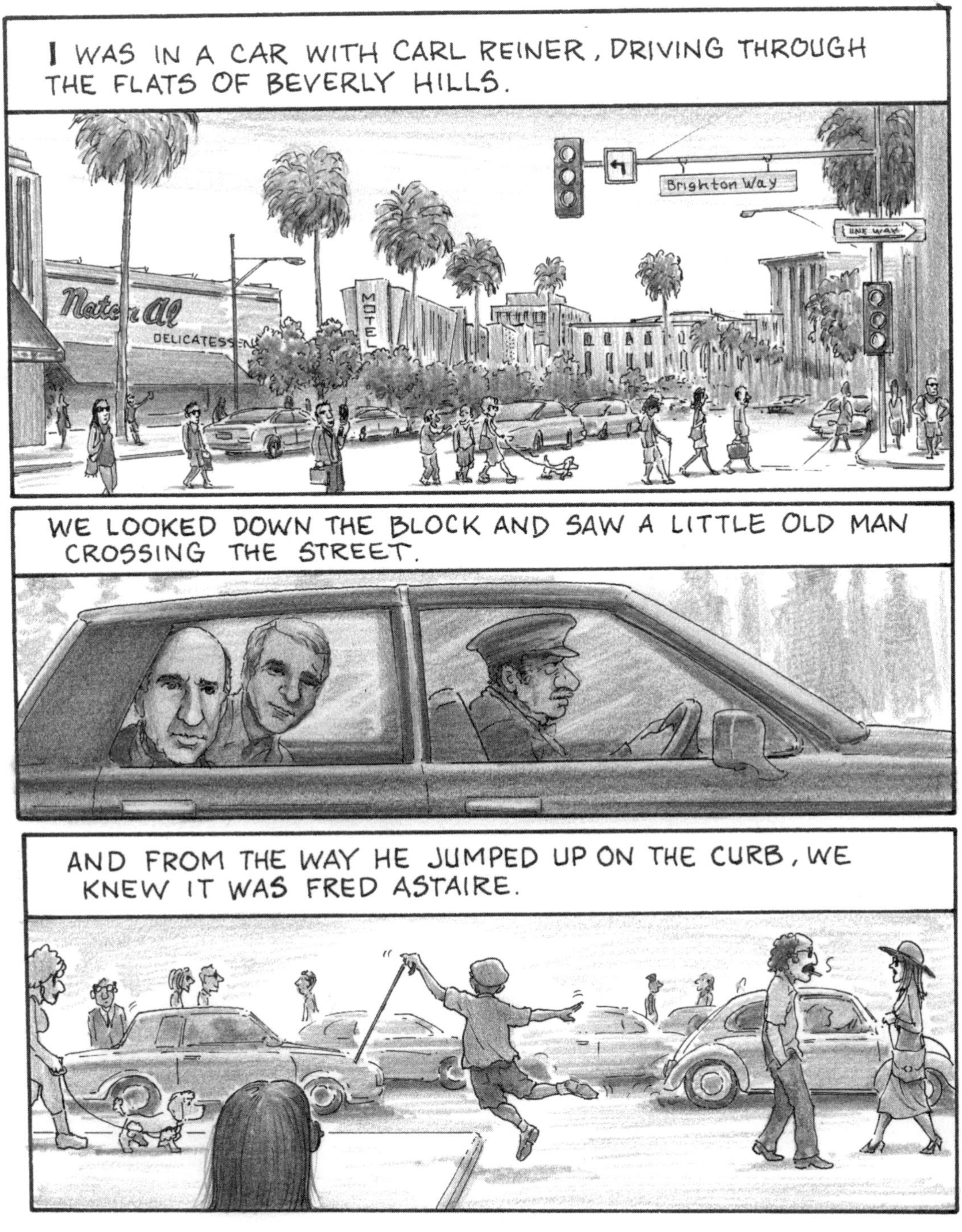
I WAS IN A CAR WITH CARL REINER, DRIVING THROUGH THE FLATS OF BEVERLY HILLS.
Brighton Way
MOTEL
WE LOOKED DOWN THE BLOCK AND SAW A LITTLE OLD MAN CROSSING THE STREET.
AND FROM THE WAY HE JUMPED UP ON THE CURB, WE KNEW IT WAS FRED ASTAIRE.

ALL of ME

AFTER THE SUCCESS OF *THE JERK*, I WAS FEELING ADRIFT. MY FOLLOWING THREE MOVIES DIDN'T PERFORM AS I HOPED. BUT CARL REINER APPROACHED ME WITH A SCRIPT, *ALL OF ME*. I COULDN'T MAKE UP MY MIND.

I WAS FLYING FROM LOS ANGELES TO NEW YORK AND I DECIDED TO TAKE THE SCRIPT WITH ME AND MAKE A DECISION BEFORE I LANDED.

HEY, YOU'RE THAT GUY ON *THE TONIGHT SHOW*! YUCK.

I READ IT THREE TIMES ON THE PLANE. I SAID TO MYSELF...

THIS IS FUNNY, AND FUNNY IS WHAT I SHOULD BE DOING.

I'M IN!

ONCE A MOVIE IS GREEN-LIT, IT'S LIKE AN UNSTOPPABLE LOCOMOTIVE. THE POWERHOUSE LILY TOMLIN SIGNED ON, AS WELL AS THE HILARIOUS DICK LIBERTINI. THE ENGLISH ACTRESS, VICTORIA TENNANT, SIGNED ON, AND WE ENDED UP MARRIED FOR A GOOD WHILE.

BACK IN BOWL!

GREAT!

CARL REINER

WHEN SHOOTING WAS OVER, LILY AND I ATTENDED A SMALL PRIVATE SCREENING OF A ROUGH CUT. WE COULD TELL THAT THE MOVIE WORKED.

YOU'RE FANTASTIC HERE.

AND SO AM I.

WHEN IT WAS OVER, LILY STOOD UP AND CONGRATULATED EVERYONE.

AS SHE EXITED, SHE LEFT US WITH A TINY BIT OF SHOW BUSINESS WISDOM...

DON'T FORGET TO LEAVE IN THE BORING PARTS.

AT A TEST SCREENING FOR "REAL PEOPLE," AS WE SAY IN SHOW BUSINESS, THE MOVIE PLAYED WELL.

HA HA   HA HA   HA HA

I WATCHED FROM THE BACK OF THE AUDIENCE, GAUGING EVERY LAUGH.
SCENE 11: BIG LAUGHS FOLLOWED BY LIGHT CHUCKLES, 3 GUFFAWS, AND SOMEONE CHOKING ON POPCORN...
AFTERWARD, AS THE AUDIENCE EXITED, A COUPLE SPOTTED ME. THEY APPROACHED AND THE WIFE SAID...
I LOVED THIS MOVIE. AND MY HUSBAND LOVED IT. AND HE HATES YOU!
THIS MOVIE PUT ME BACK IN THE WINNER'S COLUMN.
FISH FILLET
FREEZE KING

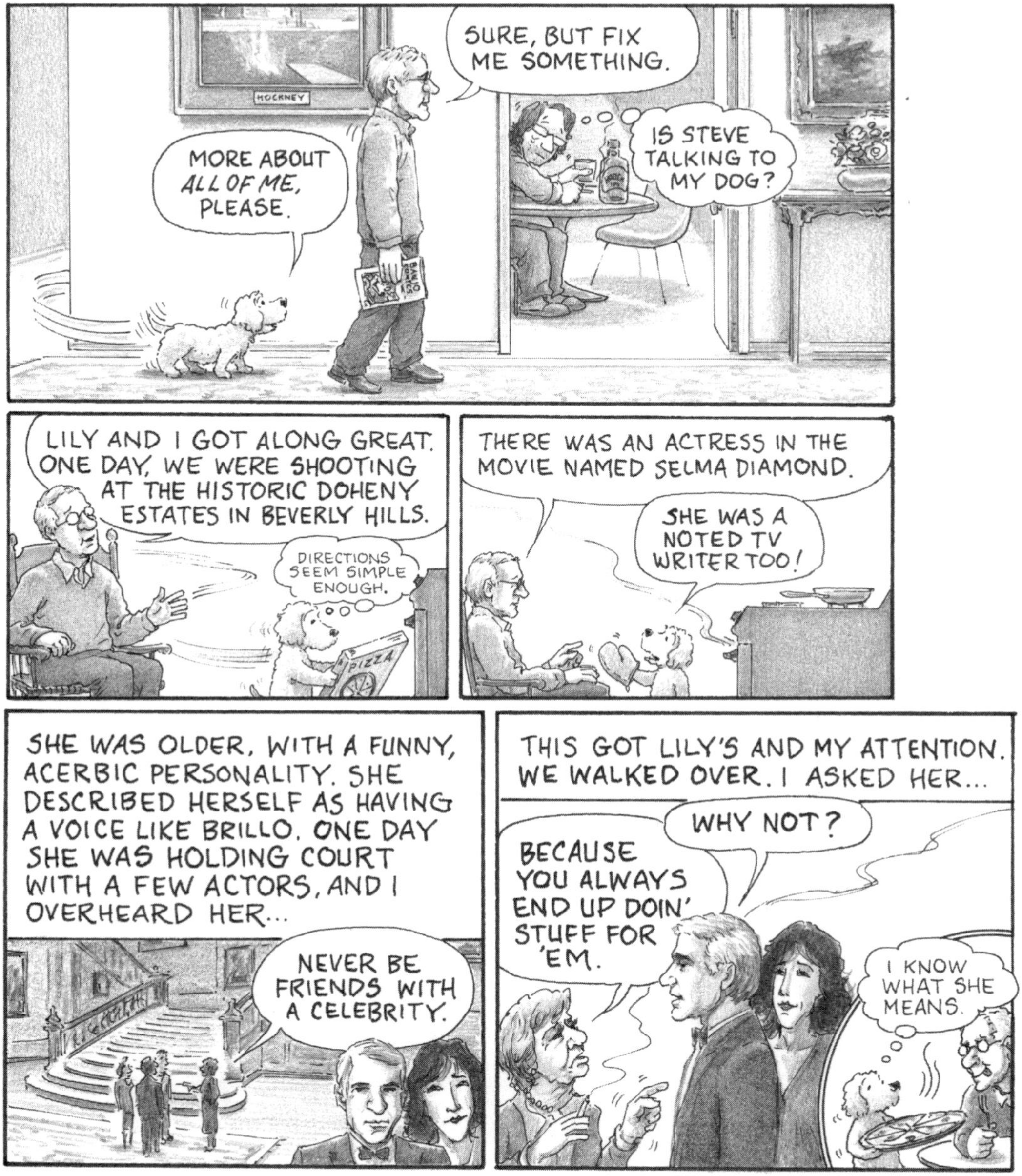
SURE, BUT FIX ME SOMETHING.
MORE ABOUT *ALL OF ME*, PLEASE.
IS STEVE TALKING TO MY DOG?
LILY AND I GOT ALONG GREAT. ONE DAY, WE WERE SHOOTING AT THE HISTORIC DOHENY ESTATES IN BEVERLY HILLS.
DIRECTIONS SEEM SIMPLE ENOUGH.
PIZZA
THERE WAS AN ACTRESS IN THE MOVIE NAMED SELMA DIAMOND.
SHE WAS A NOTED TV WRITER TOO!
SHE WAS OLDER, WITH A FUNNY, ACERBIC PERSONALITY. SHE DESCRIBED HERSELF AS HAVING A VOICE LIKE BRILLO. ONE DAY SHE WAS HOLDING COURT WITH A FEW ACTORS, AND I OVERHEARD HER...
NEVER BE FRIENDS WITH A CELEBRITY.
THIS GOT LILY'S AND MY ATTENTION. WE WALKED OVER. I ASKED HER...
WHY NOT?
BECAUSE YOU ALWAYS END UP DOIN' STUFF FOR 'EM.
I KNOW WHAT SHE MEANS.

THE WRITING OF ¡THREE AMIGOS!

HARRY, PENNY, WAKE UP. I REMEMBERED A *THREE AMIGOS* STORY... GUYS?

WHA? WHO?

MARTIN!

WHEN I WAS TWELVE, I WORKED AT DISNEYLAND IN FRONTIERLAND DOING COWBOY TRICK-ROPING.

ACROSS FROM MY STAND, DOING AT LEAST A DOZEN SHOWS A DAY, WORKED THREE SENSATIONAL MUSICIANS CALLED...

THE TRIO
Gonzalez,
Gonzalez
+
Gonzalez

STEVE

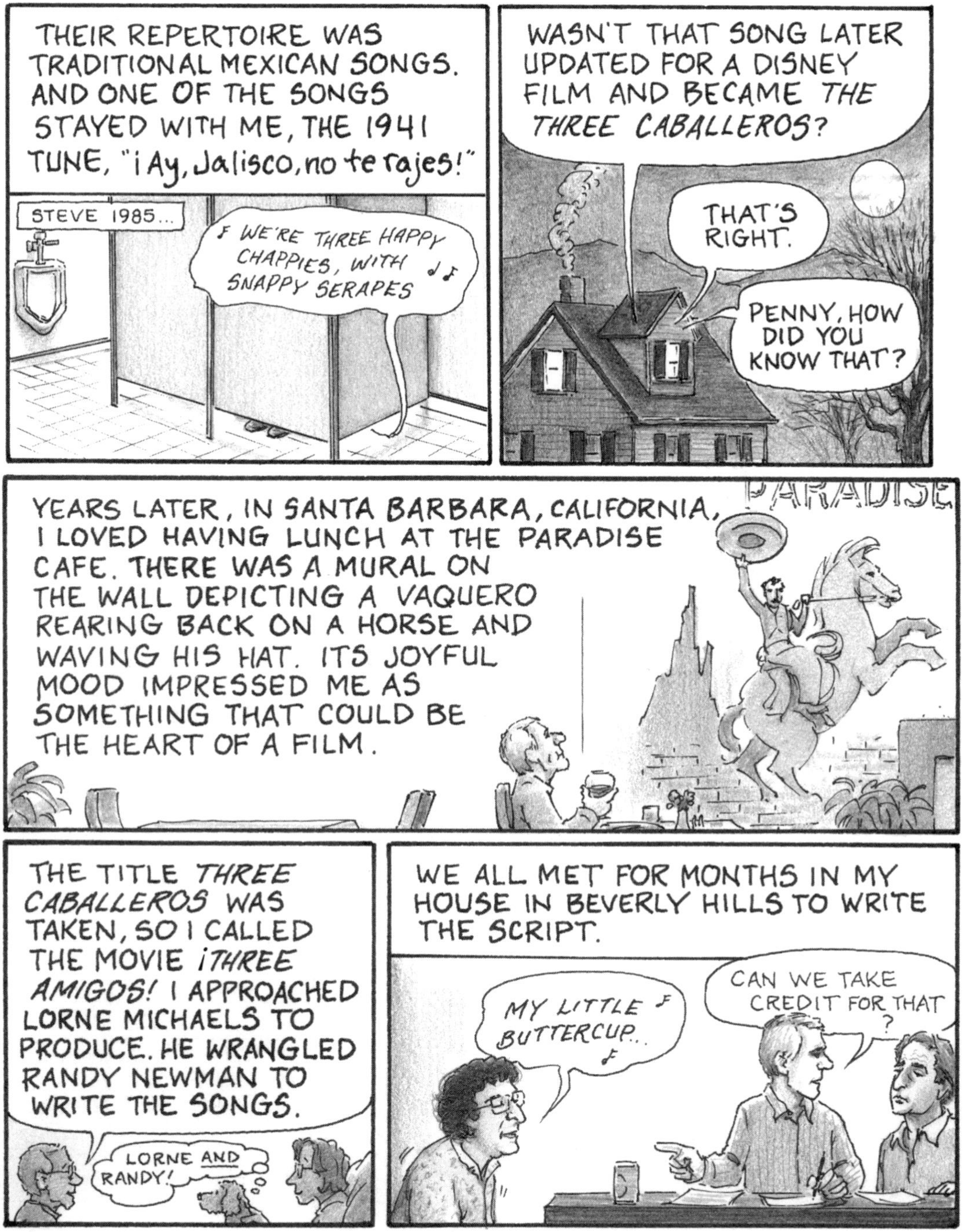
THEIR REPERTOIRE WAS TRADITIONAL MEXICAN SONGS. AND ONE OF THE SONGS STAYED WITH ME, THE 1941 TUNE, "¡Ay, Jalisco, no te rajes!"
STEVE 1985...
WE'RE THREE HAPPY CHAPPIES, WITH SNAPPY SERAPES
WASN'T THAT SONG LATER UPDATED FOR A DISNEY FILM AND BECAME *THE THREE CABALLEROS*?
THAT'S RIGHT.
PENNY, HOW DID YOU KNOW THAT?
YEARS LATER, IN SANTA BARBARA, CALIFORNIA, I LOVED HAVING LUNCH AT THE PARADISE CAFE. THERE WAS A MURAL ON THE WALL DEPICTING A VAQUERO REARING BACK ON A HORSE AND WAVING HIS HAT. ITS JOYFUL MOOD IMPRESSED ME AS SOMETHING THAT COULD BE THE HEART OF A FILM.
PARADISE
THE TITLE *THREE CABALLEROS* WAS TAKEN, SO I CALLED THE MOVIE *¡THREE AMIGOS!* I APPROACHED LORNE MICHAELS TO PRODUCE. HE WRANGLED RANDY NEWMAN TO WRITE THE SONGS.
LORNE AND RANDY!
WE ALL MET FOR MONTHS IN MY HOUSE IN BEVERLY HILLS TO WRITE THE SCRIPT.
MY LITTLE BUTTERCUP...
CAN WE TAKE CREDIT FOR THAT?

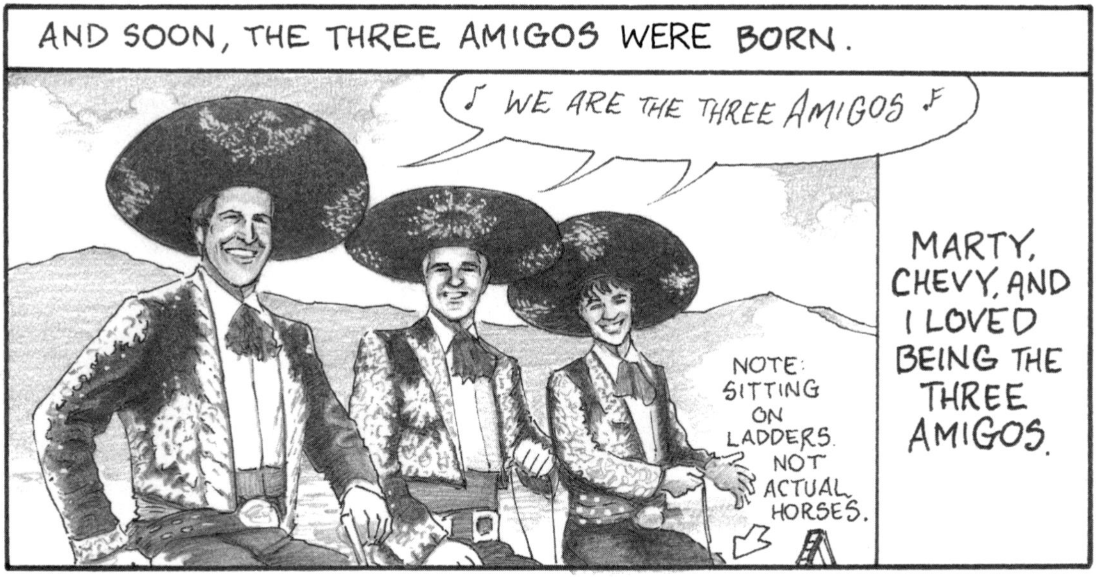
AND SOON, THE THREE AMIGOS WERE BORN.
♪ WE ARE THE THREE AMIGOS ♪
NOTE: SITTING ON LADDERS. NOT ACTUAL HORSES.
MARTY, CHEVY, AND I LOVED BEING THE THREE AMIGOS.

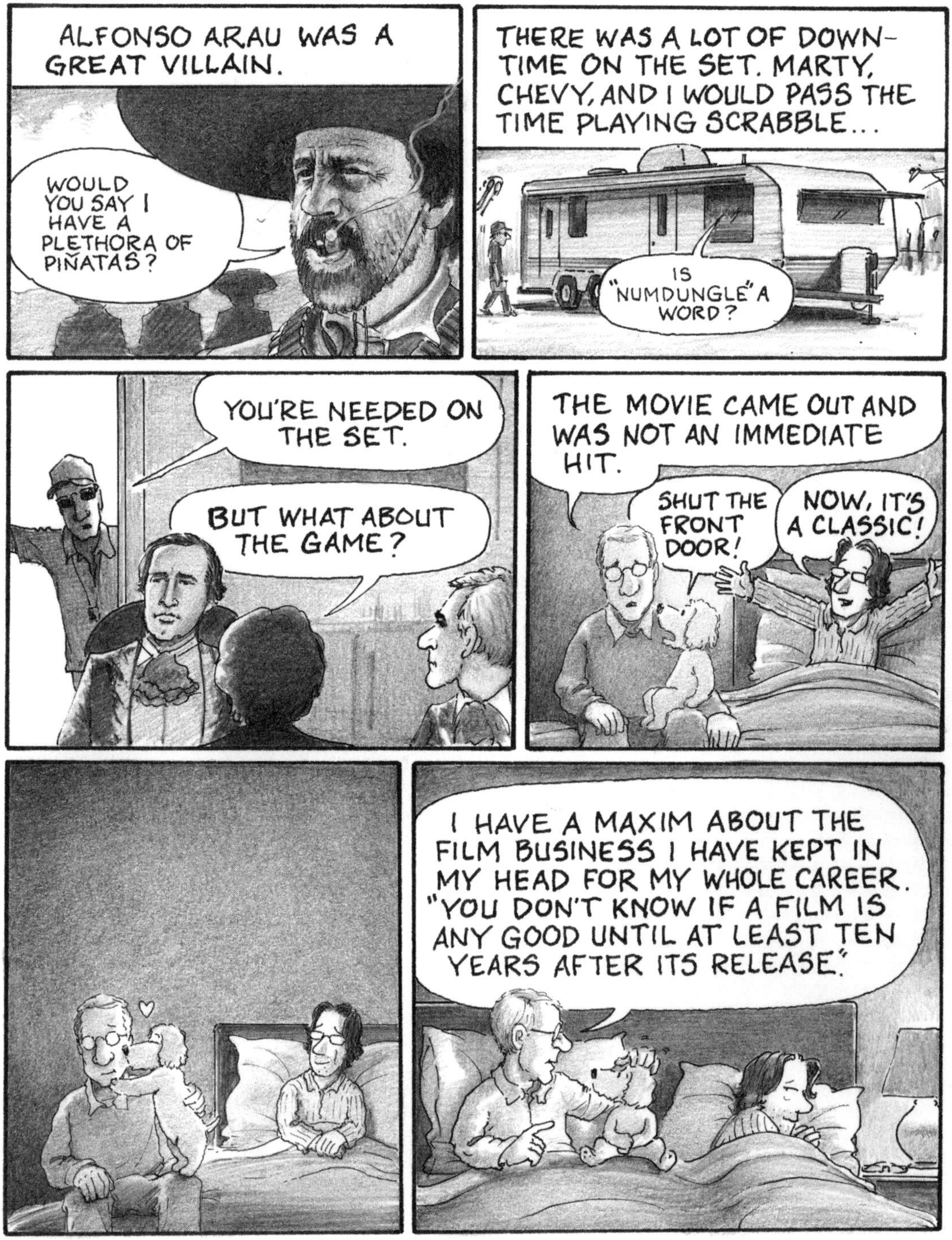
ALFONSO ARAU WAS A GREAT VILLAIN.
WOULD YOU SAY I HAVE A PLETHORA OF PIÑATAS?
THERE WAS A LOT OF DOWN-TIME ON THE SET. MARTY, CHEVY, AND I WOULD PASS THE TIME PLAYING SCRABBLE...
IS "NUMDUNGLE" A WORD?
YOU'RE NEEDED ON THE SET.
BUT WHAT ABOUT THE GAME?
THE MOVIE CAME OUT AND WAS NOT AN IMMEDIATE HIT.
SHUT THE FRONT DOOR!
NOW, IT'S A CLASSIC!
I HAVE A MAXIM ABOUT THE FILM BUSINESS I HAVE KEPT IN MY HEAD FOR MY WHOLE CAREER. "YOU DON'T KNOW IF A FILM IS ANY GOOD UNTIL AT LEAST TEN YEARS AFTER ITS RELEASE."

GENE
KELLY

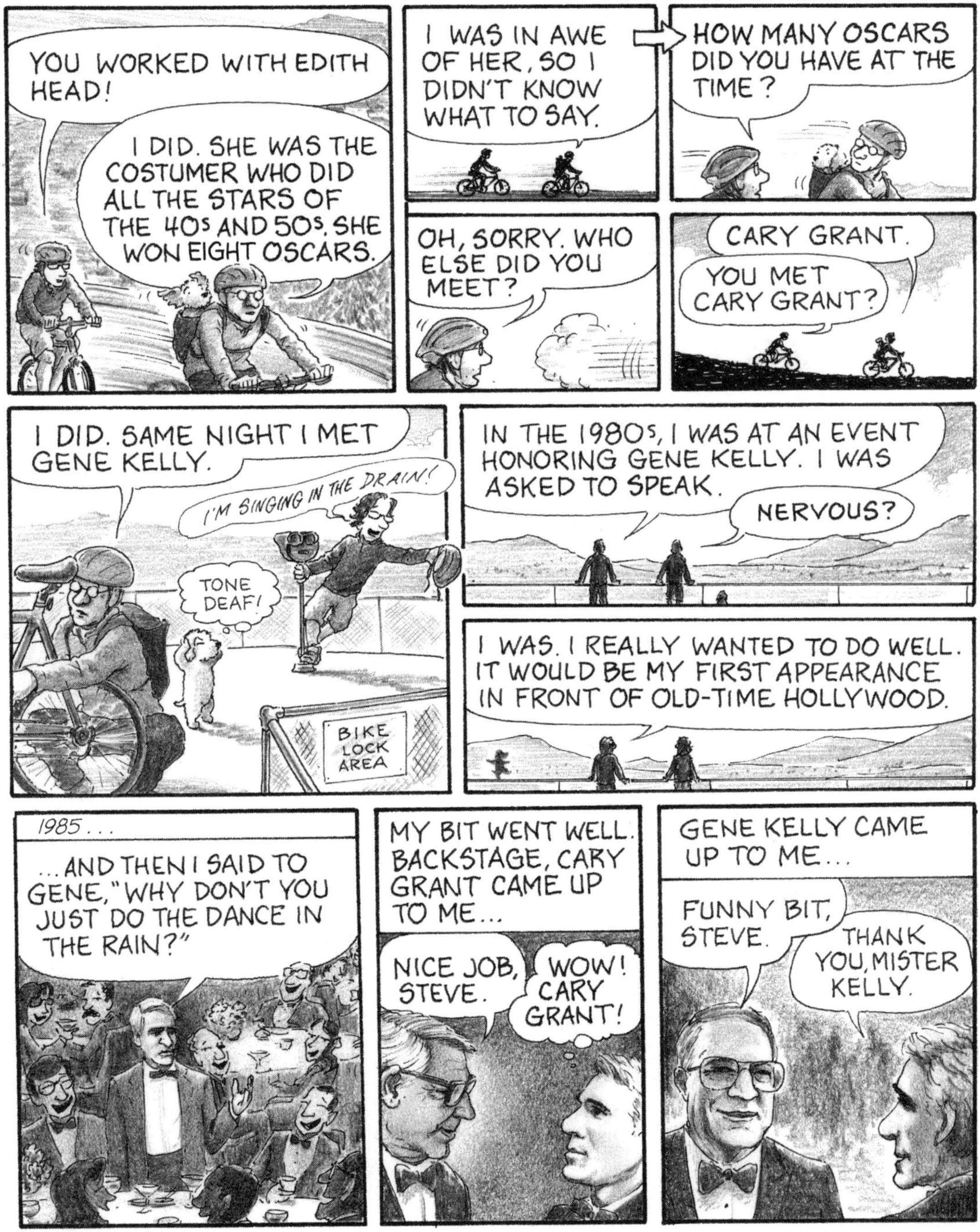
YOU WORKED WITH EDITH HEAD!
I DID. SHE WAS THE COSTUMER WHO DID ALL THE STARS OF THE 40s AND 50s. SHE WON EIGHT OSCARS.
I WAS IN AWE OF HER, SO I DIDN'T KNOW WHAT TO SAY.
HOW MANY OSCARS DID YOU HAVE AT THE TIME?
OH, SORRY. WHO ELSE DID YOU MEET?
CARY GRANT.
YOU MET CARY GRANT?
I DID. SAME NIGHT I MET GENE KELLY.
I'M SINGING IN THE DRAIN!
TONE DEAF!
BIKE LOCK AREA
IN THE 1980s, I WAS AT AN EVENT HONORING GENE KELLY. I WAS ASKED TO SPEAK.
NERVOUS?
I WAS. I REALLY WANTED TO DO WELL. IT WOULD BE MY FIRST APPEARANCE IN FRONT OF OLD-TIME HOLLYWOOD.
1985 . . .
. . . AND THEN I SAID TO GENE, "WHY DON'T YOU JUST DO THE DANCE IN THE RAIN?"
MY BIT WENT WELL. BACKSTAGE, CARY GRANT CAME UP TO ME . . .
NICE JOB, STEVE.
WOW! CARY GRANT!
GENE KELLY CAME UP TO ME . . .
FUNNY BIT, STEVE.
THANK YOU, MISTER KELLY.

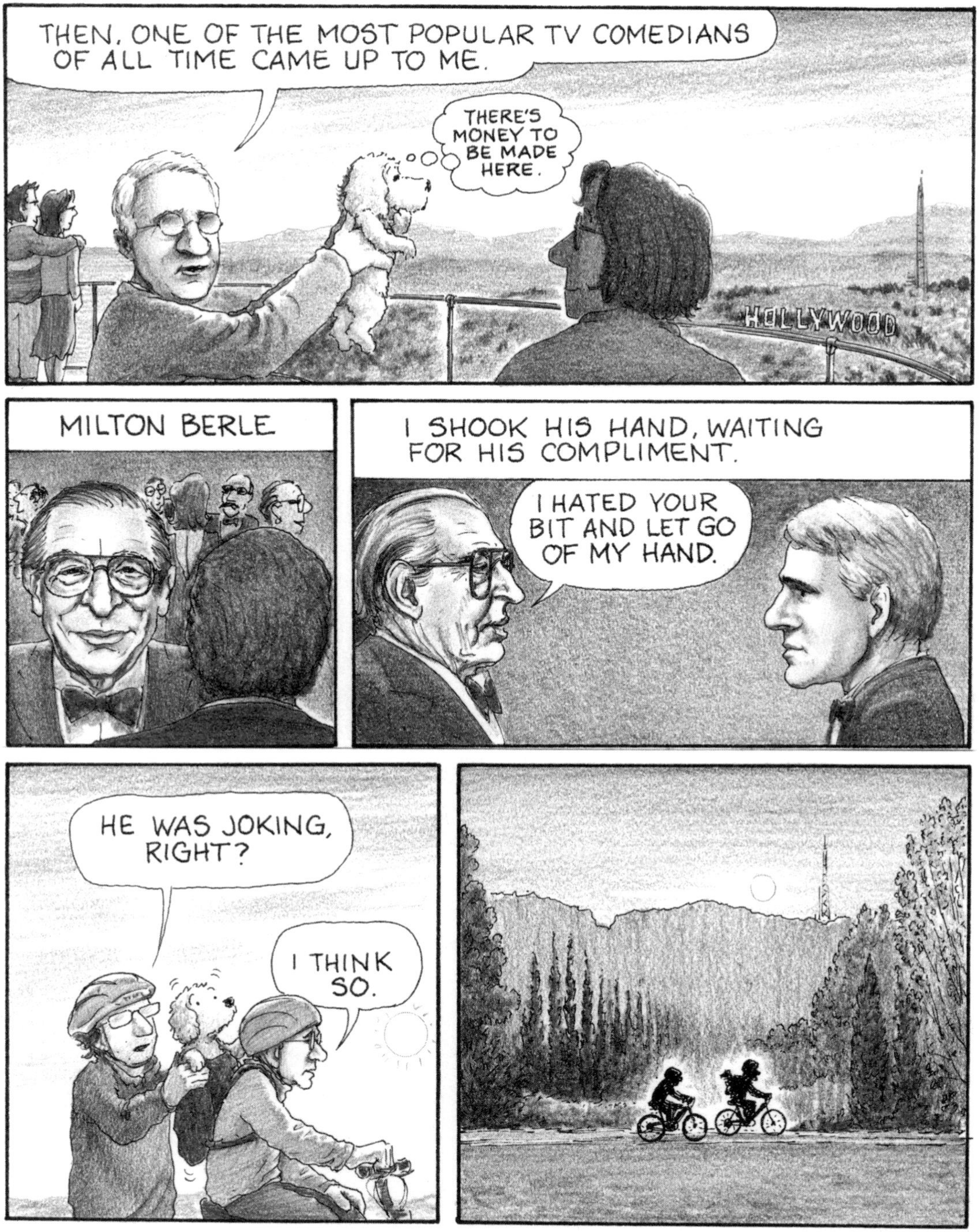
THEN, ONE OF THE MOST POPULAR TV COMEDIANS OF ALL TIME CAME UP TO ME.
THERE'S MONEY TO BE MADE HERE.
HOLLYWOOD
MILTON BERLE
I SHOOK HIS HAND, WAITING FOR HIS COMPLIMENT.
I HATED YOUR BIT AND LET GO OF MY HAND.
HE WAS JOKING, RIGHT?
I THINK SO.

PLANES TRAINS AND AUTOMOBILES

I FIRST MET JOHN CANDY IN HIS HOTEL ROOM IN CHICAGO...

HEY, JOHN.

YESSIR!

HE COULD MAKE ME LAUGH EVERY TIME WITH AN IMPRESSION OF AN ITALIAN GLADIATOR MOVIE, COMPLETE WITH BAD DUBBING.

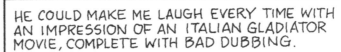

KNEEL BEFORE YOUR QUEEN, CENTURION!

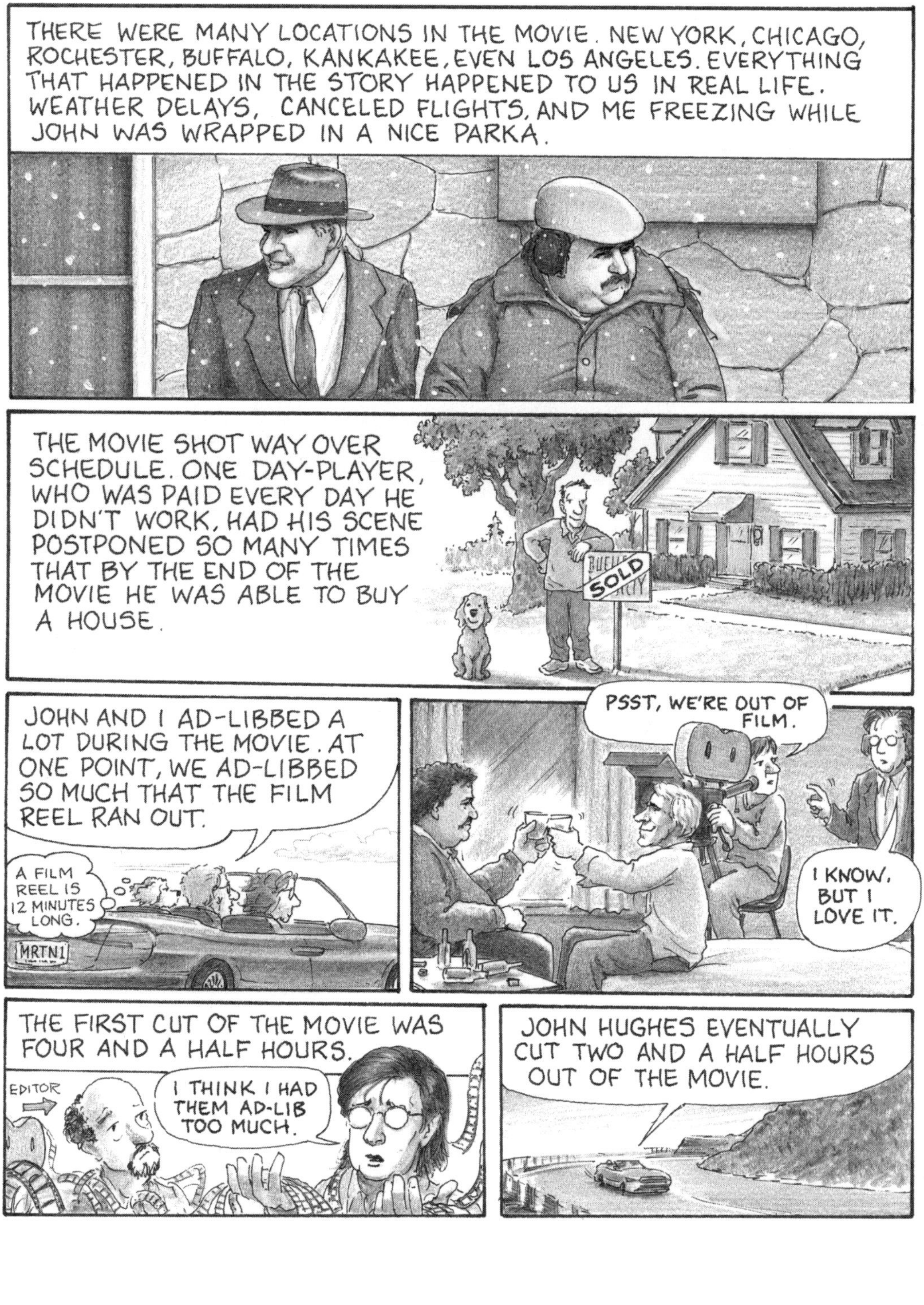
THERE WERE MANY LOCATIONS IN THE MOVIE. NEW YORK, CHICAGO, ROCHESTER, BUFFALO, KANKAKEE, EVEN LOS ANGELES. EVERYTHING THAT HAPPENED IN THE STORY HAPPENED TO US IN REAL LIFE. WEATHER DELAYS, CANCELED FLIGHTS, AND ME FREEZING WHILE JOHN WAS WRAPPED IN A NICE PARKA.
THE MOVIE SHOT WAY OVER SCHEDULE. ONE DAY-PLAYER, WHO WAS PAID EVERY DAY HE DIDN'T WORK, HAD HIS SCENE POSTPONED SO MANY TIMES THAT BY THE END OF THE MOVIE HE WAS ABLE TO BUY A HOUSE.
SOLD
JOHN AND I AD-LIBBED A LOT DURING THE MOVIE. AT ONE POINT, WE AD-LIBBED SO MUCH THAT THE FILM REEL RAN OUT.
A FILM REEL IS 12 MINUTES LONG.
MRTN1
PSST, WE'RE OUT OF FILM.
I KNOW, BUT I LOVE IT.
THE FIRST CUT OF THE MOVIE WAS FOUR AND A HALF HOURS.
EDITOR
I THINK I HAD THEM AD-LIB TOO MUCH.
JOHN HUGHES EVENTUALLY CUT TWO AND A HALF HOURS OUT OF THE MOVIE.

AT THE END OF THE MOVIE, JOHN'S CHARACTER EXPLAINED OUR FRIENDSHIP...

I SORT OF ATTACH MYSELF TO PEOPLE FROM TIME TO TIME... BUT THIS TIME, I JUST COULDN'T LET GO.

EVERY TIME JOHN SAID THE LINE, I WEPT OFF-SCREEN. STRANGELY, THE LINE WAS CUT, BUT THE ENDING STILL WORKED. WHEN I SAW THE MOVIE WITH AN AUDIENCE, THEY WEPT TOO.

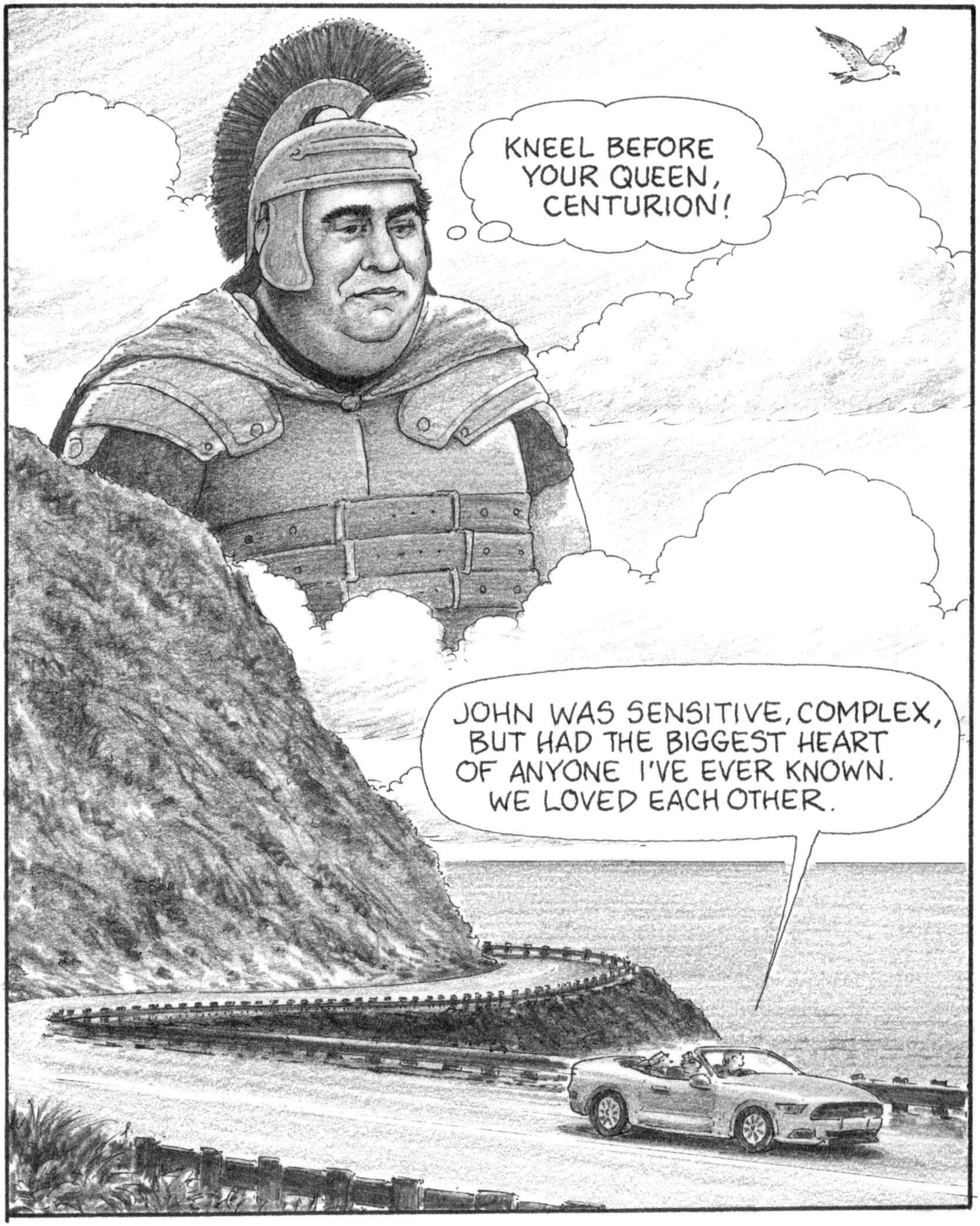
KNEEL BEFORE YOUR QUEEN, CENTURION!
JOHN WAS SENSITIVE, COMPLEX, BUT HAD THE BIGGEST HEART OF ANYONE I'VE EVER KNOWN. WE LOVED EACH OTHER.

The F-BOMB

THERE IS A SCENE IN *PLANES, TRAINS AND AUTOMOBILES* WHERE MY CHARACTER EXPRESSES EXTREME TRAVEL FRUSTRATION TO A RENTAL CAR AGENT. THE SPEECH IS VENTILATED WITH EIGHTEEN F–BOMBS.

I WANT A F***ING CAR RIGHT F***ING NOW. FOUR F***ING WHEELS AND A SEAT...

IT HAS BECOME ONE OF THE MOST NOTORIOUS SCENES IN THE MOVIE.

IT WAS FUN TO SHOOT.

THE FILM WAS SHOT IN 1987, WHEN STANDARDS WERE TIGHTER THAN THEY ARE NOW. I WORRIED THAT THE SCENE WOULD GIVE THE MOVIE AN UNTENABLE RATING FOR AN OSTENSIBLY WHOLESOME FAMILY MOVIE.

I LOVED THE F–BOMB SCENE, BUT ALSO BEING PRACTICAL, I WENT TO THE DIRECTOR, JOHN HUGHES, AND REQUESTED WE SHOOT A CLEANED–UP VERSION OF THE SCENE JUST IN CASE OF TROUBLES DOWN THE LINE.

R | **RESTRICTED**
UNDER 17 REQUIRES BOTH PARENTS – TOO MANY F-BOMBS

SORRY, TIMMY.

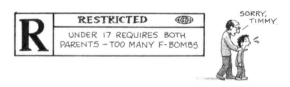

I WANT A CAR RIGHT NOW!

THE SCENE WAS DEAD WITHOUT THE F-BOMBS, BUT BOTH JOHN AND I KNEW THE AIRLINES WOULD WANT VANILLA–EDITED VERSIONS TO SHOW ON CROSS-COUNTRY FLIGHTS.

I DON'T KNOW IF THE SANITIZED VERSION WAS EVER USED, BUT SOMEWHERE IN AN EDITOR'S DRAWER IS THE SQUEAKY–CLEAN VERSION OF THE SCENE.

CLEAN VERSION OF *LAST TANGO IN PARIS*

CLEAN VERSION OF *THE EXORCIST*

PULP FICTION CLEAN...

THERE ARE RUMORS OF A HALLOWED DIRECTOR'S CUT OF *PLANES, TRAINS AND AUTOMOBILES*. IT DOESN'T EXIST. "DIRECTOR'S" CUT IMPLIES THERE IS A DIRECTOR-ENDORSED VERSION THAT THE STUDIO NIXED AND THEN REPLACED WITH THEIR OWN CUT.

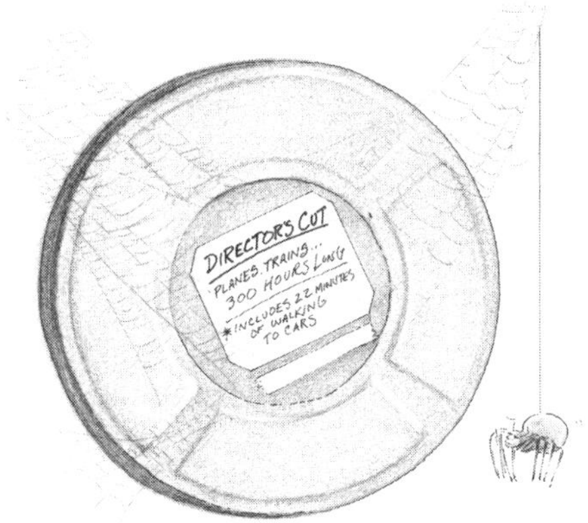
DIRECTOR'S CUT
PLANES, TRAINS...
300 HOURS LONG
*INCLUDES 22 MINUTES OF WALKING TO CARS

JOHN HUGHES WAS IN CHARGE OF ALL THE CUTS OF THE MOVIE, TRIMMING IT DOWN FOR TIME IN EVERY VERSION UNTIL HIS FINAL CUT WAS ACHIEVED. HE WAS AN AVID SCREENER OF THE FILM IN FRONT OF AUDIENCES, LISTENING CLOSELY TO THEIR RESPONSES AND CUTTING ACCORDINGLY.

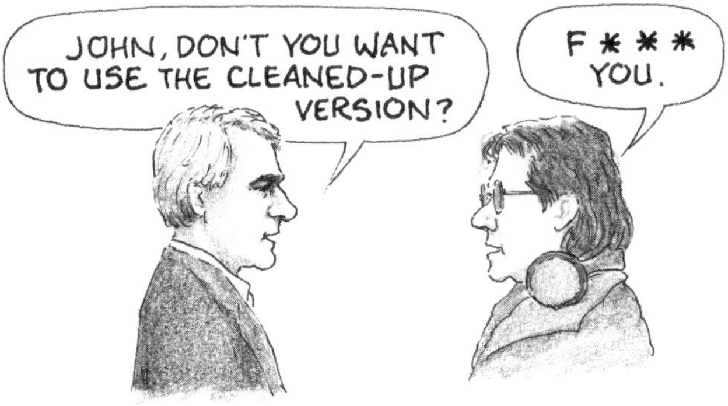
JOHN, DON'T YOU WANT TO USE THE CLEANED-UP VERSION?
F*** YOU.

"STEVE, I CAN CONTROL THE AUDIENCE RESPONSE LIKE A CONDUCTOR, DEPENDING IF CERTAIN SCENES ARE LEFT IN OR OUT."

ACT ING

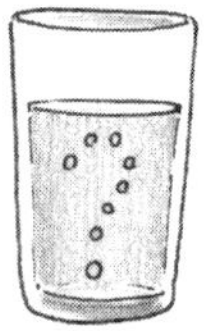

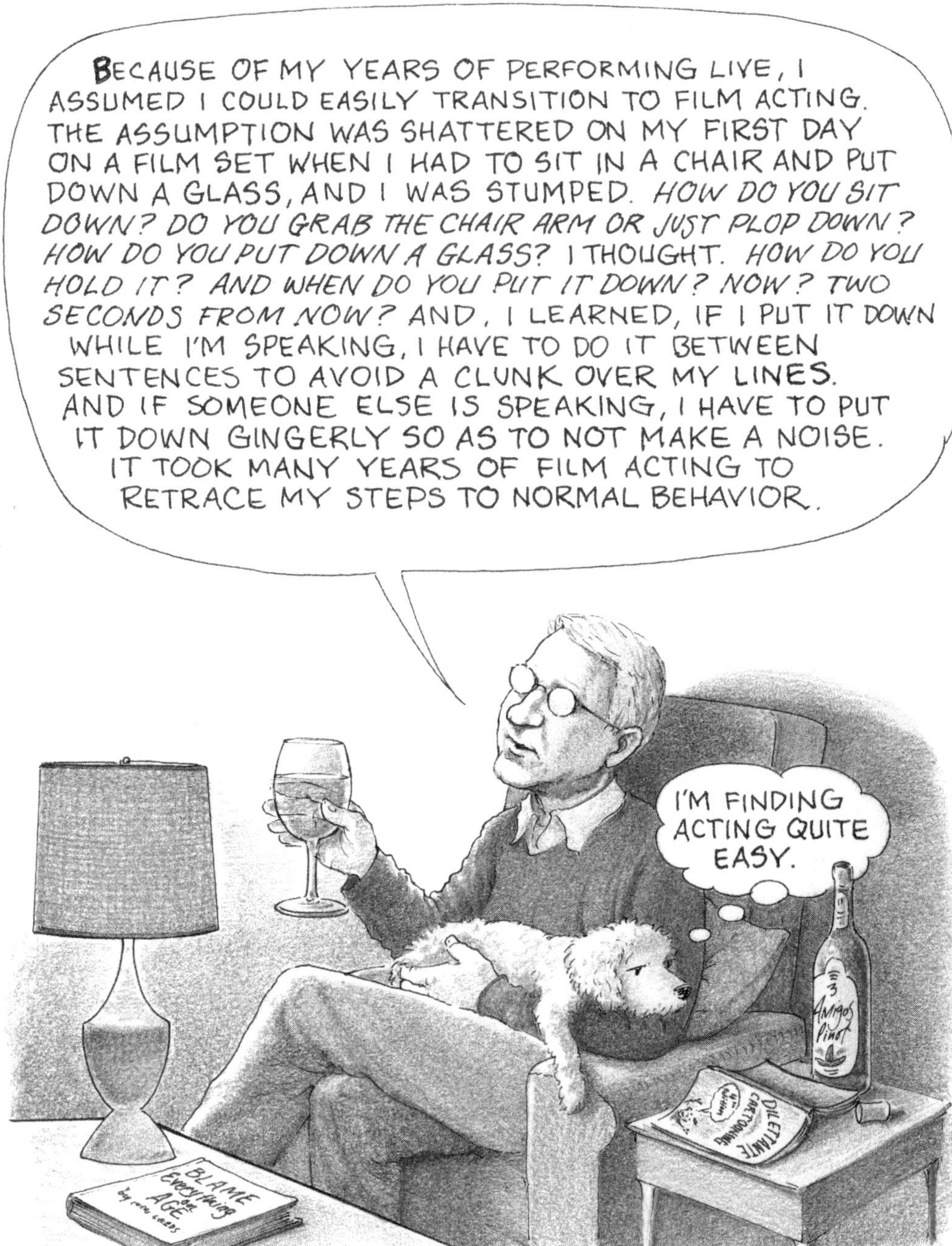
BECAUSE OF MY YEARS OF PERFORMING LIVE, I ASSUMED I COULD EASILY TRANSITION TO FILM ACTING. THE ASSUMPTION WAS SHATTERED ON MY FIRST DAY ON A FILM SET WHEN I HAD TO SIT IN A CHAIR AND PUT DOWN A GLASS, AND I WAS STUMPED. *HOW DO YOU SIT DOWN? DO YOU GRAB THE CHAIR ARM OR JUST PLOP DOWN? HOW DO YOU PUT DOWN A GLASS?* I THOUGHT. *HOW DO YOU HOLD IT? AND WHEN DO YOU PUT IT DOWN? NOW? TWO SECONDS FROM NOW?* AND, I LEARNED, IF I PUT IT DOWN WHILE I'M SPEAKING, I HAVE TO DO IT BETWEEN SENTENCES TO AVOID A CLUNK OVER MY LINES. AND IF SOMEONE ELSE IS SPEAKING, I HAVE TO PUT IT DOWN GINGERLY SO AS TO NOT MAKE A NOISE. IT TOOK MANY YEARS OF FILM ACTING TO RETRACE MY STEPS TO NORMAL BEHAVIOR.
I'M FINDING ACTING QUITE EASY.
3 Amigos Pinot
DILETTANTE CARTOONING
BLAME Everything on AGE

ROXANNE

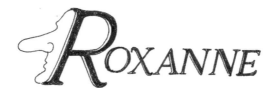

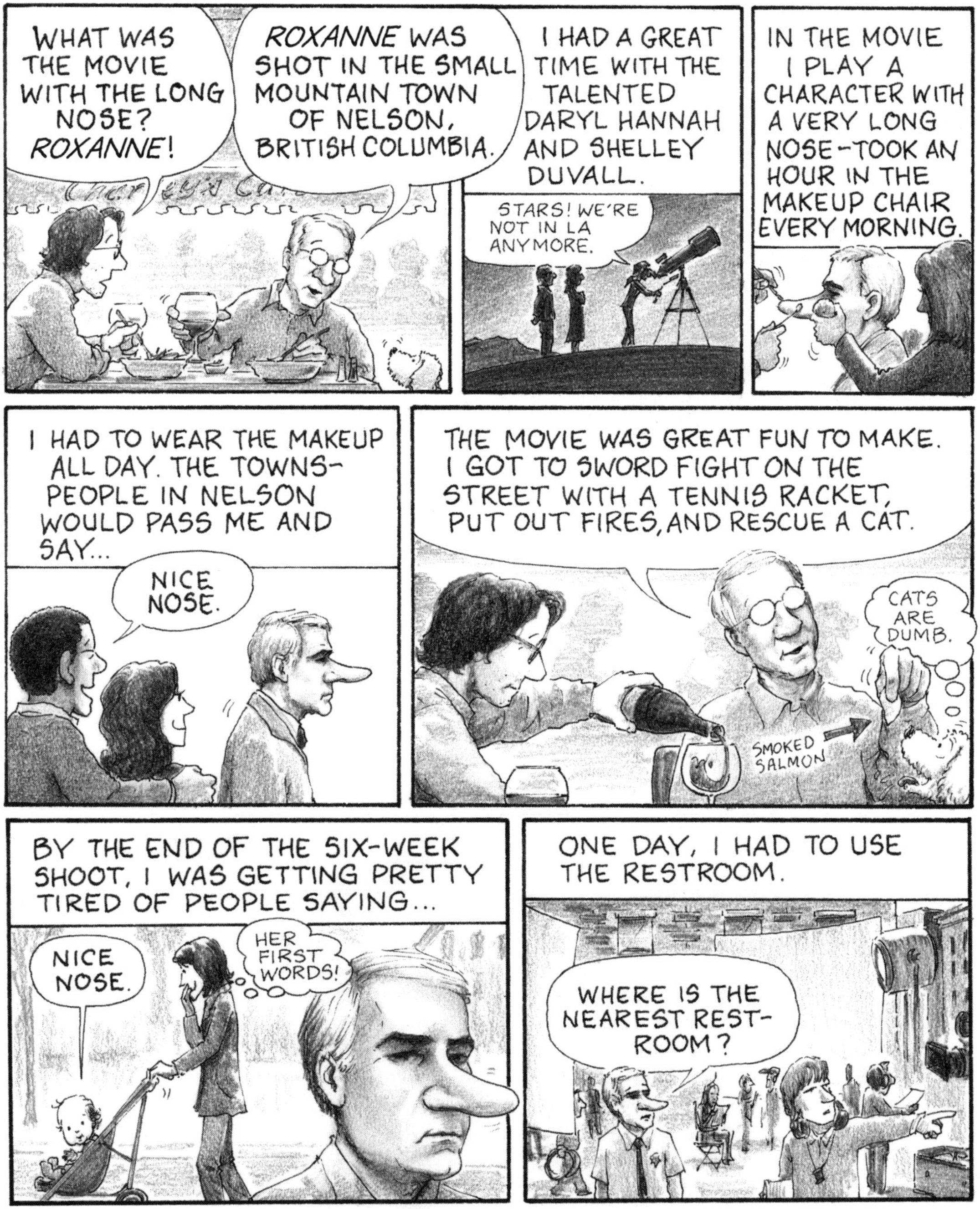
WHAT WAS THE MOVIE WITH THE LONG NOSE? *ROXANNE*!
ROXANNE WAS SHOT IN THE SMALL MOUNTAIN TOWN OF NELSON, BRITISH COLUMBIA.
I HAD A GREAT TIME WITH THE TALENTED DARYL HANNAH AND SHELLEY DUVALL.
STARS! WE'RE NOT IN LA ANYMORE.
IN THE MOVIE I PLAY A CHARACTER WITH A VERY LONG NOSE—TOOK AN HOUR IN THE MAKEUP CHAIR EVERY MORNING.
I HAD TO WEAR THE MAKEUP ALL DAY. THE TOWNS-PEOPLE IN NELSON WOULD PASS ME AND SAY...
NICE NOSE.
THE MOVIE WAS GREAT FUN TO MAKE. I GOT TO SWORD FIGHT ON THE STREET WITH A TENNIS RACKET, PUT OUT FIRES, AND RESCUE A CAT.
CATS ARE DUMB.
SMOKED SALMON
BY THE END OF THE SIX-WEEK SHOOT, I WAS GETTING PRETTY TIRED OF PEOPLE SAYING...
NICE NOSE.
HER FIRST WORDS!
ONE DAY, I HAD TO USE THE RESTROOM.
WHERE IS THE NEAREST REST-ROOM?

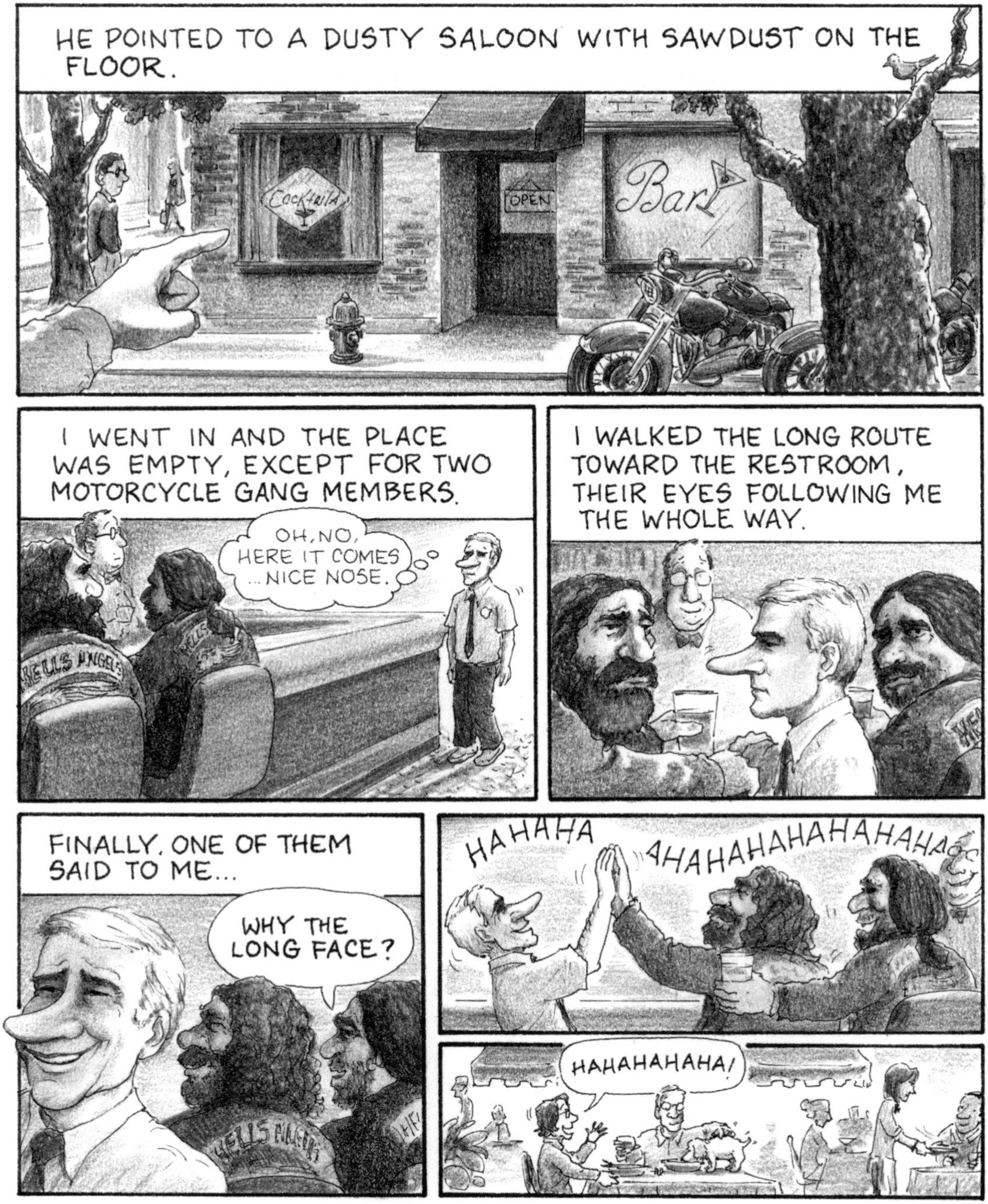

HE POINTED TO A DUSTY SALOON WITH SAWDUST ON THE FLOOR.
Cocktails
OPEN
Bar
I WENT IN AND THE PLACE WAS EMPTY, EXCEPT FOR TWO MOTORCYCLE GANG MEMBERS.
OH, NO, HERE IT COMES ...NICE NOSE.
HELLS ANGELS
I WALKED THE LONG ROUTE TOWARD THE RESTROOM, THEIR EYES FOLLOWING ME THE WHOLE WAY.
FINALLY, ONE OF THEM SAID TO ME...
WHY THE LONG FACE?
HELLS ANGELS
HAHAHA
AHAHAHAHAHAHAHAHA
HAHAHAHAHA!

The Writing of Roxanne

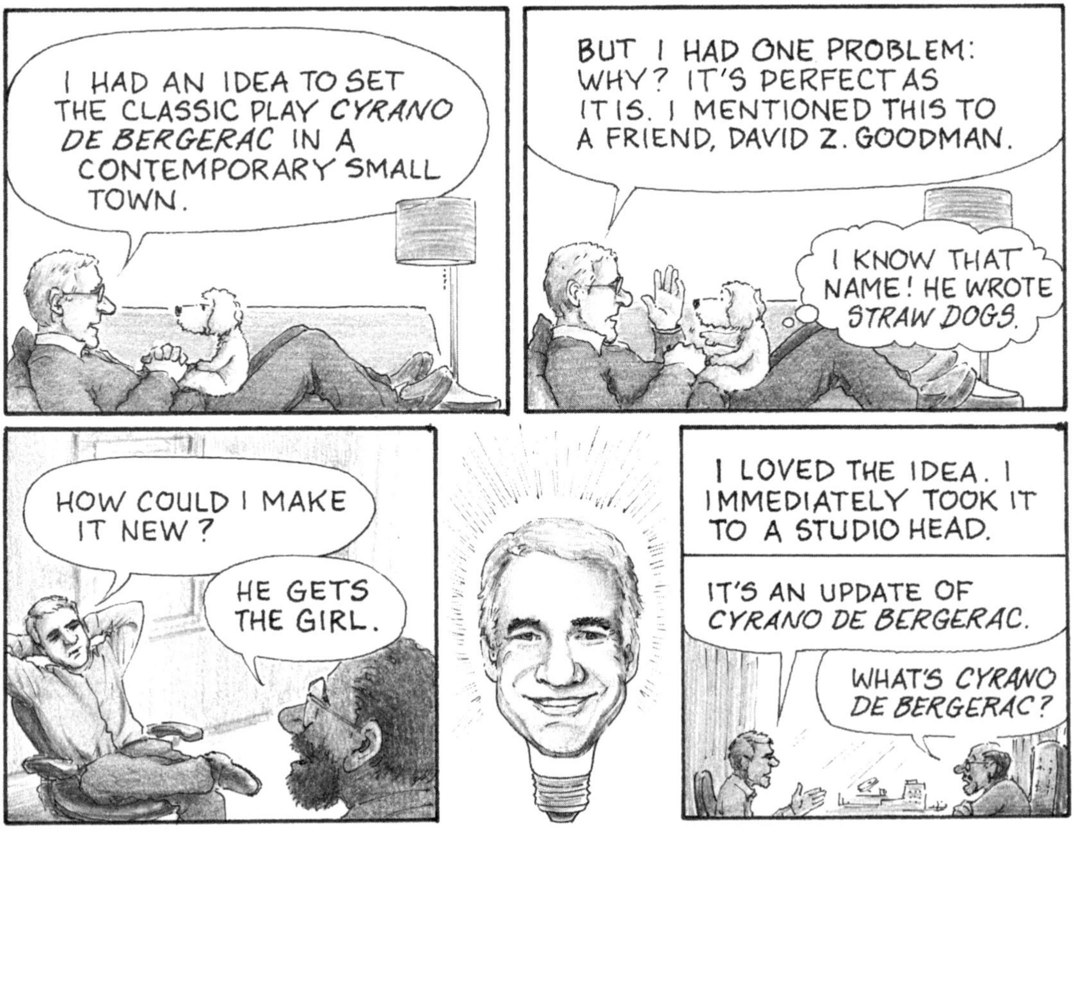

I HAD AN IDEA TO SET THE CLASSIC PLAY *CYRANO DE BERGERAC* IN A CONTEMPORARY SMALL TOWN.
BUT I HAD ONE PROBLEM: WHY? IT'S PERFECT AS IT IS. I MENTIONED THIS TO A FRIEND, DAVID Z. GOODMAN.
I KNOW THAT NAME! HE WROTE *STRAW DOGS*.
HOW COULD I MAKE IT NEW?
HE GETS THE GIRL.
I LOVED THE IDEA. I IMMEDIATELY TOOK IT TO A STUDIO HEAD.
IT'S AN UPDATE OF *CYRANO DE BERGERAC*.
WHAT'S *CYRANO DE BERGERAC*?

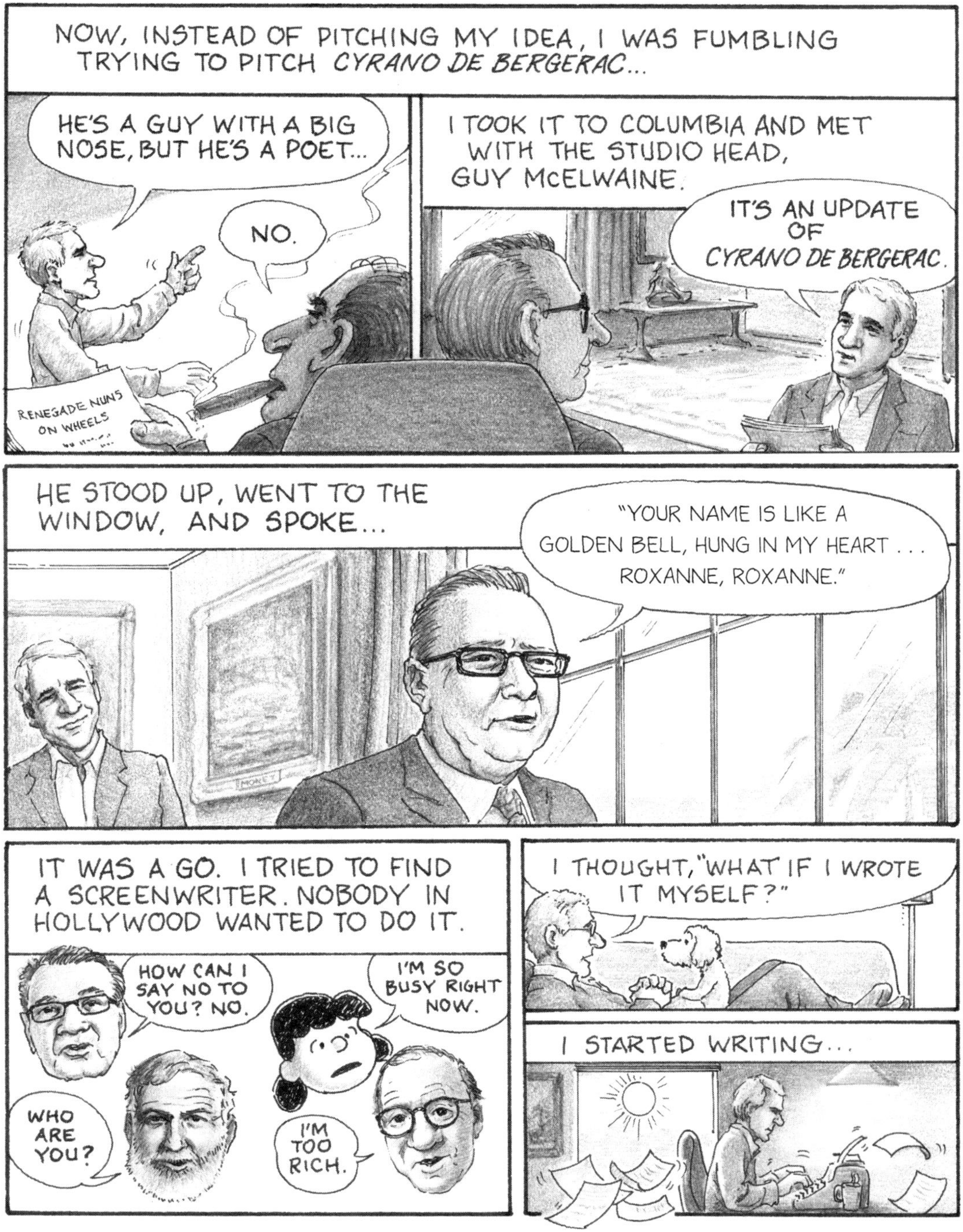
NOW, INSTEAD OF PITCHING MY IDEA, I WAS FUMBLING TRYING TO PITCH *CYRANO DE BERGERAC*...
HE'S A GUY WITH A BIG NOSE, BUT HE'S A POET...
NO.
RENEGADE NUNS ON WHEELS
I TOOK IT TO COLUMBIA AND MET WITH THE STUDIO HEAD, GUY McELWAINE.
IT'S AN UPDATE OF *CYRANO DE BERGERAC*.
HE STOOD UP, WENT TO THE WINDOW, AND SPOKE...
"YOUR NAME IS LIKE A GOLDEN BELL, HUNG IN MY HEART . . . ROXANNE, ROXANNE."
IT WAS A GO. I TRIED TO FIND A SCREENWRITER. NOBODY IN HOLLYWOOD WANTED TO DO IT.
HOW CAN I SAY NO TO YOU? NO.
I'M SO BUSY RIGHT NOW.
WHO ARE YOU?
I'M TOO RICH.
I THOUGHT, "WHAT IF I WROTE IT MYSELF?"
I STARTED WRITING...

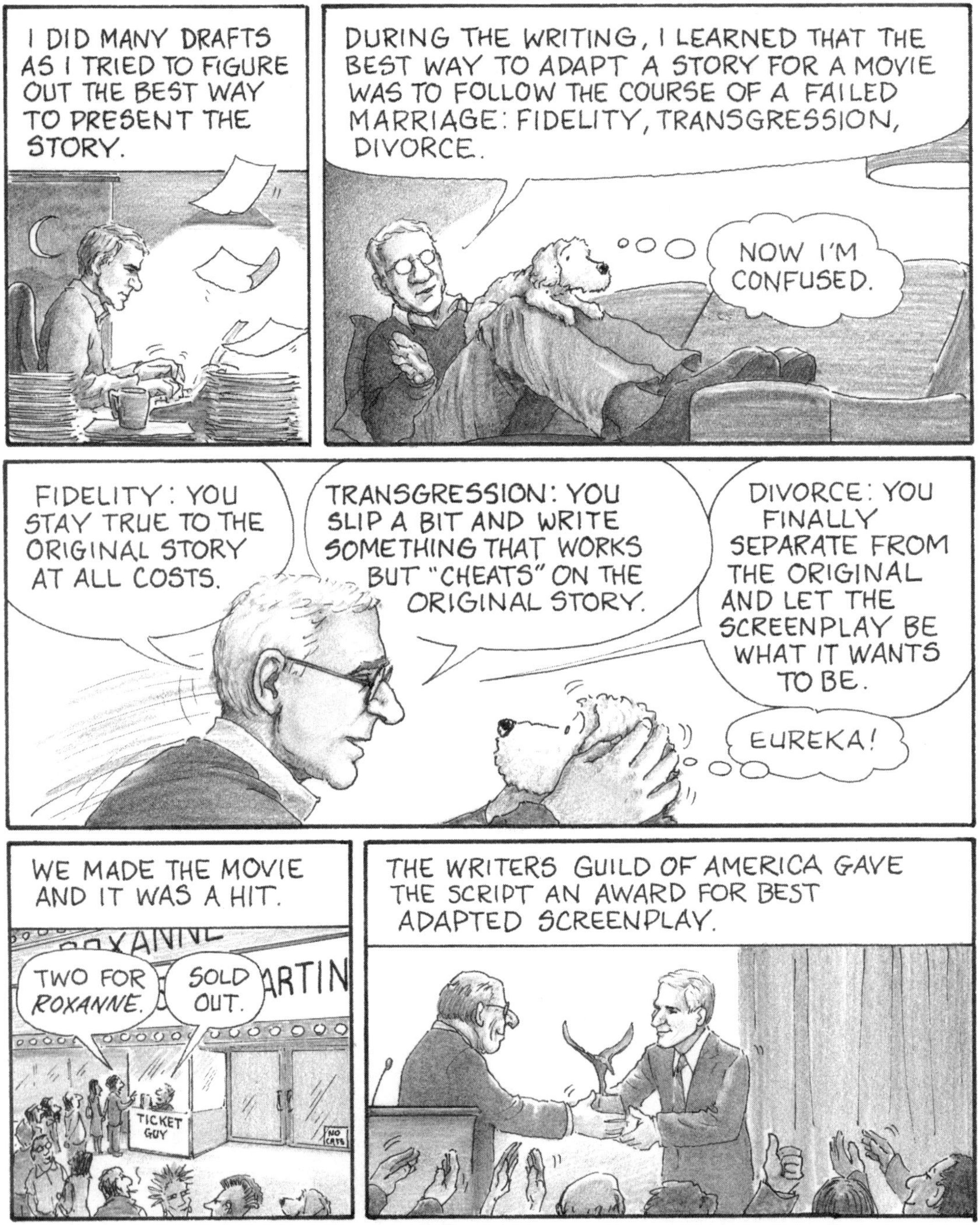
I DID MANY DRAFTS AS I TRIED TO FIGURE OUT THE BEST WAY TO PRESENT THE STORY.
DURING THE WRITING, I LEARNED THAT THE BEST WAY TO ADAPT A STORY FOR A MOVIE WAS TO FOLLOW THE COURSE OF A FAILED MARRIAGE: FIDELITY, TRANSGRESSION, DIVORCE.
NOW I'M CONFUSED.
FIDELITY: YOU STAY TRUE TO THE ORIGINAL STORY AT ALL COSTS.
TRANSGRESSION: YOU SLIP A BIT AND WRITE SOMETHING THAT WORKS BUT "CHEATS" ON THE ORIGINAL STORY.
DIVORCE: YOU FINALLY SEPARATE FROM THE ORIGINAL AND LET THE SCREENPLAY BE WHAT IT WANTS TO BE.
EUREKA!
WE MADE THE MOVIE AND IT WAS A HIT.
TWO FOR *ROXANNE*.
SOLD OUT.
TICKET GUY
THE WRITERS GUILD OF AMERICA GAVE THE SCRIPT AN AWARD FOR BEST ADAPTED SCREENPLAY.

I GAVE A SPEECH...
TO BE READ IF I WIN: "THANK YOU SO MUCH FOR THIS GREAT HONOR."
TO BE READ IF I LOSE: "YOU IDIOTS, YOU MORONS. YOU WOULDN'T KNOW A GOOD SCREENPLAY IF IT VOMITED ON YOUR SHOES."
ROXANNE by STEVE MARTIN

PEOPLE I'VE MET

DID YOU MEET KATHARINE HEPBURN?
NOPE.
DID YOU MEET "THE ROCK"?
NOPE.
DID YOU MEET LADY GAGA?
NOPE.

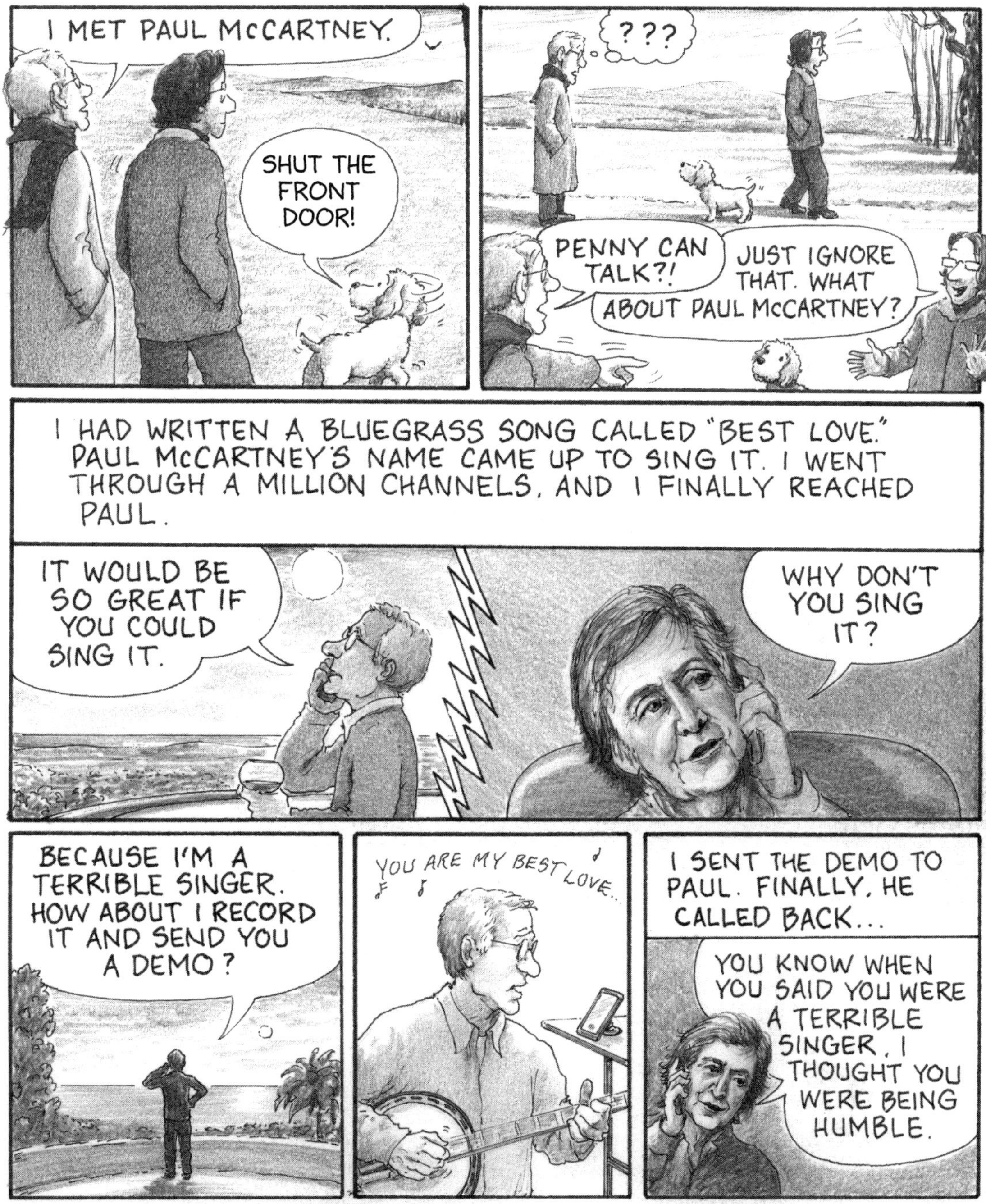

I MET PAUL McCARTNEY.
SHUT THE FRONT DOOR!
???
PENNY CAN TALK?!
JUST IGNORE THAT. WHAT ABOUT PAUL McCARTNEY?
I HAD WRITTEN A BLUEGRASS SONG CALLED "BEST LOVE." PAUL McCARTNEY'S NAME CAME UP TO SING IT. I WENT THROUGH A MILLION CHANNELS, AND I FINALLY REACHED PAUL.
IT WOULD BE SO GREAT IF YOU COULD SING IT.
WHY DON'T YOU SING IT?
BECAUSE I'M A TERRIBLE SINGER. HOW ABOUT I RECORD IT AND SEND YOU A DEMO?
YOU ARE MY BEST LOVE...
I SENT THE DEMO TO PAUL. FINALLY, HE CALLED BACK...
YOU KNOW WHEN YOU SAID YOU WERE A TERRIBLE SINGER, I THOUGHT YOU WERE BEING HUMBLE.

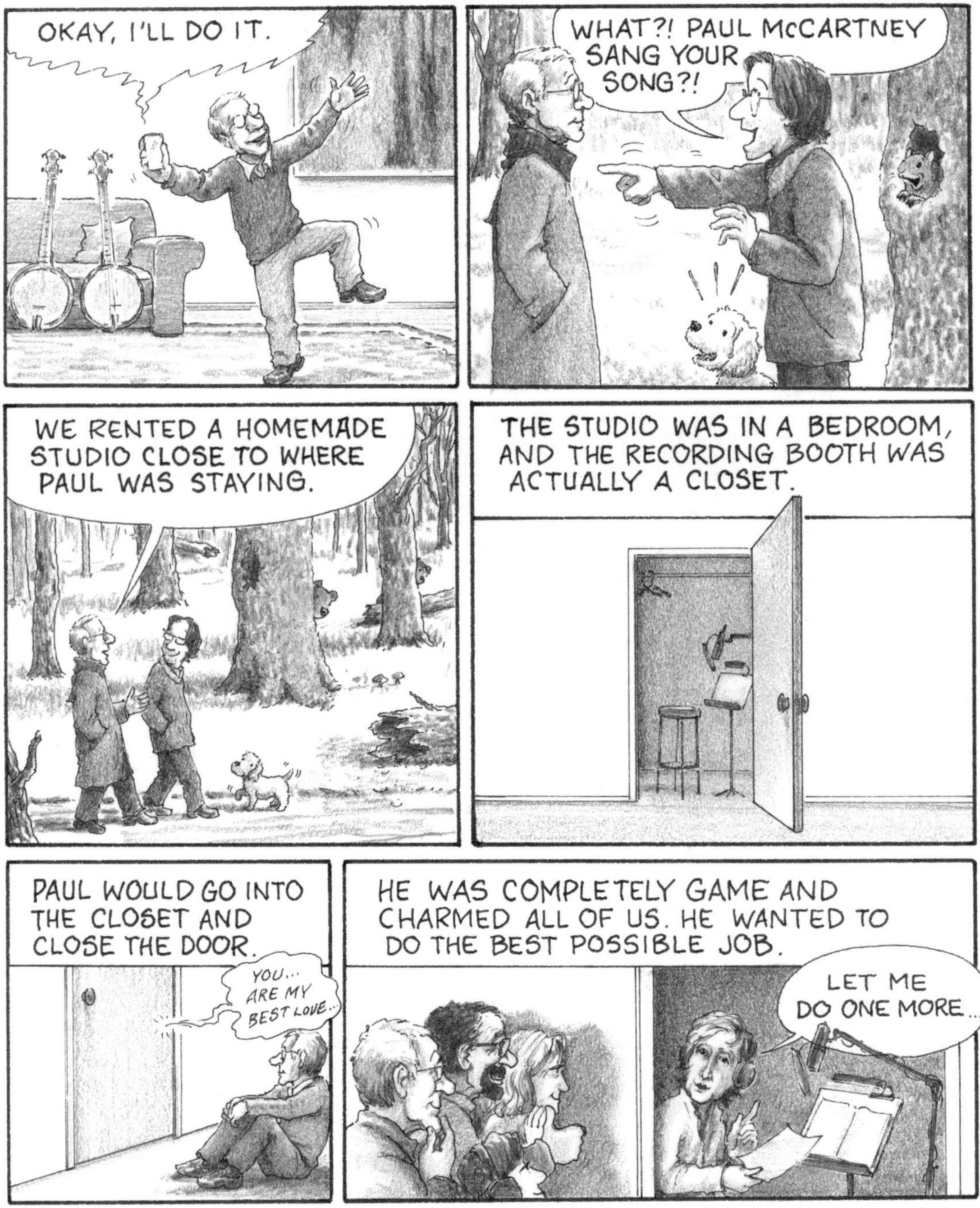
OKAY, I'LL DO IT.
WHAT?! PAUL McCARTNEY SANG YOUR SONG?!
WE RENTED A HOMEMADE STUDIO CLOSE TO WHERE PAUL WAS STAYING.
THE STUDIO WAS IN A BEDROOM, AND THE RECORDING BOOTH WAS ACTUALLY A CLOSET.
PAUL WOULD GO INTO THE CLOSET AND CLOSE THE DOOR.
YOU... ARE MY BEST LOVE...
HE WAS COMPLETELY GAME AND CHARMED ALL OF US. HE WANTED TO DO THE BEST POSSIBLE JOB.
LET ME DO ONE MORE...

THEN HE POSED FOR PICTURES WITH THE CREW. WE SAT OUTSIDE AND HAD LUNCH.

IS THAT PAUL?

IT'S DEFINITELY NOT HIM.

HE'S ONE OF THE MOST RECOGNIZABLE PEOPLE IN THE WORLD.

IS THAT ANDERSON COOPER?

WOW, HE GOT OLD.

AN ASIDE

IN THE EARLY 1970S, MY FRIEND JOHN McEUEN AND I ATTENDED A BIG BLUEGRASS MUSIC FESTIVAL NEAR SAN FRANCISCO. THERE WAS A STAGE, BUT EVERYONE BROUGHT THEIR INSTRUMENTS SO WE ALL COULD JAM ON THE GRASSY LAWN. JOHN AND I PICKED OUR BANJOS, AND A THIRD BANJO PLAYER SPONTANEOUSLY JOINED US. I DIDN'T KNOW WHO HE WAS, BUT I THOUGHT, "THIS GUY'S PRETTY GOOD." RANDOM PHOTOGRAPHERS SNAPPED AWAY AT THE FOLKSY CROWD.

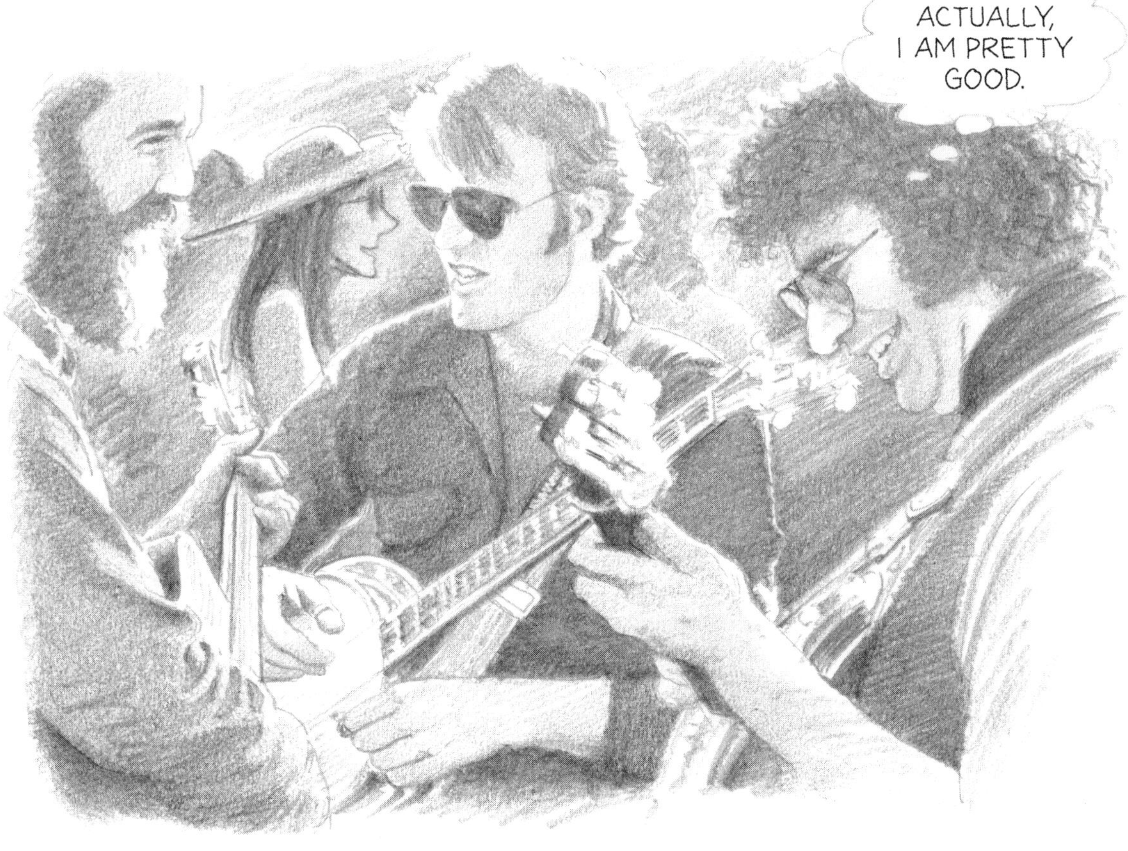
ACTUALLY, I AM PRETTY GOOD.

PROBABLY TWENTY YEARS LATER, I SAW A PHOTO OF US AT THE EVENT. THERE WAS JOHN, ME, AND A BANJO-PLAYING JERRY GARCIA.

DIRTY ROTTEN SCOUNDRELS

SO, HARRY, HOW DID YOU GET STARTED CARTOONING?

WELL, I...

THAT REMINDS ME OF WHEN I DID THE MOVIE *DIRTY ROTTEN SCOUNDRELS*...

OH, THAT WAS A GOOD MOVIE.

WHY, THANK YOU!

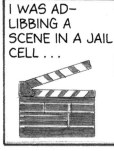

I WAS AD-LIBBING A SCENE IN A JAIL CELL...

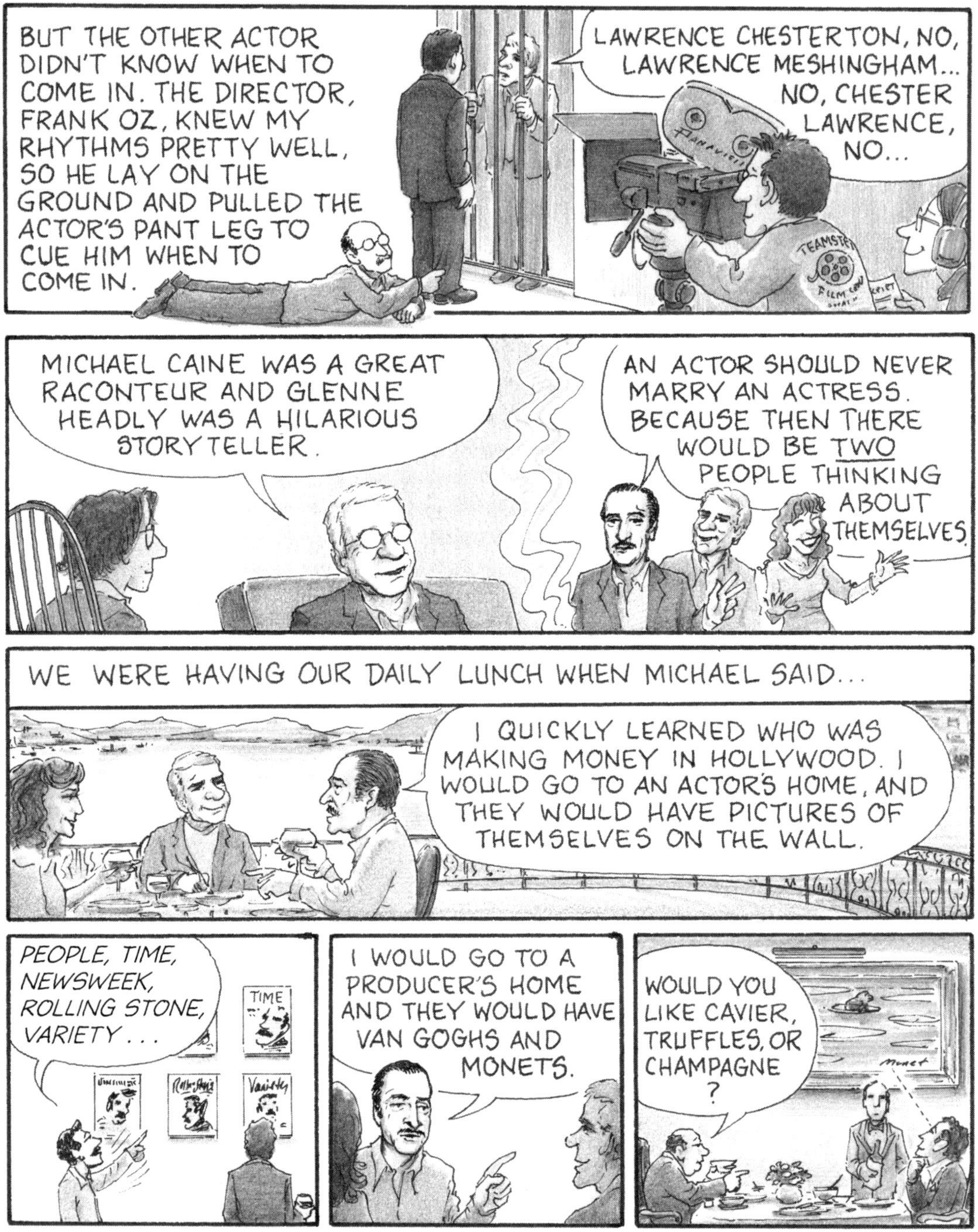
BUT THE OTHER ACTOR DIDN'T KNOW WHEN TO COME IN. THE DIRECTOR, FRANK OZ, KNEW MY RHYTHMS PRETTY WELL, SO HE LAY ON THE GROUND AND PULLED THE ACTOR'S PANT LEG TO CUE HIM WHEN TO COME IN.
LAWRENCE CHESTERTON, NO, LAWRENCE MESHINGHAM... NO, CHESTER LAWRENCE, NO...
MICHAEL CAINE WAS A GREAT RACONTEUR AND GLENNE HEADLY WAS A HILARIOUS STORYTELLER.
AN ACTOR SHOULD NEVER MARRY AN ACTRESS. BECAUSE THEN THERE WOULD BE TWO PEOPLE THINKING ABOUT THEMSELVES.
WE WERE HAVING OUR DAILY LUNCH WHEN MICHAEL SAID...
I QUICKLY LEARNED WHO WAS MAKING MONEY IN HOLLYWOOD. I WOULD GO TO AN ACTOR'S HOME, AND THEY WOULD HAVE PICTURES OF THEMSELVES ON THE WALL.
PEOPLE, TIME, NEWSWEEK, ROLLING STONE, VARIETY . . .
TIME
I WOULD GO TO A PRODUCER'S HOME AND THEY WOULD HAVE VAN GOGHS AND MONETS.
WOULD YOU LIKE CAVIER, TRUFFLES, OR CHAMPAGNE ?

HAHAHAHA!
SO, YOU WERE TALKING ABOUT HOW YOU GOT STARTED...
OH, YEAH, I WAS...
WELP, BEDTIME.

The Pink Panther in Paris

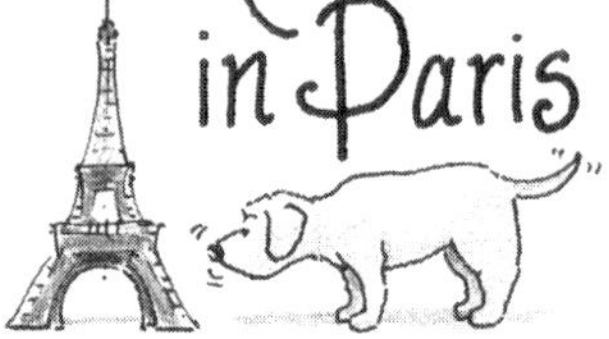

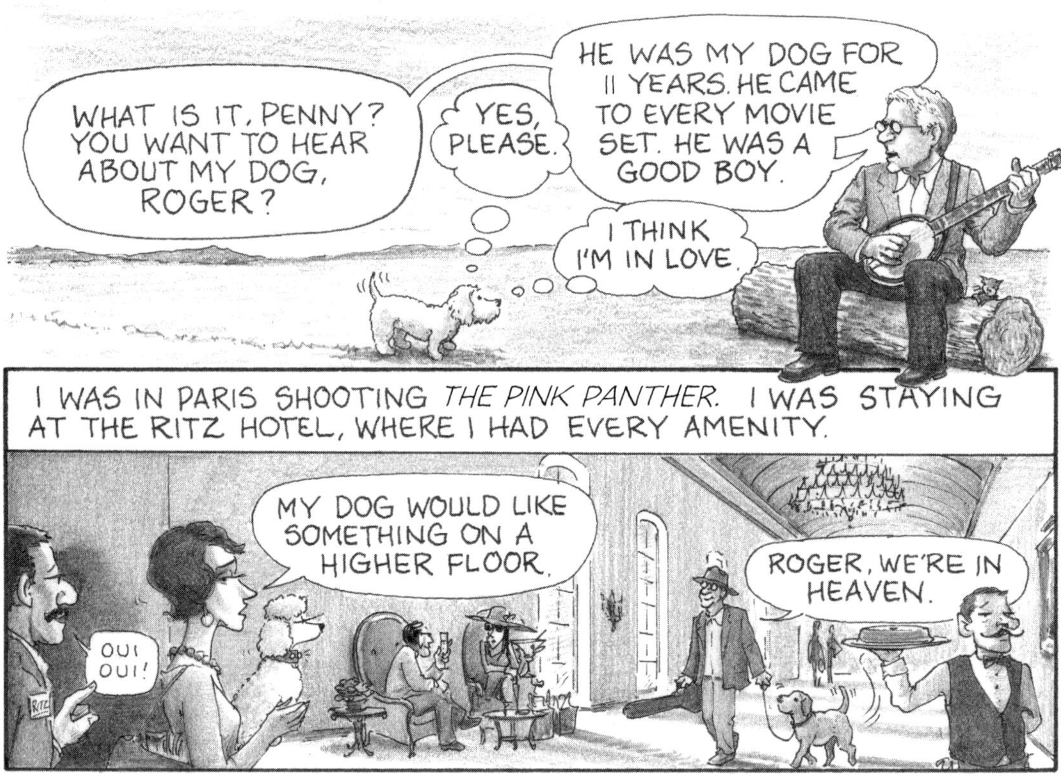
WHAT IS IT, PENNY? YOU WANT TO HEAR ABOUT MY DOG, ROGER?
YES, PLEASE.
HE WAS MY DOG FOR 11 YEARS. HE CAME TO EVERY MOVIE SET. HE WAS A GOOD BOY.
I THINK I'M IN LOVE.
I WAS IN PARIS SHOOTING *THE PINK PANTHER.* I WAS STAYING AT THE RITZ HOTEL, WHERE I HAD EVERY AMENITY.
MY DOG WOULD LIKE SOMETHING ON A HIGHER FLOOR.
OUI OUI!
RITZ
ROGER, WE'RE IN HEAVEN.

ONE DAY, I RAN OUT OF DOG FOOD. SO I CALLED DOWN TO ROOM SERVICE AND ASKED IF THEY HAD ANY. THEY PROMPTLY DELIVERED CHICKEN WITH RICE IN A BOWL.

VOILA.

LATER, I CHECKED THE BILL. IT WAS NINETY EUROS!

I CALLED THE FRONT DESK. I SAID, "I'VE HAPPILY PAID ALL MY BILLS AT THE RITZ, BUT THIS SEEMS EXTRAVAGANT." THEY AGREED AND ALL FUTURE DOG FOOD FOR MY BUDDY, ROGER, WAS ON THE HOUSE.

HEY, YOU TWO, WHAT'S GOIN' ON?

YOU NEVER TAKE ME ANYWHERE.

DURING MY TIME WITH ROGER, I DID FOURTEEN MOVIES, INCLUDING *THE SPANISH PRISONER* (WORKING WITH DAVID MAMET WAS A THRILL), *BOWFINGER* (EDDIE MURPHY SHOULD HAVE GOTTEN AN OSCAR NOMINATION), *THE OUT-OF-TOWNERS* (WITH THE SUPREMELY LUMINOUS GOLDIE HAWN), *BRINGING DOWN THE HOUSE* (WE LAUGHED EVERY DAY), A QUIRKY LITTLE FILM CALLED *NOVOCAINE* (MY SECOND DENTIST ROLE), *CHEAPER BY THE DOZEN* (LOVELY FAMILY FARE), AND *SHOPGIRL* (FROM MY NOVEL). WHEN I WAS PICKED UP IN THE MORNING BY THE TEAMSTER DRIVER, I WOULD SIT IN THE BACK SEAT WITH ROGER, AND HE WOULD ALWAYS PUT HIS PAW ON MY ARM. I ONLY HAD ONE EXPLANATION FOR THIS ROUTINE: IT WAS A GESTURE OF AFFECTION.

ROBIN
Williams

MIGHT TURN COLD TONIGHT—
BETTER SPLIT UP SOME WOOD.

"HAHA!"

DID YOU EVER
WORK WITH
ROBIN WILLIAMS?

THWAK

I DID. ROBIN AND I DID *WAITING FOR GODOT* OFF BROADWAY.

MIKE NICHOLS DIRECTED.

MIKE DIRECTED *THE GRADUATE.*

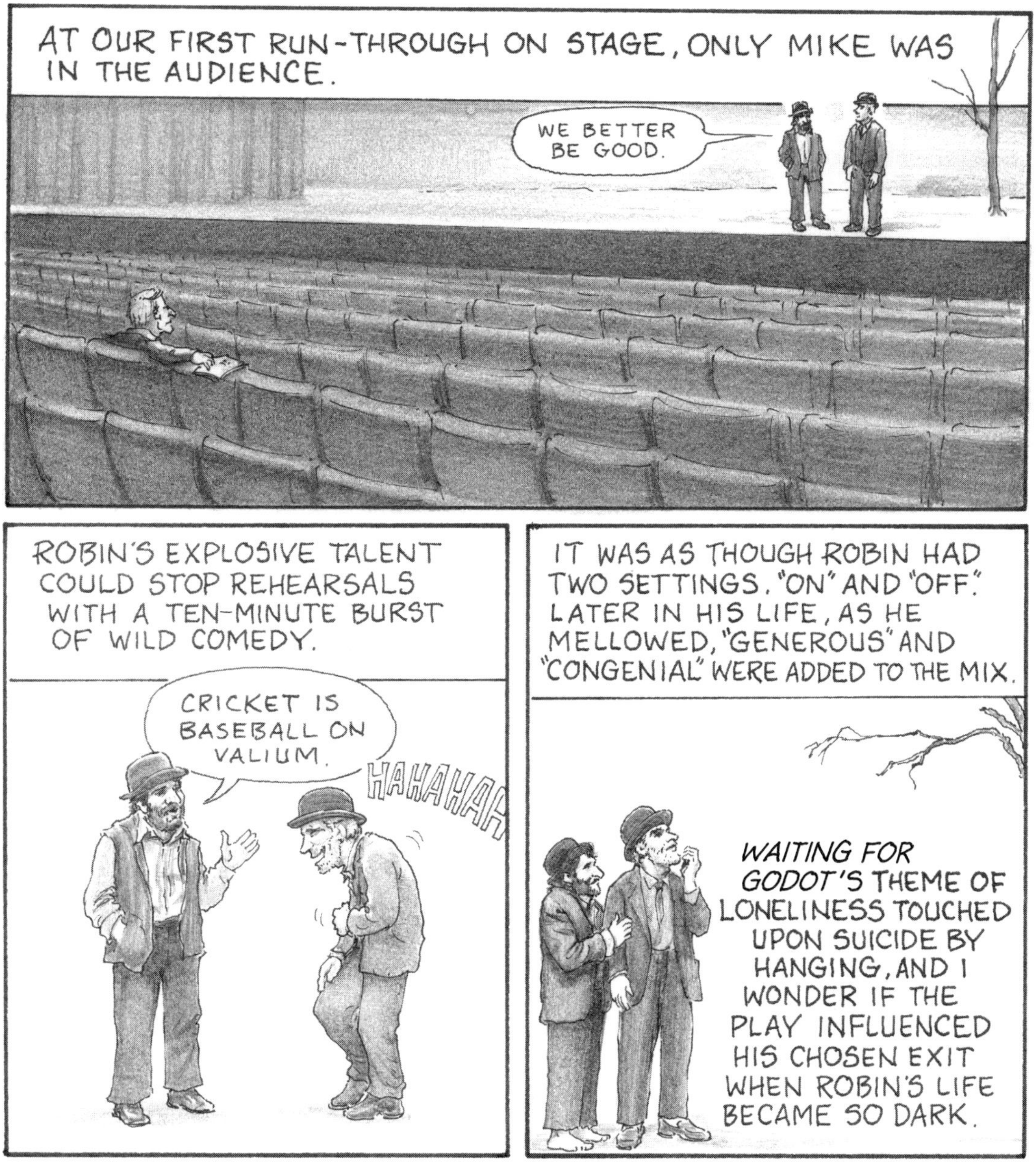
AT OUR FIRST RUN-THROUGH ON STAGE, ONLY MIKE WAS IN THE AUDIENCE.
WE BETTER BE GOOD.
ROBIN'S EXPLOSIVE TALENT COULD STOP REHEARSALS WITH A TEN-MINUTE BURST OF WILD COMEDY.
CRICKET IS BASEBALL ON VALIUM.
HAHAHAHAH
IT WAS AS THOUGH ROBIN HAD TWO SETTINGS, "ON" AND "OFF." LATER IN HIS LIFE, AS HE MELLOWED, "GENEROUS" AND "CONGENIAL" WERE ADDED TO THE MIX.
WAITING FOR GODOT'S THEME OF LONELINESS TOUCHED UPON SUICIDE BY HANGING, AND I WONDER IF THE PLAY INFLUENCED HIS CHOSEN EXIT WHEN ROBIN'S LIFE BECAME SO DARK.

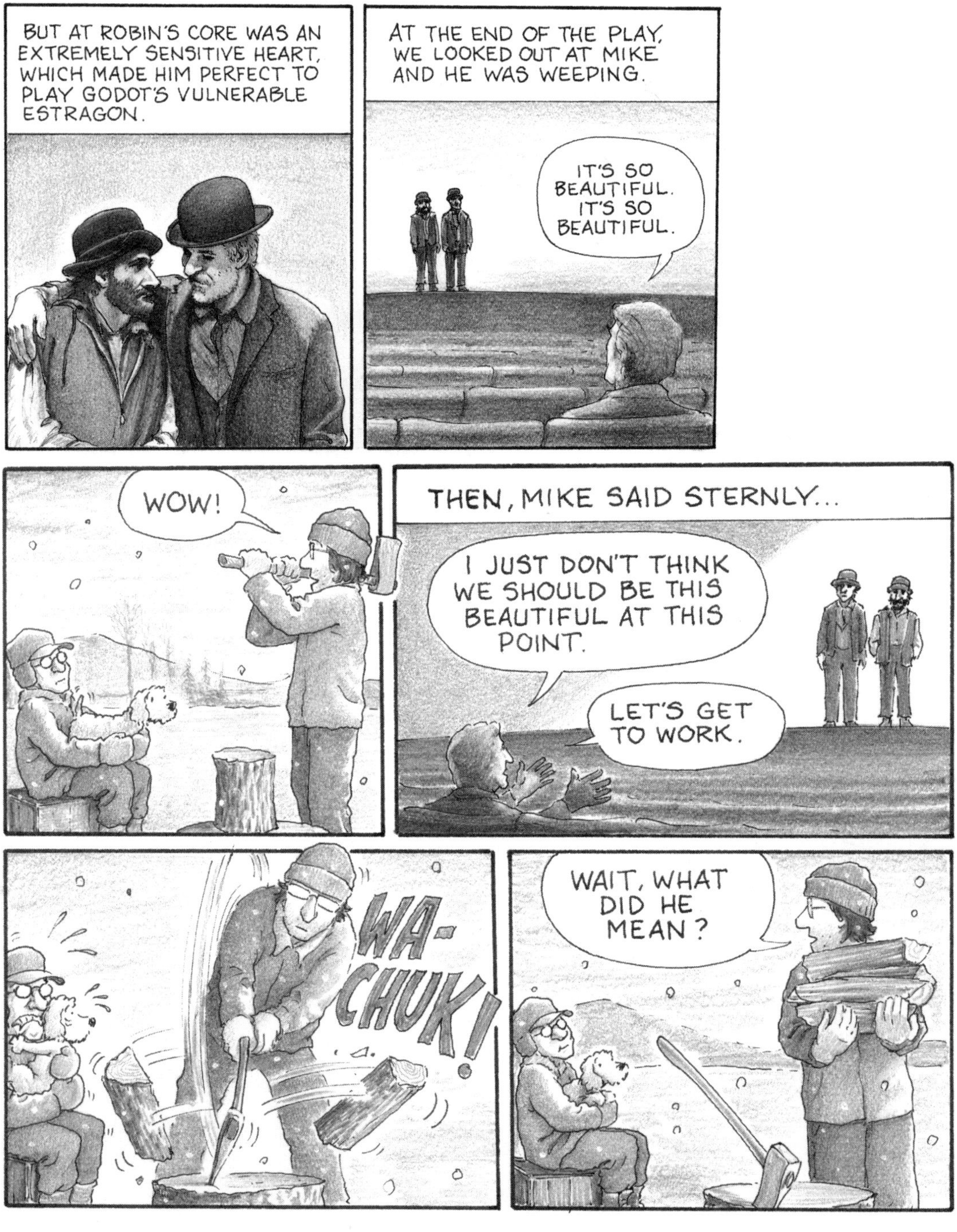

BUT AT ROBIN'S CORE WAS AN EXTREMELY SENSITIVE HEART, WHICH MADE HIM PERFECT TO PLAY GODOT'S VULNERABLE ESTRAGON.
AT THE END OF THE PLAY, WE LOOKED OUT AT MIKE AND HE WAS WEEPING.
IT'S SO BEAUTIFUL. IT'S SO BEAUTIFUL.
WOW!
THEN, MIKE SAID STERNLY...
I JUST DON'T THINK WE SHOULD BE THIS BEAUTIFUL AT THIS POINT.
LET'S GET TO WORK.
WA-CHUK!
WAIT, WHAT DID HE MEAN?

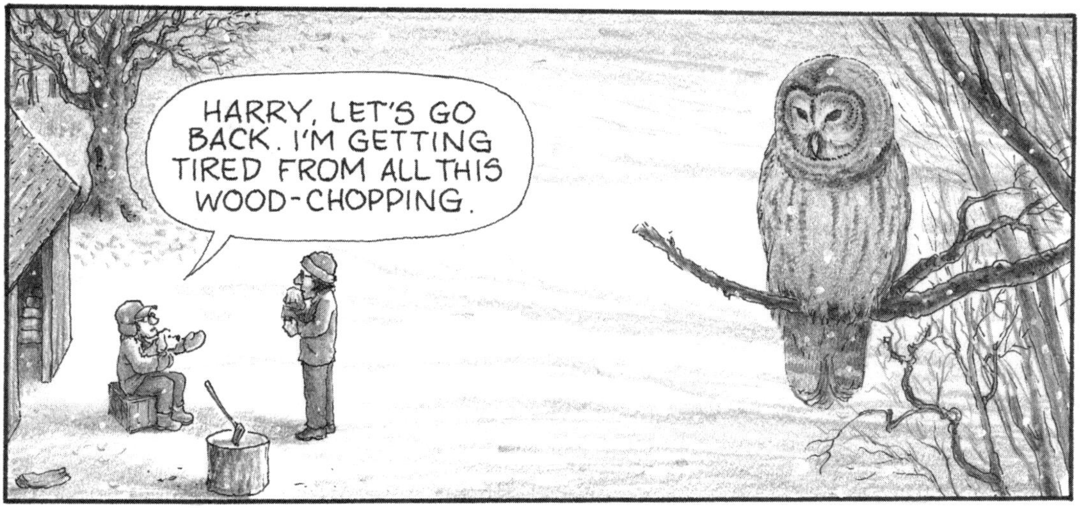
HARRY, LET'S GO BACK. I'M GETTING TIRED FROM ALL THIS WOOD-CHOPPING.

MORE waitin' for

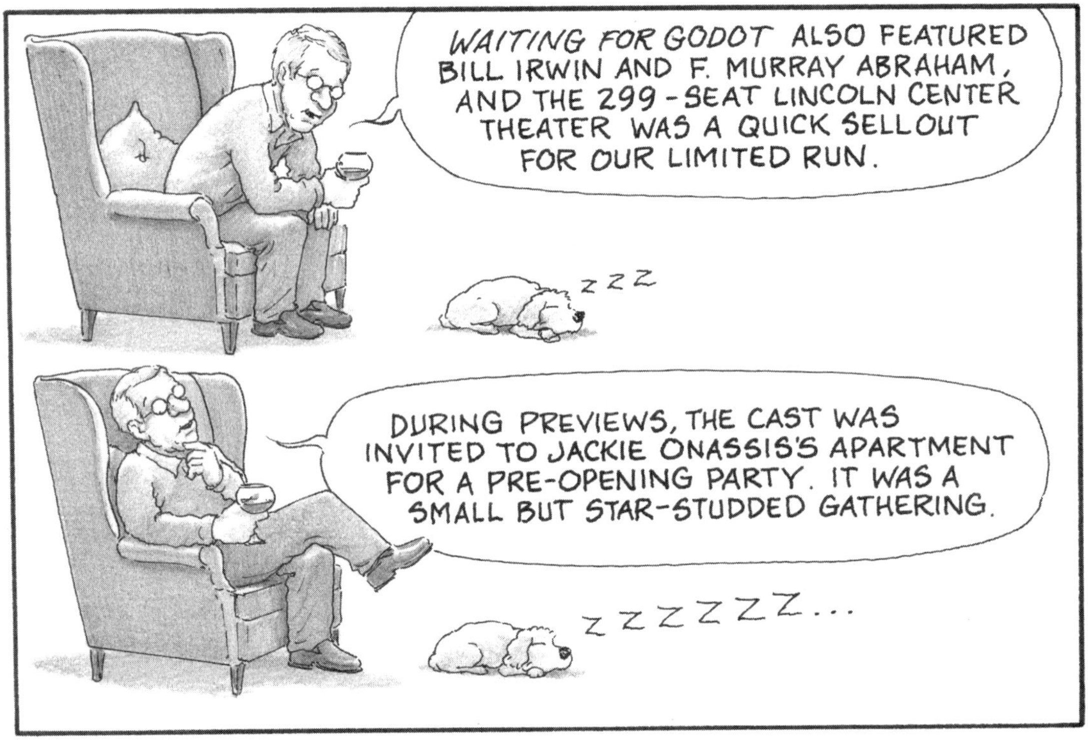
WAITING FOR GODOT ALSO FEATURED BILL IRWIN AND F. MURRAY ABRAHAM, AND THE 299-SEAT LINCOLN CENTER THEATER WAS A QUICK SELLOUT FOR OUR LIMITED RUN.
ZZZ
DURING PREVIEWS, THE CAST WAS INVITED TO JACKIE ONASSIS'S APARTMENT FOR A PRE-OPENING PARTY. IT WAS A SMALL BUT STAR-STUDDED GATHERING.
ZZZZZZ...

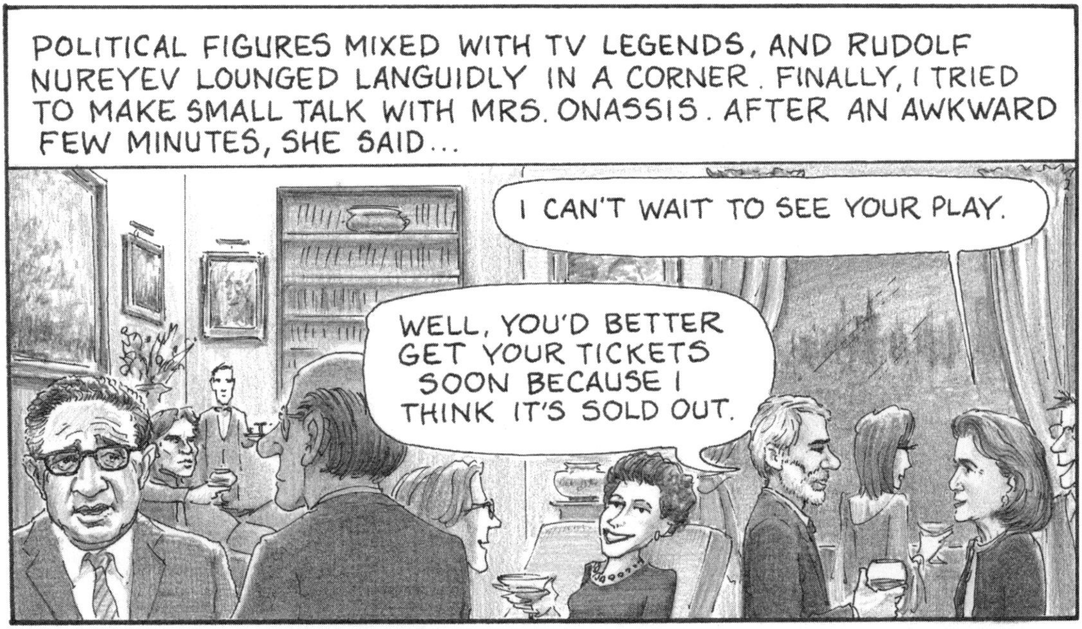
POLITICAL FIGURES MIXED WITH TV LEGENDS, AND RUDOLF NUREYEV LOUNGED LANGUIDLY IN A CORNER. FINALLY, I TRIED TO MAKE SMALL TALK WITH MRS. ONASSIS. AFTER AN AWKWARD FEW MINUTES, SHE SAID...
I CAN'T WAIT TO SEE YOUR PLAY.
WELL, YOU'D BETTER GET YOUR TICKETS SOON BECAUSE I THINK IT'S SOLD OUT.

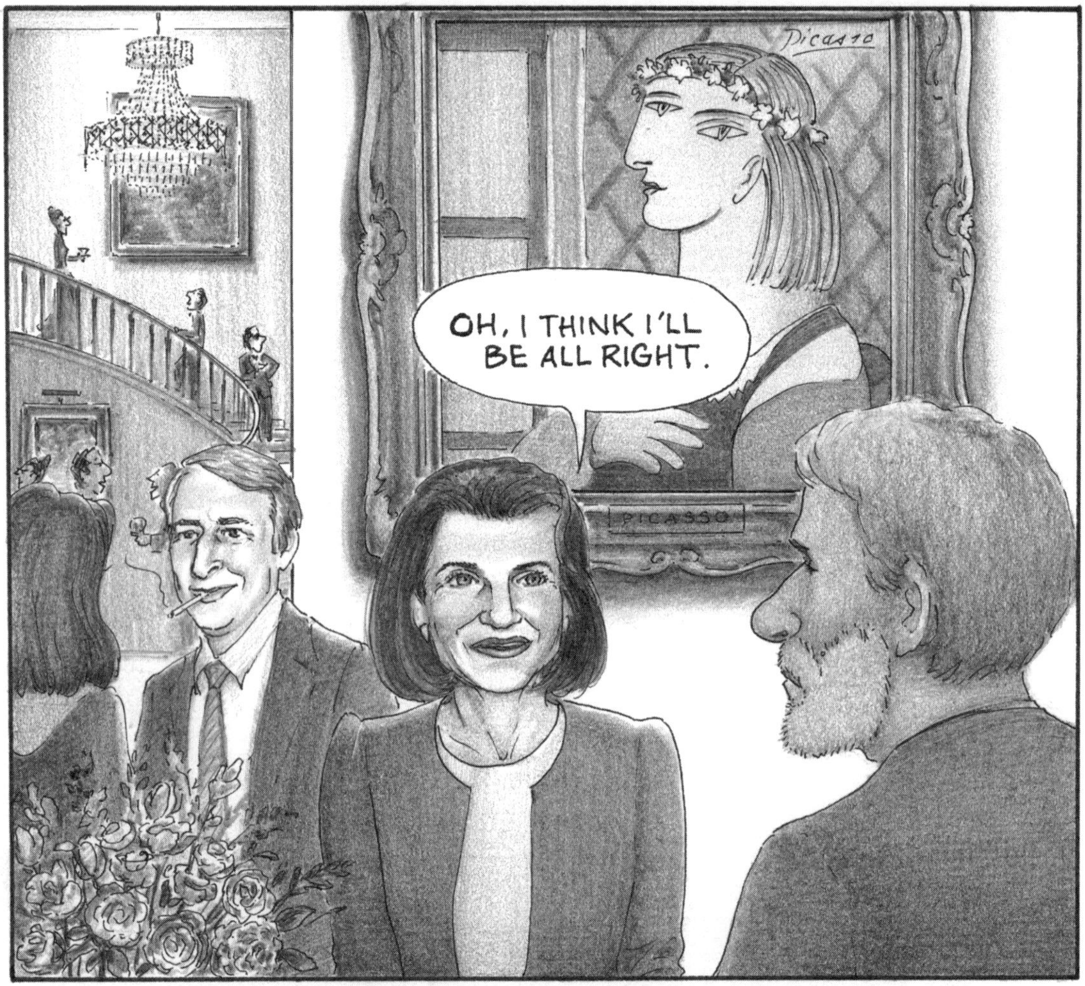
Picasso
OH, I THINK I'LL BE ALL RIGHT.
PICASSO

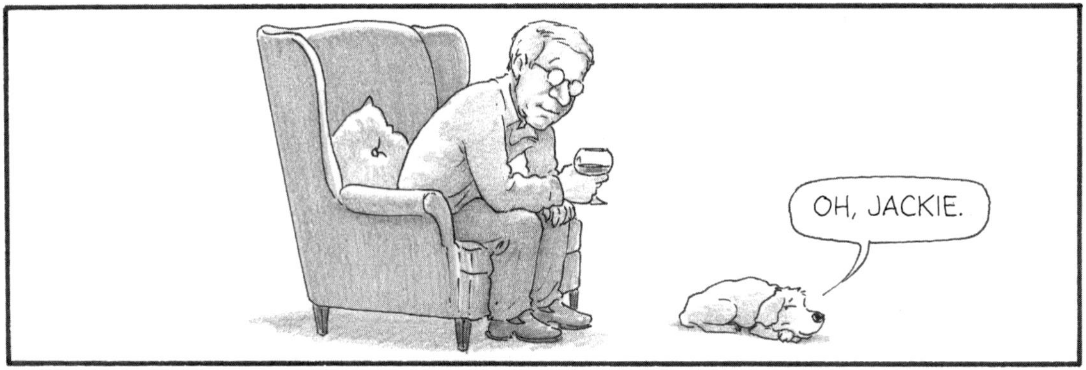
OH, JACKIE.

MIKE NICHOLS

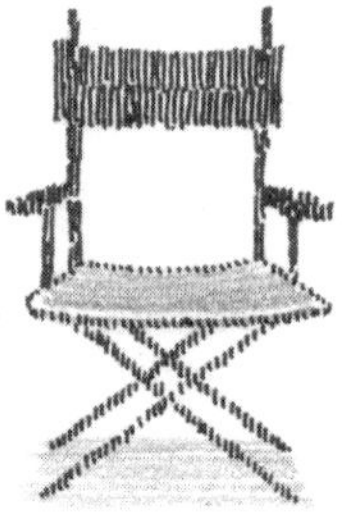

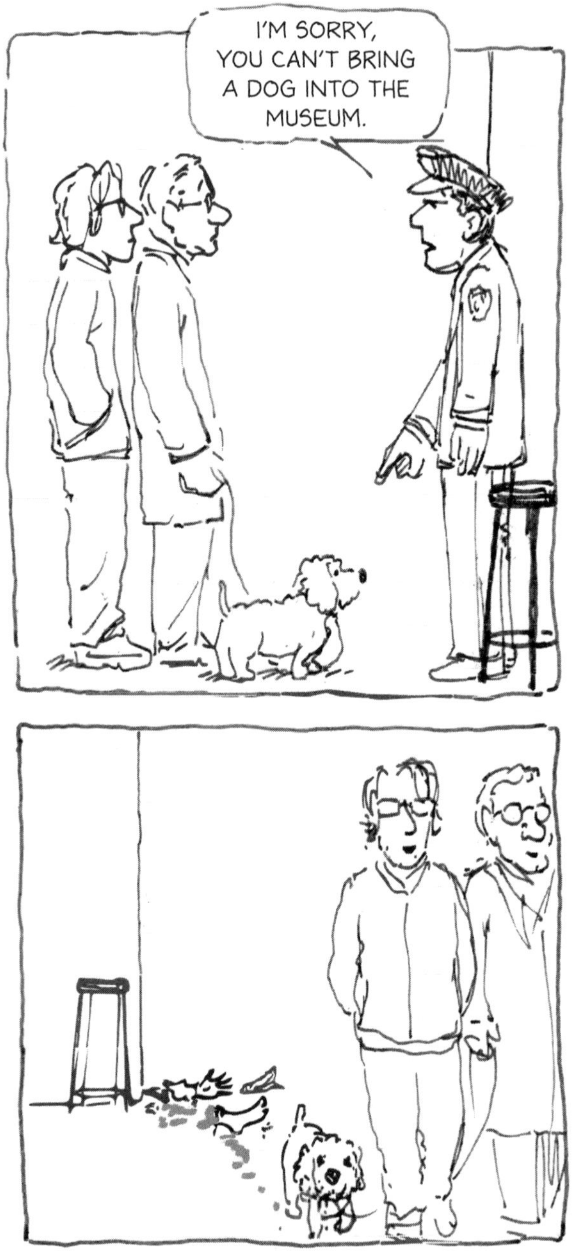
I'M SORRY, YOU CAN'T BRING A DOG INTO THE MUSEUM.

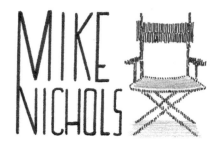

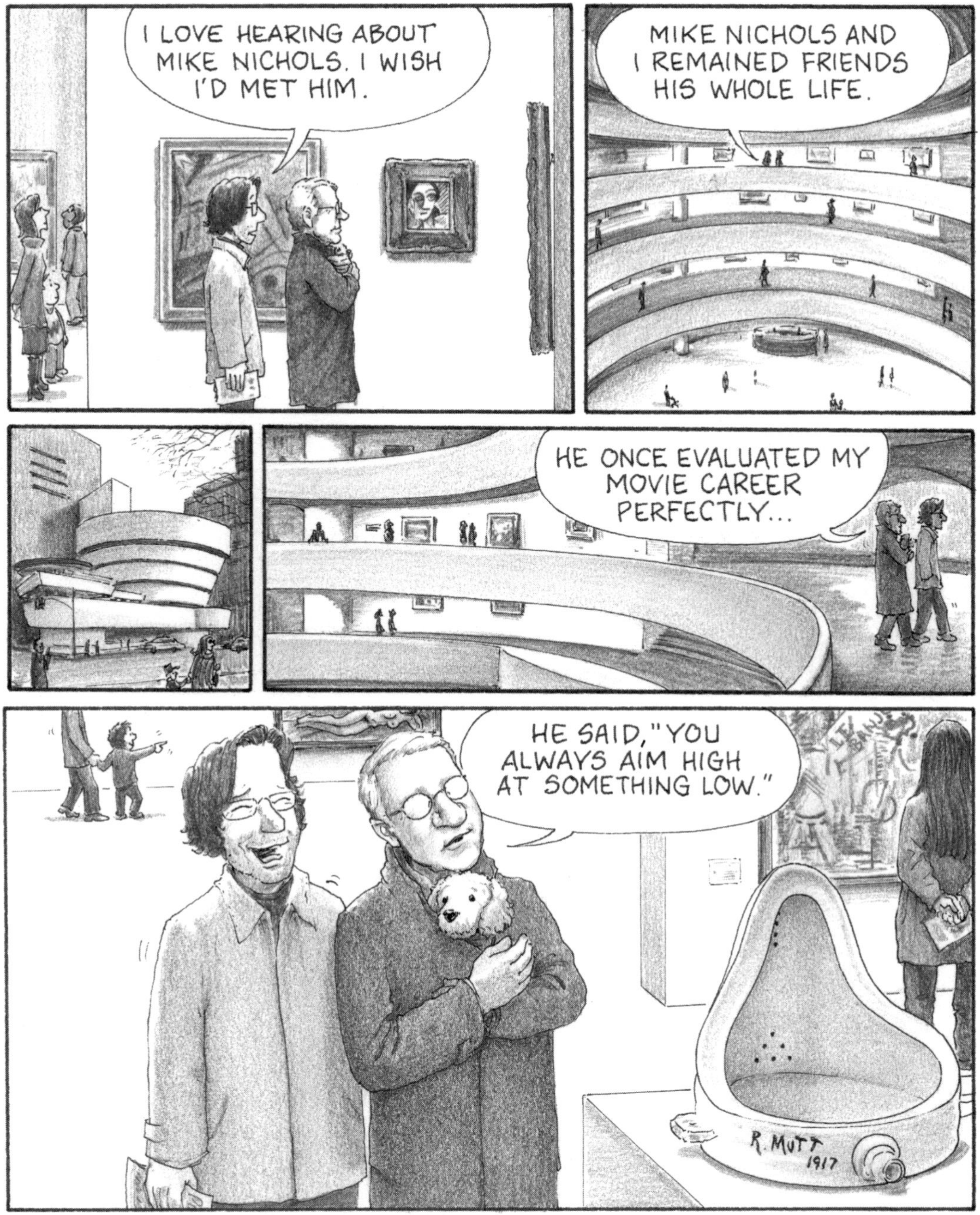
I LOVE HEARING ABOUT MIKE NICHOLS. I WISH I'D MET HIM.
MIKE NICHOLS AND I REMAINED FRIENDS HIS WHOLE LIFE.
HE ONCE EVALUATED MY MOVIE CAREER PERFECTLY...
HE SAID, "YOU ALWAYS AIM HIGH AT SOMETHING LOW."
R. MUTT 1917

PARENTHOOD

PARENTHOOD WAS DESIGNED BY ITS WRITERS AND CREATORS (RON HOWARD, BRIAN GRAZER, LOWELL GANZ, AND BABALOO MANDEL) TO TELL THE HONEST STORY OF PARENTING, WITH ALL ITS HIGHS AND LOWS.

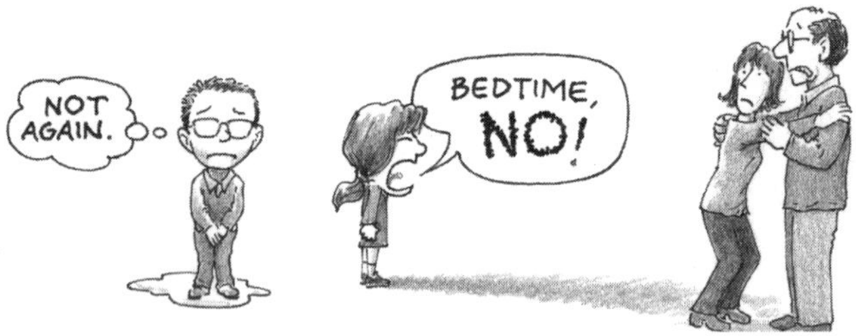
NOT AGAIN.
BEDTIME, NO!

WE SHOT IN ORLANDO, FLORIDA, HOME OF DISNEY WORLD. AMONG MY THEME-PARK ADVENTURES THERE, THE HIGHLIGHT WAS PETTING THE BABY STINGRAYS AT SEAWORLD . . .

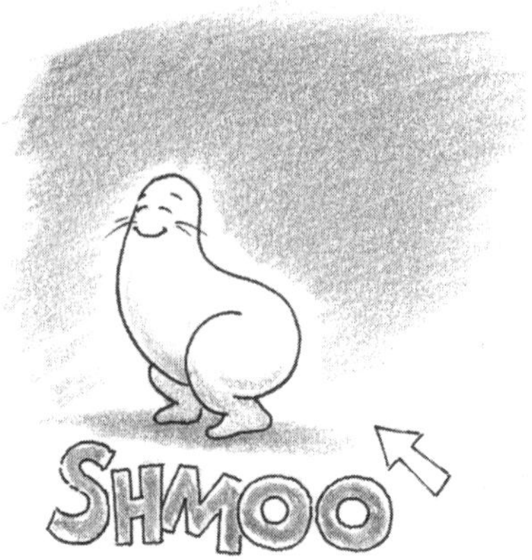
SHMOO

. . . WHO LOOKED LIKE LOVABLE SHMOOS SAYING WITH THEIR EYES, "TAKE ME HOME."

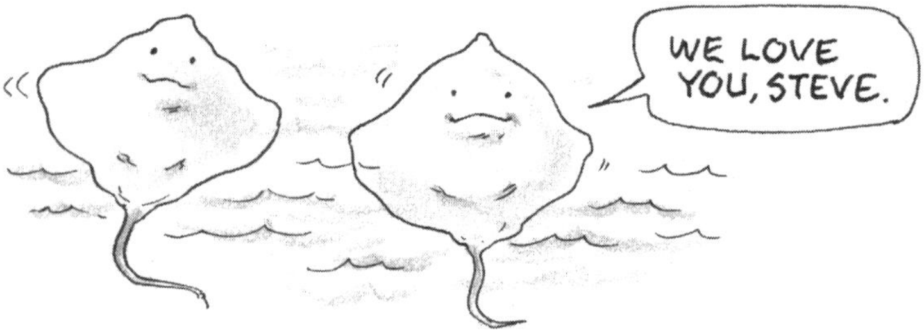
WE LOVE YOU, STEVE.

AFTER MANY MONTHS, THE MOVIE WAS SHOT AND EDITED, AND NOW I WAS TO ATTEND A FIRST AUDIENCE PREVIEW SCREENING IN LOS ANGELES.
   EARLIER THAT MONTH MY MOTHER CALLED AND SAID . . .

SOME FRIENDS OF OURS WENT TO THE MOVIES LAST WEEKEND AND THEY COULDN'T GET IN ANYWHERE, SO THEY WENT TO SEE YOURS.

SO I ENTERED THE THEATER IN A SORRY MOOD.

WHO'S THAT SAD SACK?

I WATCHED THE MOVIE FROM THE BACK OF THE HOUSE, SAW PERFECT PERFORMANCES BY MARY STEENBURGEN, DIANNE WIEST, RICK MORANIS, KEANU REEVES, AND JASON ROBARDS, AMONG OTHERS.

THE MOVIE PLAYED TO BOUNTEOUS LAUGHS AND AUDIBLE TEARS. DRIVING HOME, FEELING MOODY, I THOUGHT,

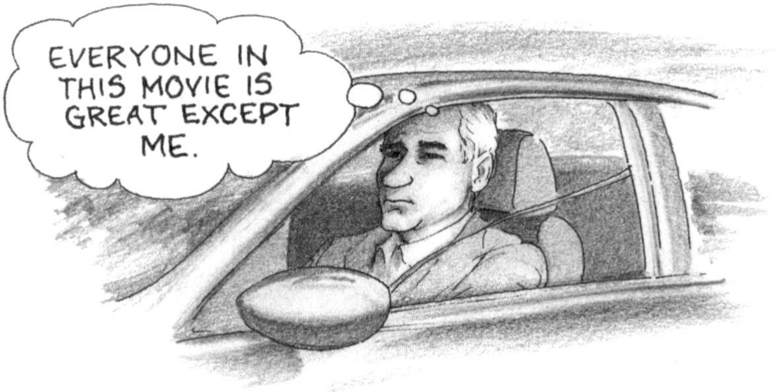
EVERYONE IN THIS MOVIE IS GREAT EXCEPT ME.

IF YOU THINK I'M BEING TOO SENSITIVE, TRY WATCHING A FILM OF YOURSELF FOR TWO HOURS IN CLOSE-UP AND COME OUT UNSCATHED.

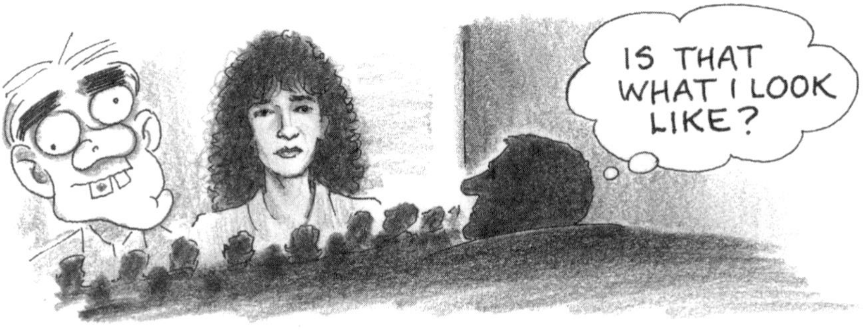
IS THAT WHAT I LOOK LIKE?

THAT NIGHT WHILE LYING IN BED, I SAID TO MYSELF, "WAIT A MINUTE, THEY DIDN'T HIRE SEVEN GREAT ACTORS AND ONE LOUSY ONE. SO I MUST BE GOOD TOO."

GOOD NIGHT, STEVE.

DIANE KEATON

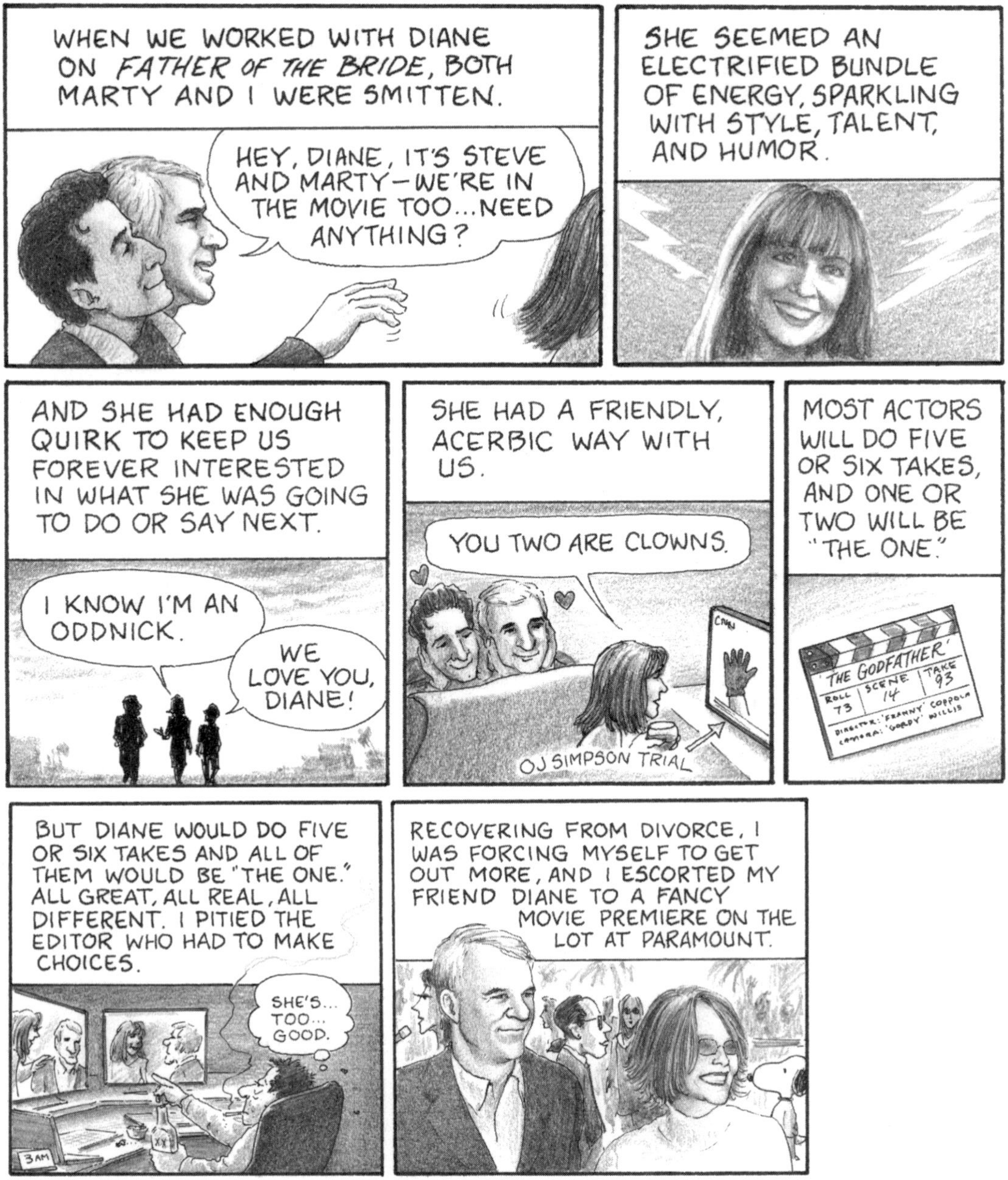
WHEN WE WORKED WITH DIANE ON *FATHER OF THE BRIDE*, BOTH MARTY AND I WERE SMITTEN.
HEY, DIANE, IT'S STEVE AND MARTY—WE'RE IN THE MOVIE TOO...NEED ANYTHING?
SHE SEEMED AN ELECTRIFIED BUNDLE OF ENERGY, SPARKLING WITH STYLE, TALENT, AND HUMOR.
AND SHE HAD ENOUGH QUIRK TO KEEP US FOREVER INTERESTED IN WHAT SHE WAS GOING TO DO OR SAY NEXT.
I KNOW I'M AN ODDNICK.
WE LOVE YOU, DIANE!
SHE HAD A FRIENDLY, ACERBIC WAY WITH US.
YOU TWO ARE CLOWNS.
OJ SIMPSON TRIAL
MOST ACTORS WILL DO FIVE OR SIX TAKES, AND ONE OR TWO WILL BE "THE ONE."
THE GODFATHER
SCENE 14
TAKE 93
ROLL 73
BUT DIANE WOULD DO FIVE OR SIX TAKES AND ALL OF THEM WOULD BE "THE ONE." ALL GREAT, ALL REAL, ALL DIFFERENT. I PITIED THE EDITOR WHO HAD TO MAKE CHOICES.
SHE'S... TOO... GOOD.
3AM
RECOVERING FROM DIVORCE, I WAS FORCING MYSELF TO GET OUT MORE, AND I ESCORTED MY FRIEND DIANE TO A FANCY MOVIE PREMIERE ON THE LOT AT PARAMOUNT.

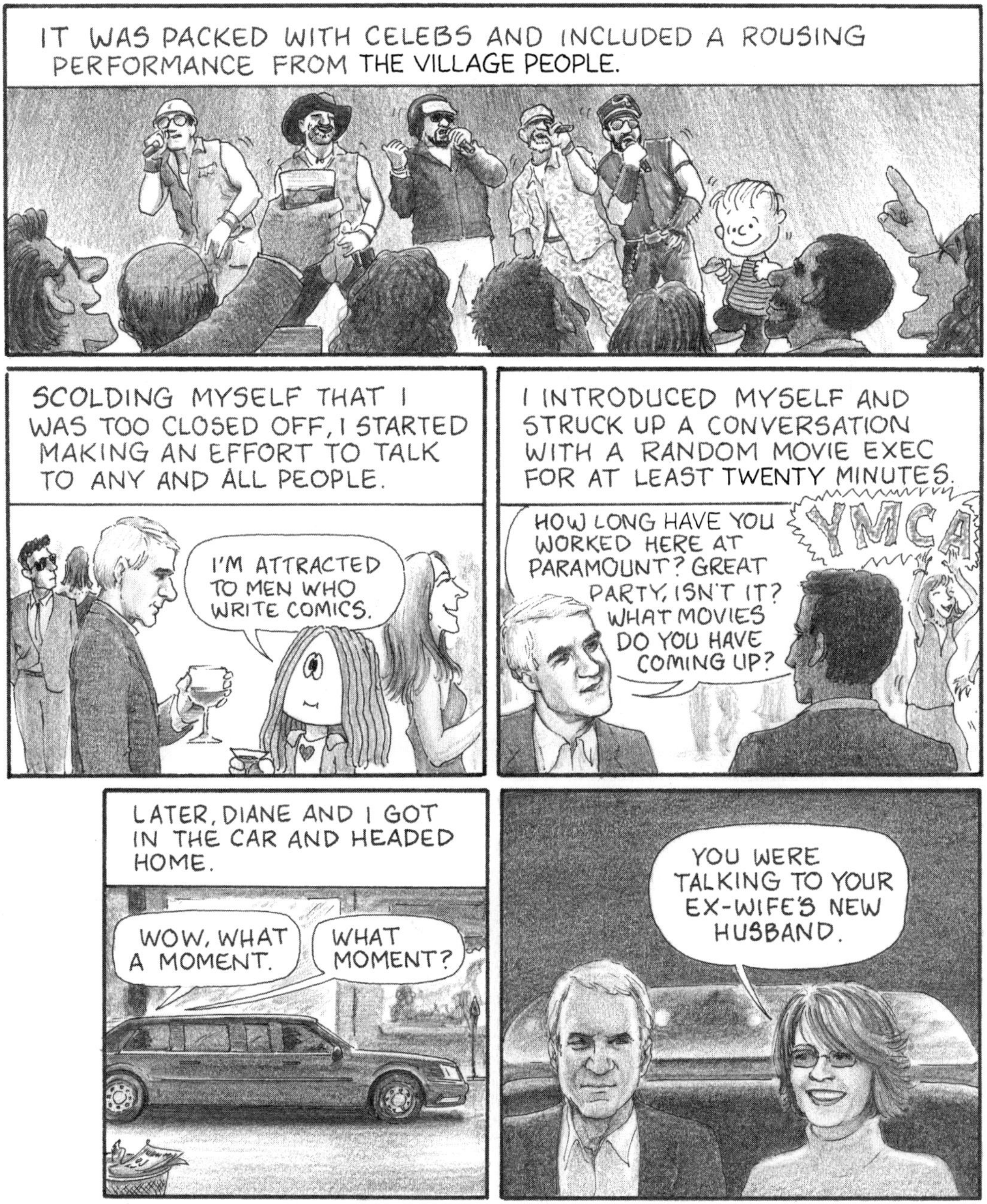

IT WAS PACKED WITH CELEBS AND INCLUDED A ROUSING PERFORMANCE FROM THE VILLAGE PEOPLE.
SCOLDING MYSELF THAT I WAS TOO CLOSED OFF, I STARTED MAKING AN EFFORT TO TALK TO ANY AND ALL PEOPLE.
I'M ATTRACTED TO MEN WHO WRITE COMICS.
I INTRODUCED MYSELF AND STRUCK UP A CONVERSATION WITH A RANDOM MOVIE EXEC FOR AT LEAST TWENTY MINUTES.
HOW LONG HAVE YOU WORKED HERE AT PARAMOUNT? GREAT PARTY, ISN'T IT? WHAT MOVIES DO YOU HAVE COMING UP?
YMCA
LATER, DIANE AND I GOT IN THE CAR AND HEADED HOME.
WOW, WHAT A MOMENT.
WHAT MOMENT?
YOU WERE TALKING TO YOUR EX-WIFE'S NEW HUSBAND.

HOUSESITTER

HOUSESITTER WAS SHOT IN BOSTON. I WORKED WITH TWO FANTASTIC WOMEN: GOLDIE HAWN AND DANA DELANY. EVERY DAY HAD TWO SUNRISES: THE NORMAL ONE, AND THEN AGAIN WHEN GOLDIE WALKED ONTO THE SET.

HI, BABE! LET ME TELL YOU ABOUT MY TRIP TO INDIA...

DANA DELANY'S PERSONALITY WAS DIRECT AND UNABASHED. SHE WAS FUNNY, AND HER HUMOR HAD A BAWDY STREAK THAT ALWAYS KEPT US HIGHLY AMUSED. DANA AND I HAD A VERY MILD LOVE SCENE COMING UP. THE DAY BEFORE, WE HAD A MOVIE-SET LUNCH.

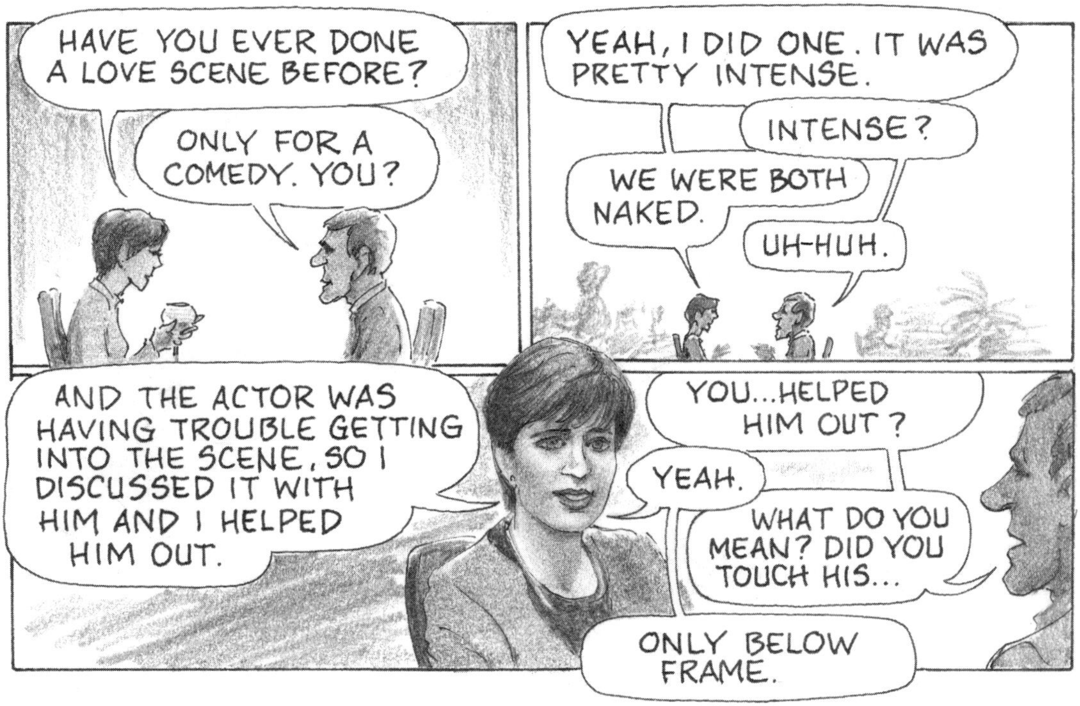
HAVE YOU EVER DONE A LOVE SCENE BEFORE?
ONLY FOR A COMEDY. YOU?
YEAH, I DID ONE. IT WAS PRETTY INTENSE.
INTENSE?
WE WERE BOTH NAKED.
UH-HUH.
AND THE ACTOR WAS HAVING TROUBLE GETTING INTO THE SCENE, SO I DISCUSSED IT WITH HIM AND I HELPED HIM OUT.
YOU...HELPED HIM OUT?
YEAH.
WHAT DO YOU MEAN? DID YOU TOUCH HIS...
ONLY BELOW FRAME.

WE DID OUR LOVE SCENE THE NEXT DAY, BUT IT WAS NOTHING COMPARED TO DANA'S.

THE SPANISH
PRISONER

DAVID MAMET WAS GREAT TO WORK WITH. HE WRITES AS PEOPLE SPEAK, WITH ALL THE *UMS* AND *AHS*, AND I HAD TO WORK HARD TO GET THEM EXACTLY RIGHT.

   HIS ONLY EVER DIRECTION TO ME WAS TO STAND UP STRAIGHT. HE WOULD INDICATE THIS BY PULLING UPWARD ON AN IMAGINARY STRING FROM THE TOP OF HIS HEAD.

I GET IT, I'M SLOUCHING.

WE SHOT IN THE FLORIDA KEYS. ONE NIGHT WHEN I WASN'T WORKING, I SAT IN A HAMMOCK, SIPPING A MAI TAI AND WATCHED A TOTAL ECLIPSE OF THE MOON.

THE MOVIE HAD A GREAT CAST, WITH CAMPBELL SCOTT, FELICITY HUFFMAN, AND BEN GAZZARA. I LOVED BEN AND HIS WIFE, ELKE. BEN WOULD REGALE ME WITH TALES OF MOVIES HE'D BEEN IN. THE FIRST NIGHT BEFORE SHOOTING, THERE WAS A PARTY ON THE BEACH.

THEN, A GUEST AT THE HOTEL WHERE WE WERE STAYING CAME UP TO BEN.

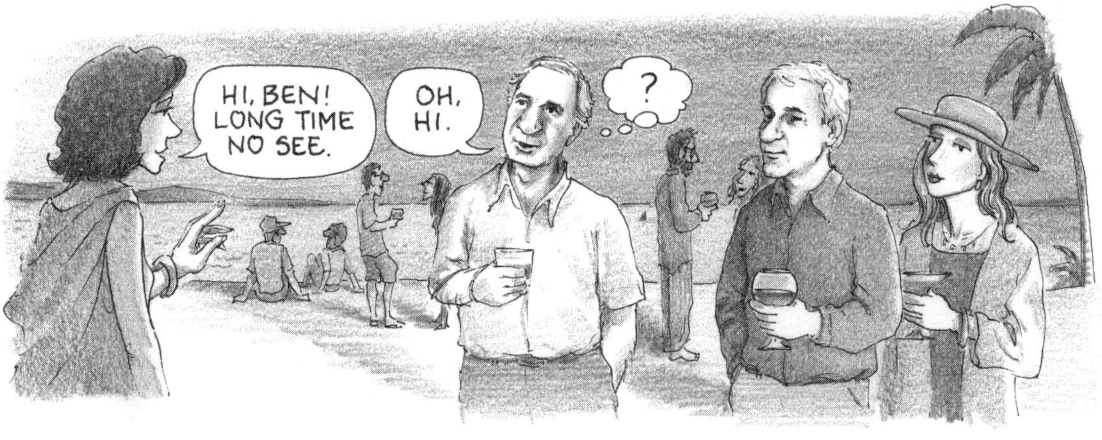
HI, BEN! LONG TIME NO SEE.
OH, HI.
?

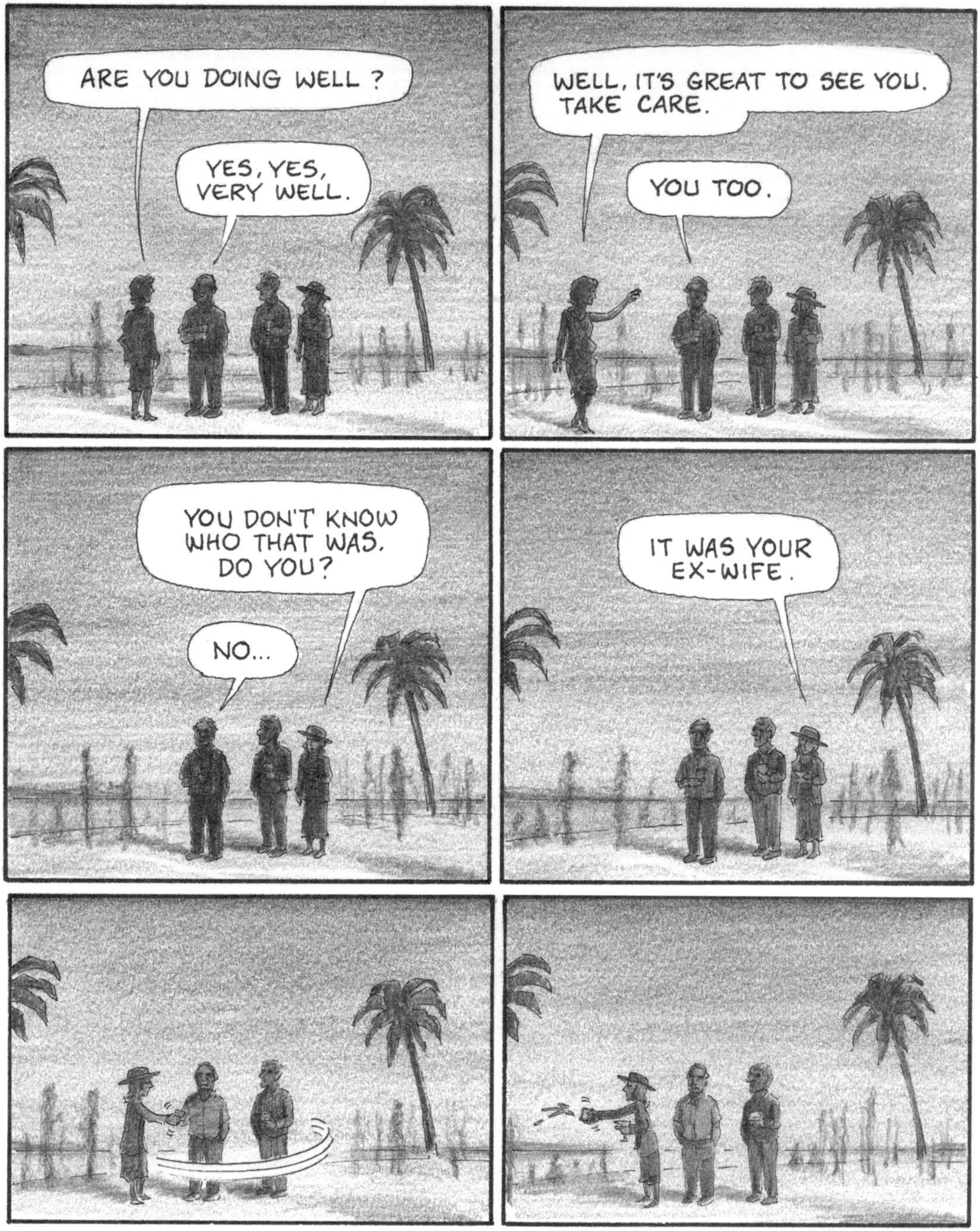
ARE YOU DOING WELL ?
YES, YES, VERY WELL.
WELL, IT'S GREAT TO SEE YOU. TAKE CARE.
YOU TOO.
YOU DON'T KNOW WHO THAT WAS. DO YOU?
NO...
IT WAS YOUR EX-WIFE.

STEVE MARTIN MADE ME AFRAID TO GO TO THE DENTIST

I AM ONE OF THE FEW ACTORS TO PLAY A SADISTIC DENTIST TWICE.
WAS STEVE IN *MARATHON MAN*?
THE FIRST WAS IN *LITTLE SHOP OF HORRORS*.
'CAUSE I'M A DENTIST!
THE SECOND WAS A SMALL, QUIRKY MOVIE CALLED *NOVOCAINE*.
I WOULD BE WORKING WITH HELENA BONHAM CARTER AND LAURA DERN, BOTH ACTRESSES I HAD LONG ADMIRED.

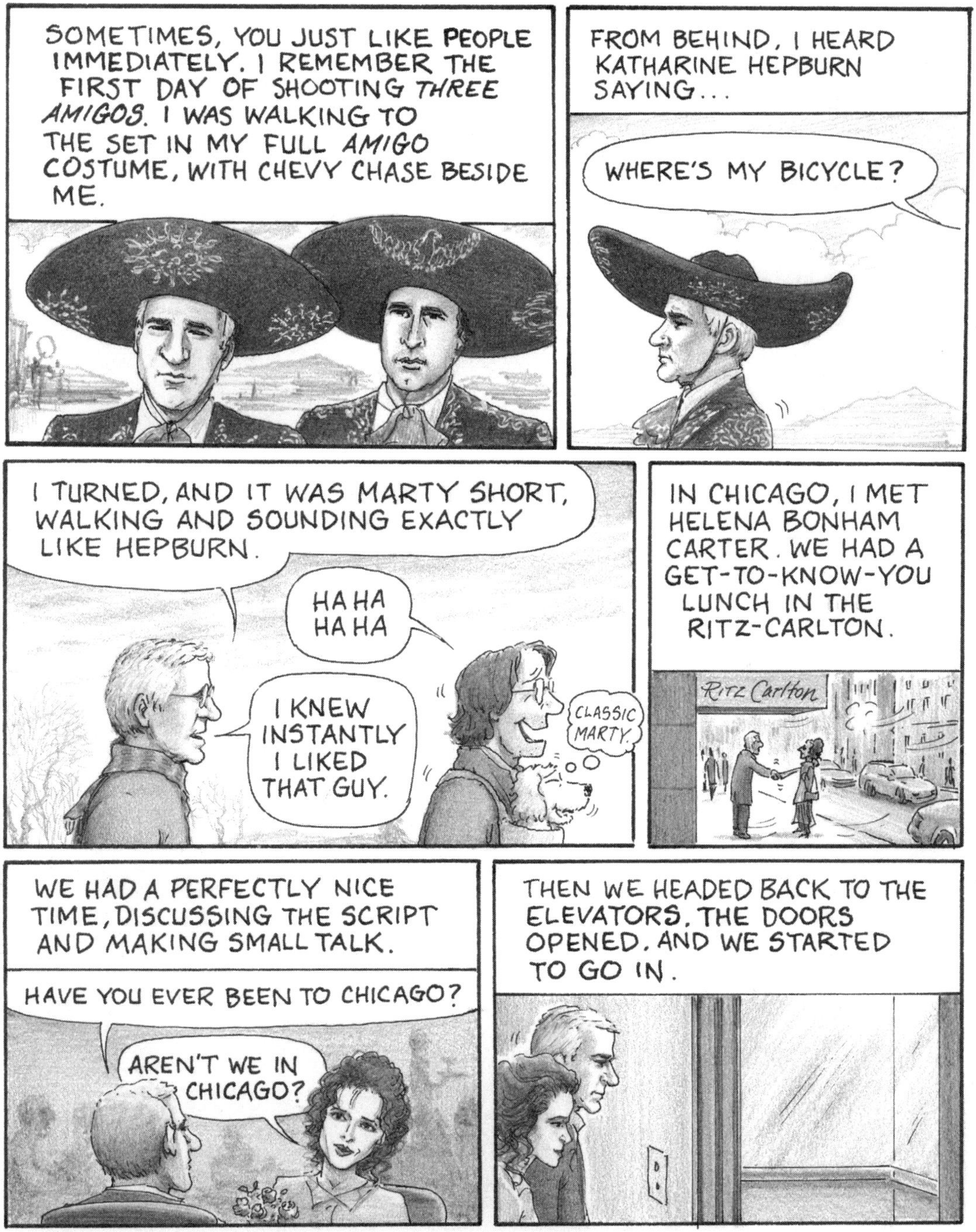
SOMETIMES, YOU JUST LIKE PEOPLE IMMEDIATELY. I REMEMBER THE FIRST DAY OF SHOOTING *THREE AMIGOS*. I WAS WALKING TO THE SET IN MY FULL *AMIGO* COSTUME, WITH CHEVY CHASE BESIDE ME.
FROM BEHIND, I HEARD KATHARINE HEPBURN SAYING...
WHERE'S MY BICYCLE?
I TURNED, AND IT WAS MARTY SHORT, WALKING AND SOUNDING EXACTLY LIKE HEPBURN.
HA HA HA HA
I KNEW INSTANTLY I LIKED THAT GUY.
CLASSIC MARTY.
IN CHICAGO, I MET HELENA BONHAM CARTER. WE HAD A GET-TO-KNOW-YOU LUNCH IN THE RITZ-CARLTON.
Ritz Carlton
WE HAD A PERFECTLY NICE TIME, DISCUSSING THE SCRIPT AND MAKING SMALL TALK.
HAVE YOU EVER BEEN TO CHICAGO?
AREN'T WE IN CHICAGO?
THEN WE HEADED BACK TO THE ELEVATORS. THE DOORS OPENED, AND WE STARTED TO GO IN.

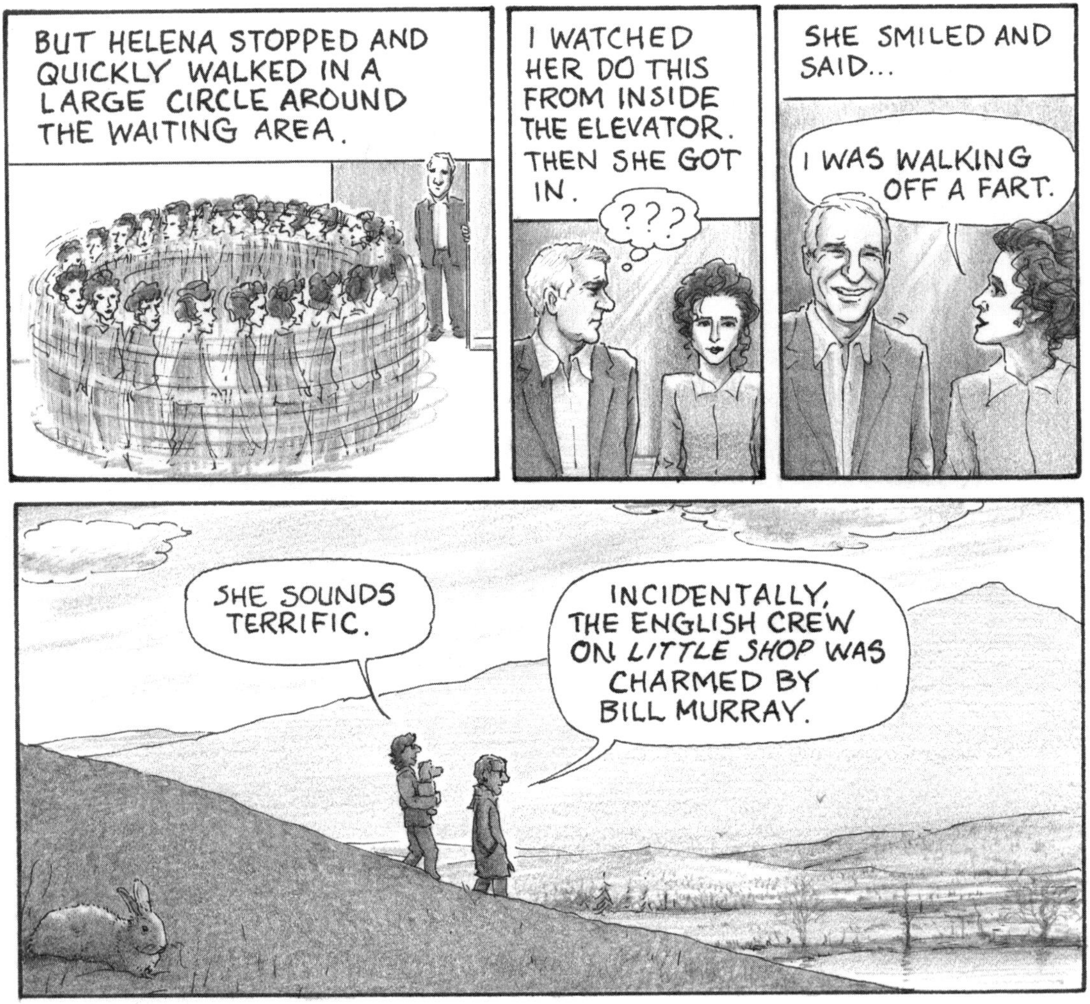
BUT HELENA STOPPED AND QUICKLY WALKED IN A LARGE CIRCLE AROUND THE WAITING AREA.
I WATCHED HER DO THIS FROM INSIDE THE ELEVATOR. THEN SHE GOT IN.
???
SHE SMILED AND SAID...
I WAS WALKING OFF A FART.
SHE SOUNDS TERRIFIC.
INCIDENTALLY, THE ENGLISH CREW ON *LITTLE SHOP* WAS CHARMED BY BILL MURRAY.

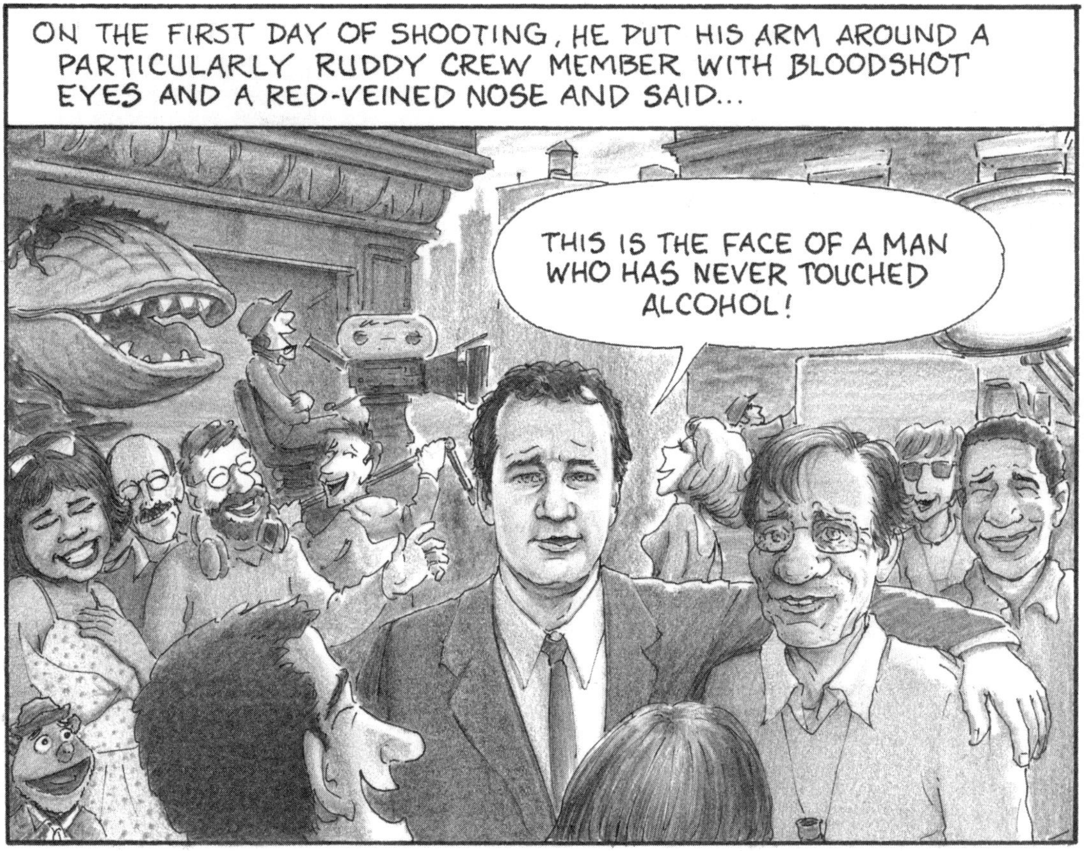
ON THE FIRST DAY OF SHOOTING, HE PUT HIS ARM AROUND A PARTICULARLY RUDDY CREW MEMBER WITH BLOODSHOT EYES AND A RED-VEINED NOSE AND SAID...
THIS IS THE FACE OF A MAN WHO HAS NEVER TOUCHED ALCOHOL!

JERRY SPRINGER

IN 2001, I WAS DOING THE *LATE SHOW WITH DAVID LETTERMAN* TO PROMOTE *CHEAPER BY THE DOZEN*. IT WAS A "TWO-SHOW DAY," MEANING THEY TAPE TWO SHOWS IN ONE DAY.

RIGHT THIS WAY, MISTER MARTIN. 14TH FLOOR.

NBC

GOING UP?

WHO'S THE GUEST ON THE OTHER SHOW?

JERRY SPRINGER.

I HAD AN INTENSE DISLIKE OF JERRY SPRINGER'S SHOW.

WOW, HIS SHOW PROMOTES VIOLENCE. HE USES PEOPLE AND MAKES THEM LOOK STUPID.

HE ELEVATES CRUDE RESOLUTIONS AND DIMINISHES RATIONAL THOUGHT.

IN FACT, JERRY SPRINGER IS RESPONSIBLE FOR PEOPLE TURNING AWAY FROM CULTURE IN AMERICA. IF I SEE JERRY, I'M GOING TO SAY SOMETHING.
DING!
IT'S HIM!
HEY, JERRY— HOW YOU DOIN'?

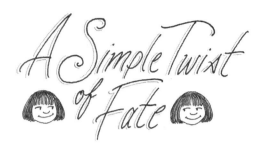

A Simple Twist of Fate

A SIMPLE TWIST OF FATE IS A LITTLE-KNOWN MOVIE OF MINE, DURING WHICH I LEARNED AN UNEXPECTED LIFE LESSON.

IN MOVIES, YOUNG CHILDREN ARE OFTEN PLAYED BY TWINS. IF ONE IS FUSSY, THE OTHER ONE CAN BE BROUGHT IN WITH NO DELAY IN PRODUCTION.

I WAS WORKING WITH TWO THREE-YEAR-OLD GIRLS. THEY WERE NEVER FUSSY. WE PUT THEM IN HOT-AIR BALLOONS, THEY NEVER FUSSED. THEY WORKED AT ODD HOURS, THEY NEVER FUSSED.

IN FACT, THEY WERE MYSTERIOUSLY, CONSTANTLY JOYFUL, AND ANY TINY TEARS WERE SOOTHED ALMOST IMMEDIATELY BY THEIR PARENTS.

ONE DAY I SAID TO THEIR PARENTS, "YOUR CHILDREN ARE SO EFFORTLESSLY HAPPY. HOW DO YOU RAISE THEM?"

THEY LOOKED BEWILDERED, AS THOUGH THEY HAD NEVER CONSIDERED IT BEFORE.

FINALLY, THE FATHER OFFERED UP A TENTATIVE ANSWER: "WELL, WE USE HUMOR."

WHEN, AT LAST, I HAD MY OWN DAUGHTER, I WAS DETERMINED TO DO THE SAME.

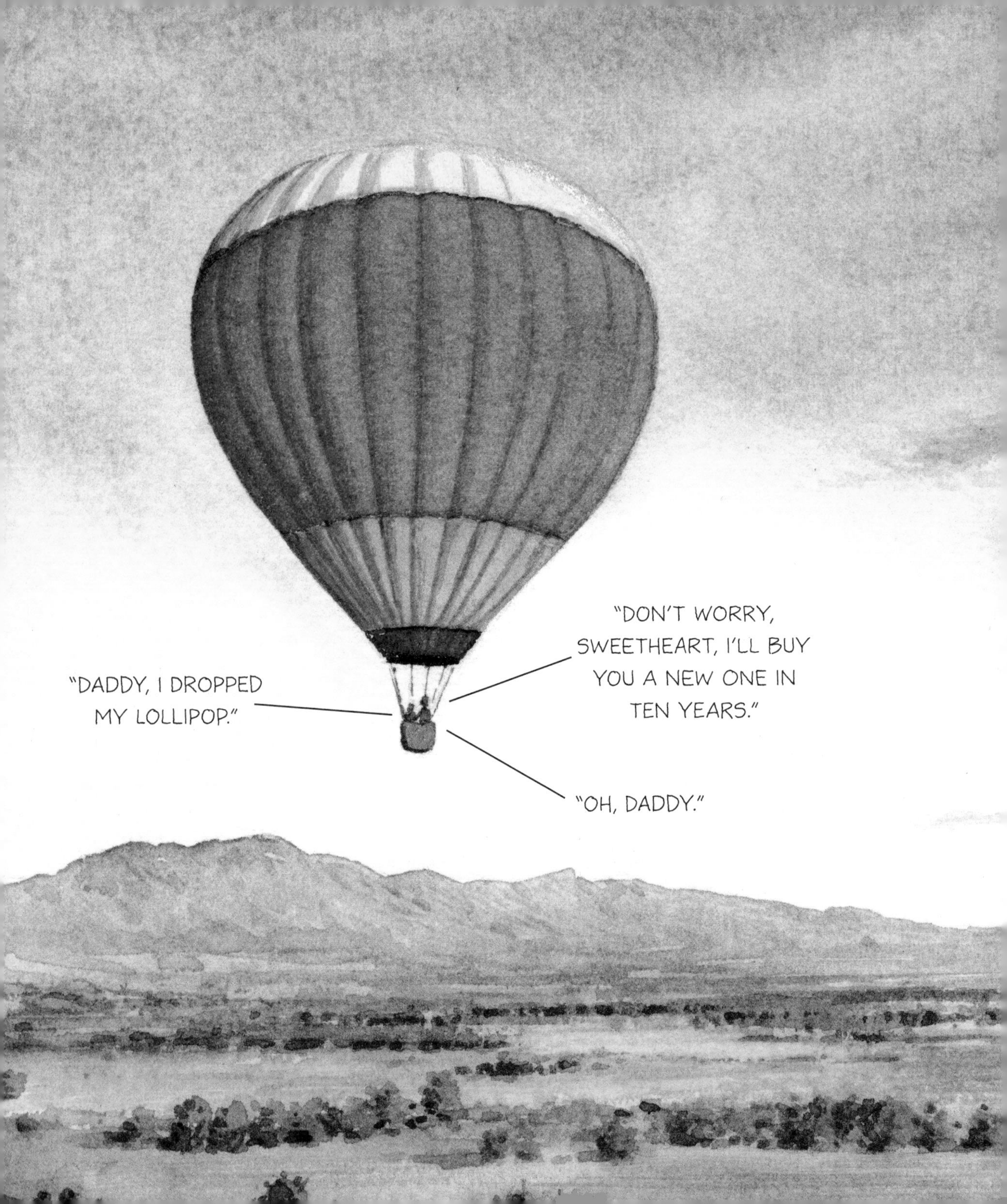
"DADDY, I DROPPED MY LOLLIPOP."
"DON'T WORRY, SWEETHEART, I'LL BUY YOU A NEW ONE IN TEN YEARS."
"OH, DADDY."

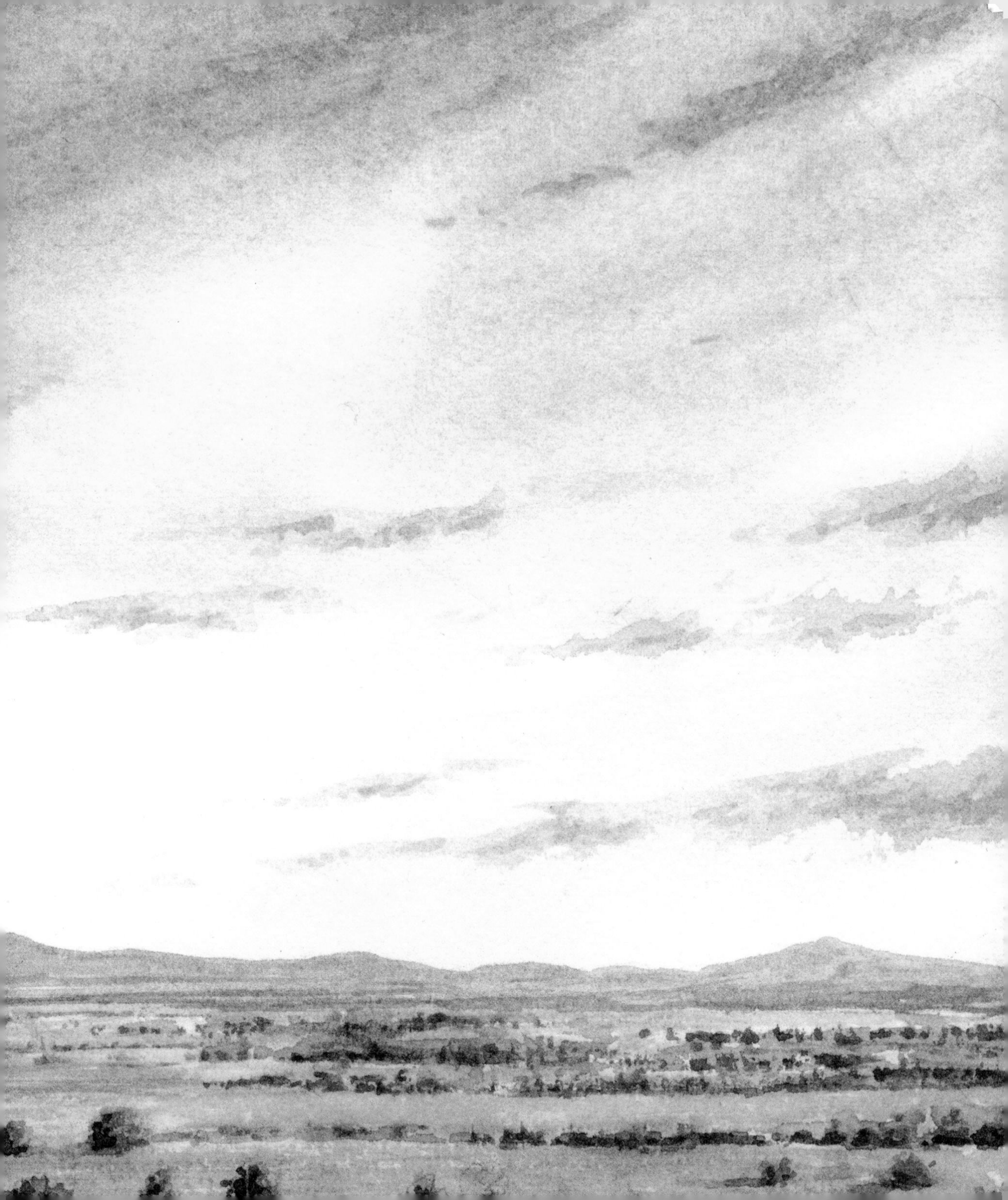

WHY I STOPPED DOING MOVIES

I LOST INTEREST IN MOVIES AT EXACTLY THE SAME TIME THE MOVIES LOST INTEREST IN ME.

FOR FOUR DECADES, MY LOVE OF MOVIES HAD BUFFERED THE PERIODIC STINGING REVIEWS, PROTECTED AGAINST THE JUDGMENT OF THE BOX OFFICE, AND JUSTIFIED THE DEMANDING TIME COMMITMENTS THAT EXCLUDED FAMILY AND FRIENDS.

BUT EVENTUALLY, YOU RUN OUT OF GAS.

I MADE MORE THAN FORTY MOVIES, BARELY PAUSING TO BREATHE, AND HERE'S WHY: I BELIEVED I HAD TO MAKE FORTY TO GET FIVE GOOD ONES.

FIFTEEN YEARS AGO, I QUIETLY EASED INTO LOWER-PROFILE AND LESS-COSTLY ENDEAVORS. RENEWING AN INTEREST IN WRITING SONGS AND PLAYING BANJO, I WENT ON THE ROAD DOING A MUSIC SHOW WITH THE STEEP CANYON RANGERS THAT HAD A BIG DOSE OF COMEDY.

YOUNG BANJO PLAYERS OFTEN ASK ME FOR ADVICE ON HOW TO GET PEOPLE TO LISTEN TO THEIR MUSIC, AND I ALWAYS TELL THEM, "BE VERY CREATIVE AND ALREADY BE FAMOUS."

I RESUMED WRITING FOR THEATRE, A BROADWAY COMEDY CALLED *METEOR SHOWER*, AND A MUSICAL WITH EDIE BRICKELL, *BRIGHT STAR*.

THEN, I FORTUITOUSLY TEAMED UP WITH MY OLD FRIEND MARTY SHORT, AND WE STARTED TOURING, DOING A BIG COMEDY SHOW ACROSS THE UNITED STATES, THE UNITED KINGDOM, AND AUSTRALIA.

MARTY AND I BECAME A FULL-TIME COMEDY TEAM. WITHOUT REALIZING IT, I HAD SLOWLY REENTERED STAND-UP, BUT THIS TIME, AS A GROWN-UP. OUR STAGE SHOW LED TO A TV SERIES, *ONLY MURDERS IN THE BUILDING*, AND MARTY AND I MADE A NEW FRIEND IN SELENA GOMEZ.

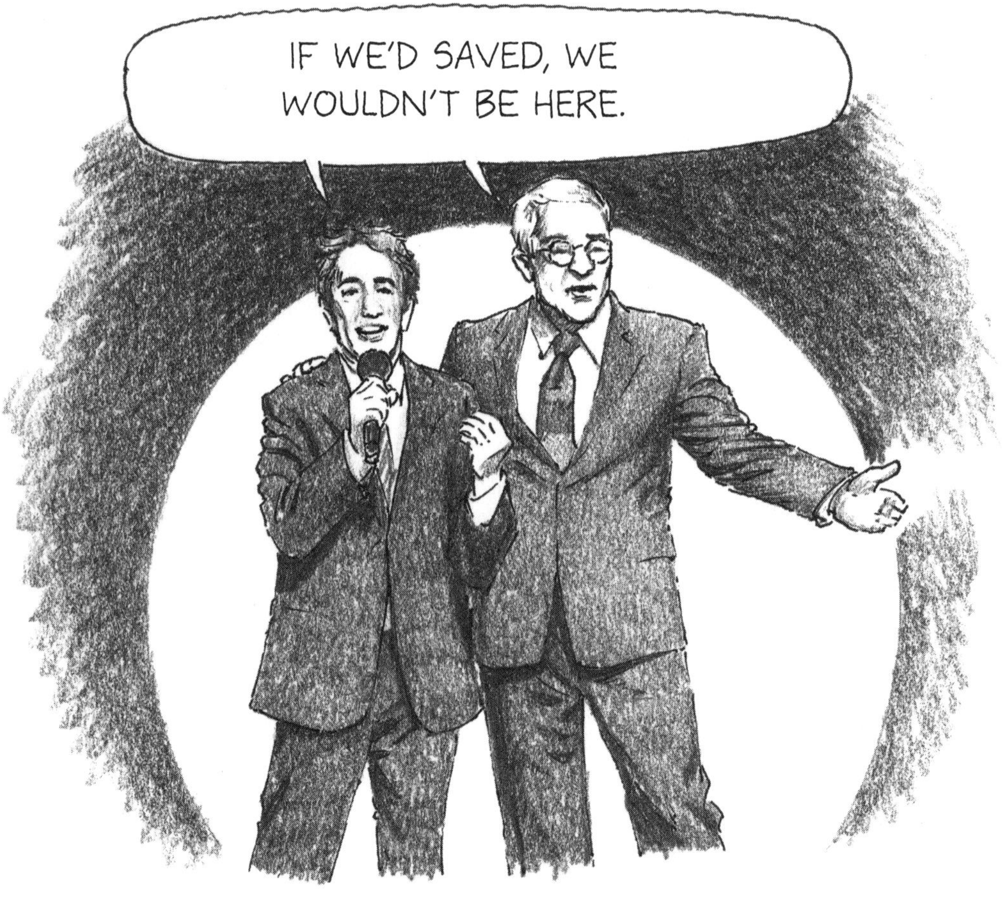
IF WE'D SAVED, WE WOULDN'T BE HERE.

THE TV SHOW BECAME MY CREATIVE OUTLET: I DIDN'T NEED MOVIES ANYMORE.

MY FRIEND, THE ACTOR CHARLES GRODIN, WAS A DEEPLY FUNNY PERSON. HE ONCE TOLD ME, WHEN HE STARTED OUT AND WAS LOOKING FOR A PUBLICIST, "I SIGNED ON WITH ELIZABETH TAYLOR'S PUBLICIST; WHO COULD BE BETTER, RIGHT?" HE FOUND OUT LATER THAT ELIZABETH HAD HIRED THE PUBLICIST TO KEEP HER NAME *OUT* OF THE PAPERS.

I DID THE SAME WHEN I CALLED MY MOVIE AGENT AND SAID, "CAN YOU NOT GET ME ANY MOVIES?"

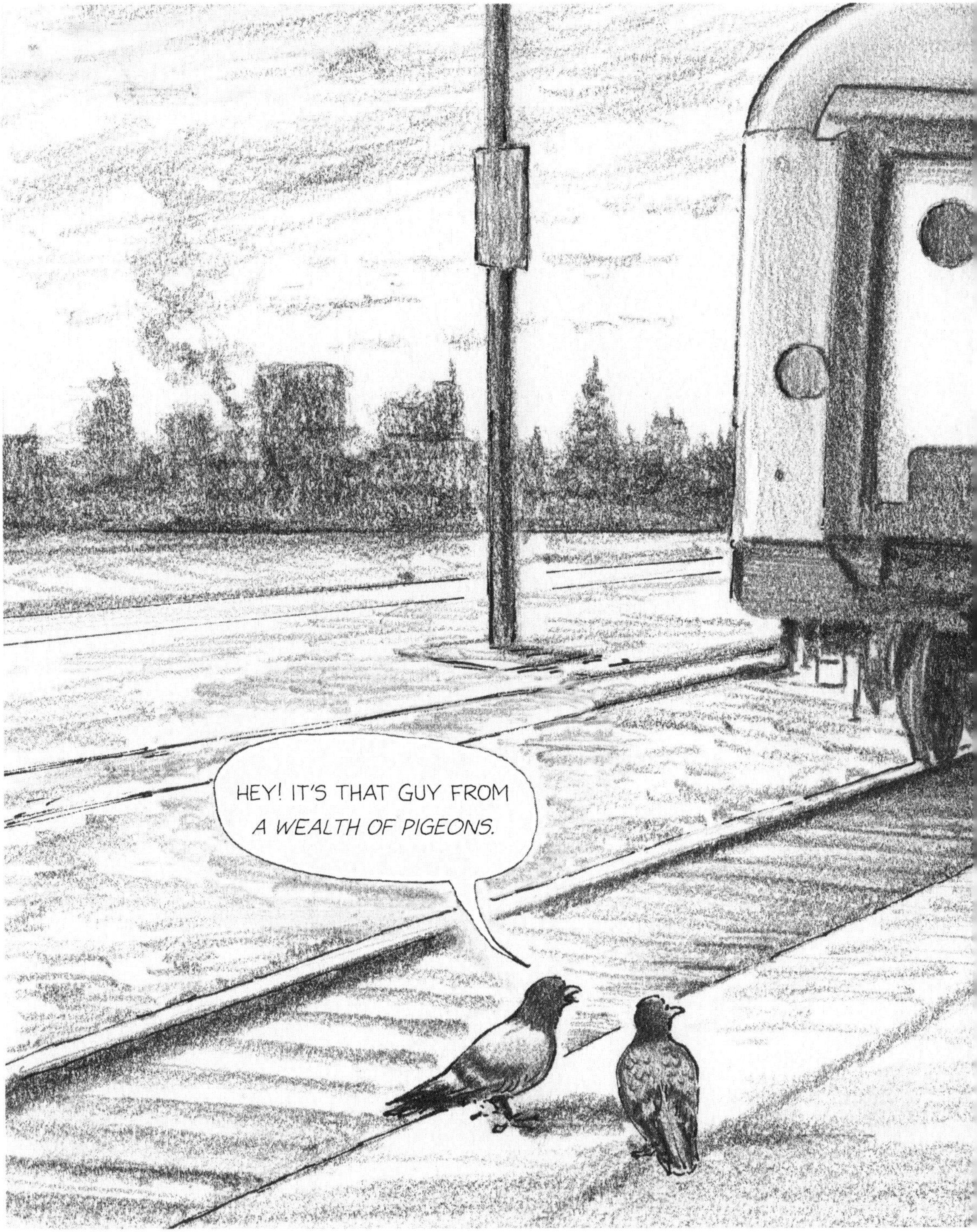
HEY! IT'S THAT GUY FROM *A WEALTH OF PIGEONS.*

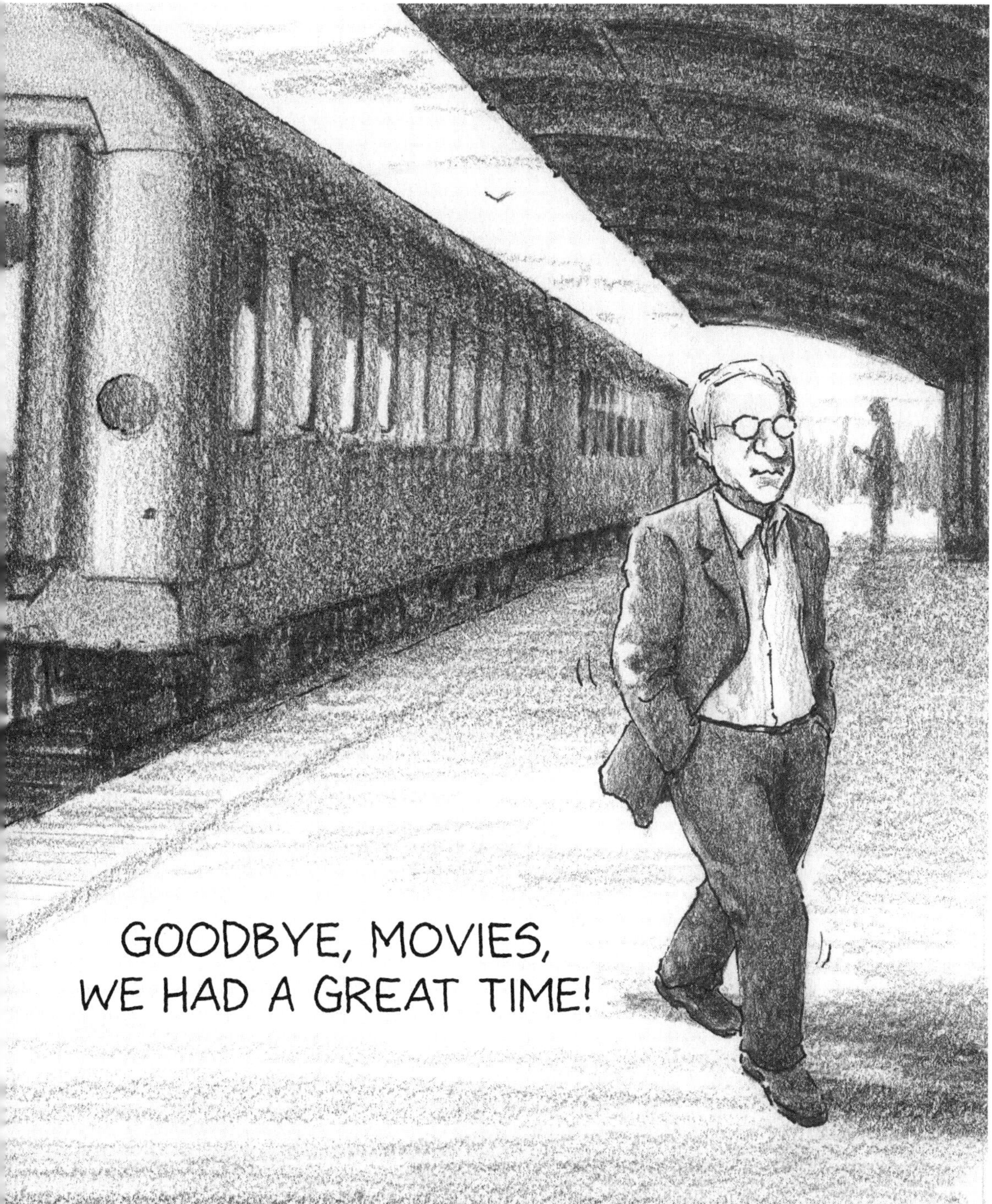
GOODBYE, MOVIES,
WE HAD A GREAT TIME!

And
OTHER
DIVERSIONS

DAN AND MAURICE WERE GREAT AT FINISHING EACH OTHER'S SENTENCES...
SO DAN SAYS, "WHAT KIND OF PIE SHOULD WE GET AND I SAID BLUEBERRY
PERIOD. END QUOTATION.
Bliss/Martin

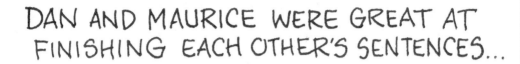

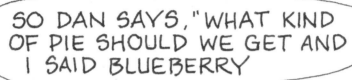

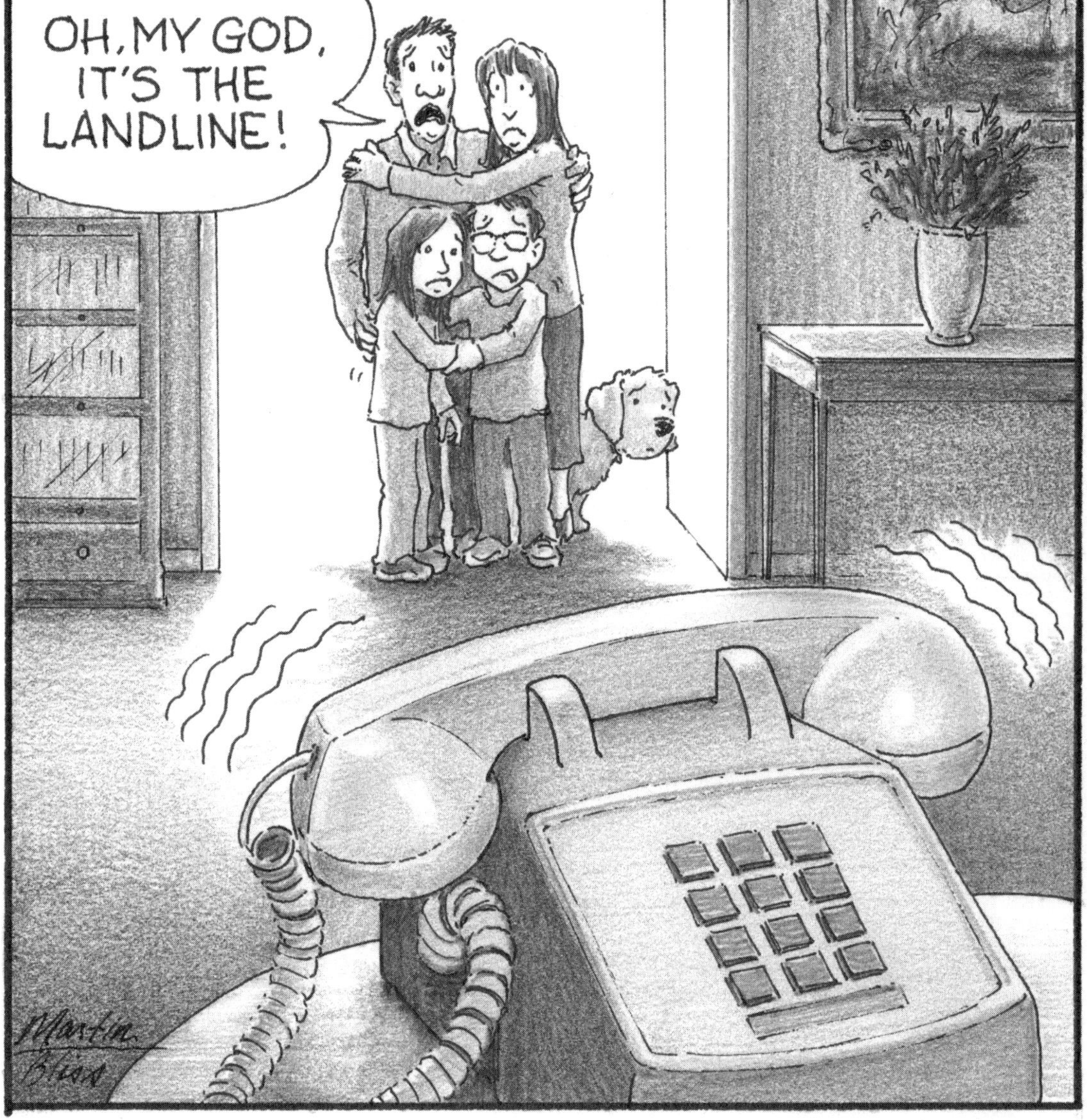
OH, MY GOD, IT'S THE LANDLINE!

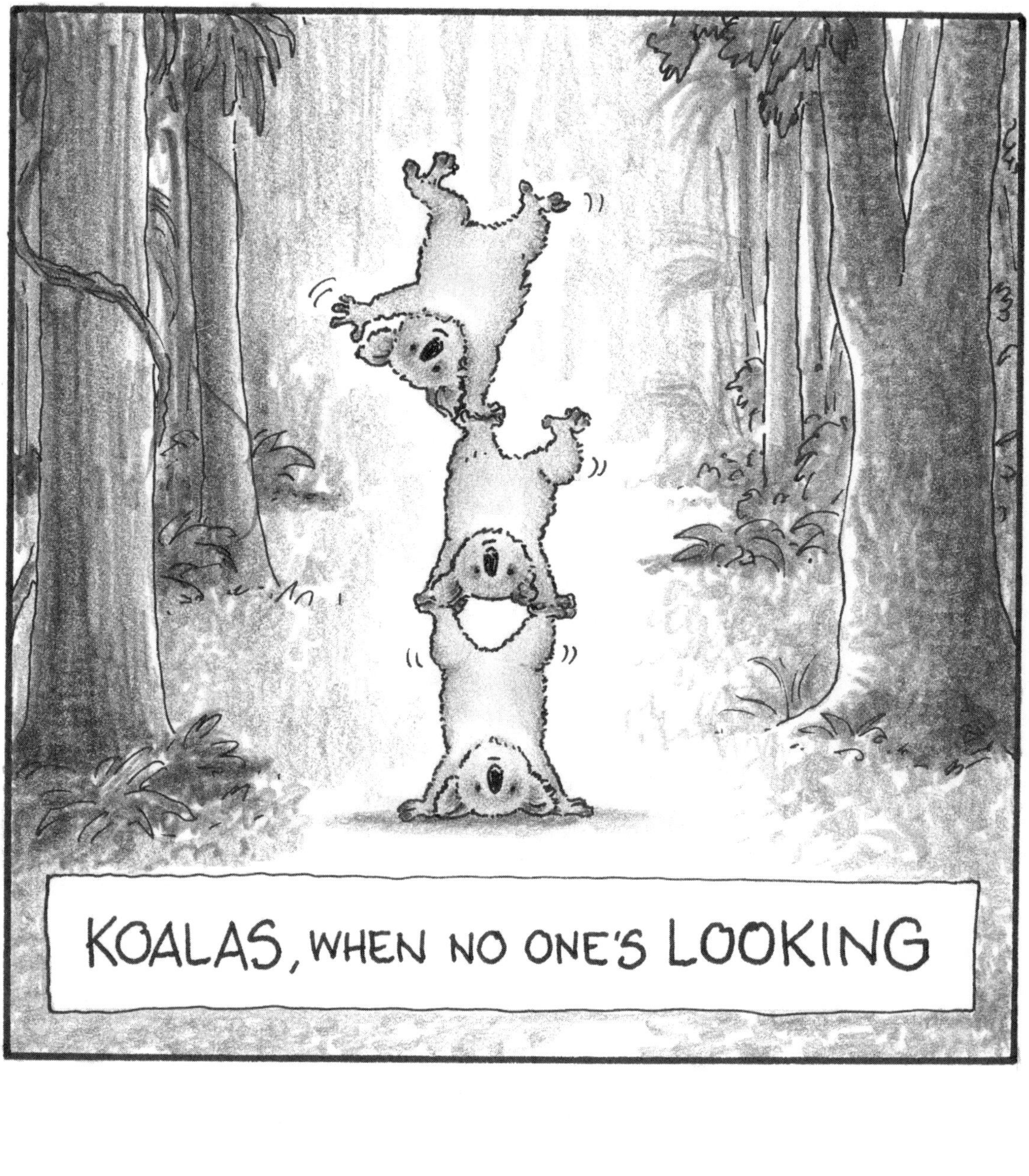
KOALAS, WHEN NO ONE'S LOOKING

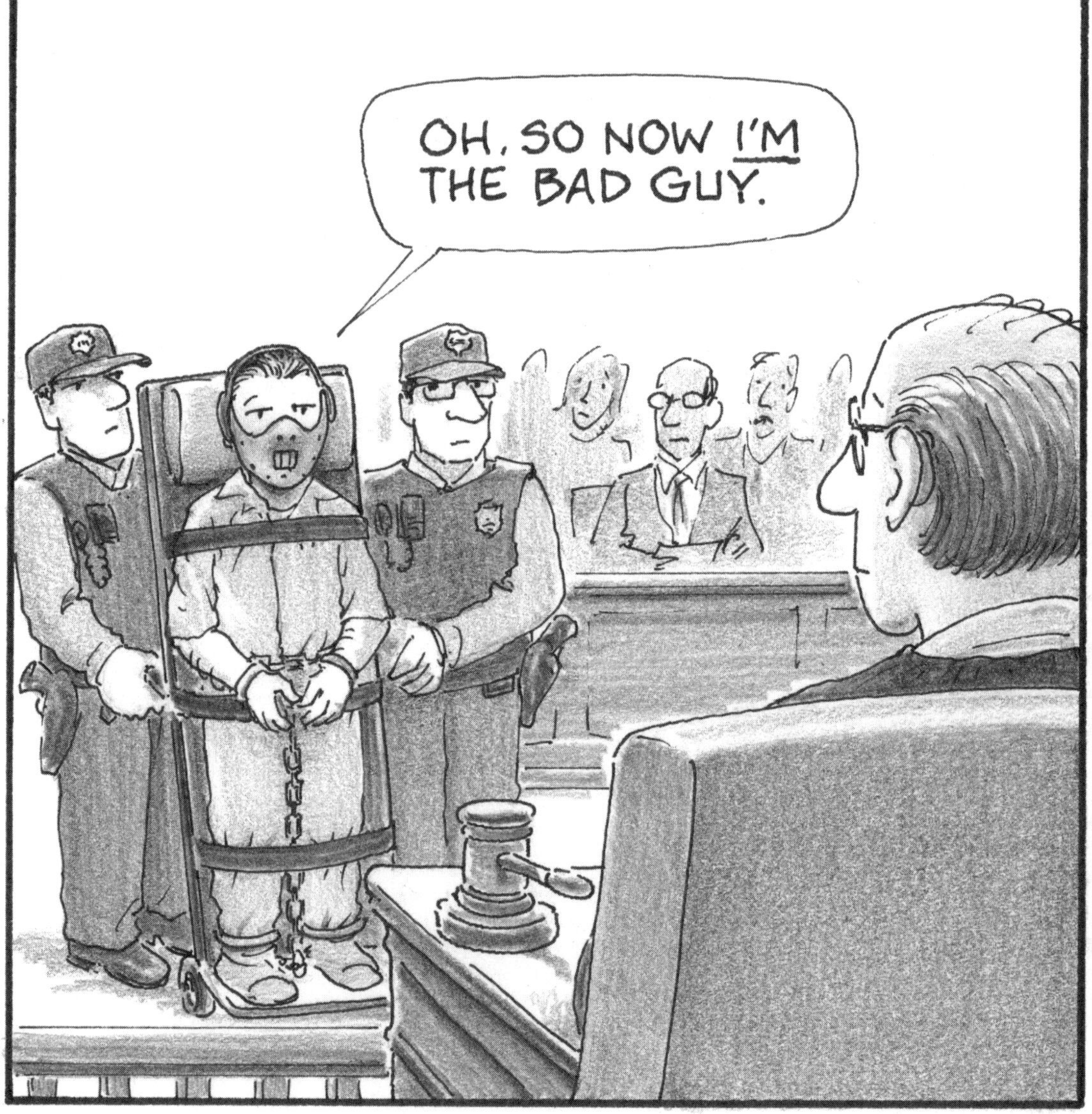
OH, SO NOW I'M THE BAD GUY.

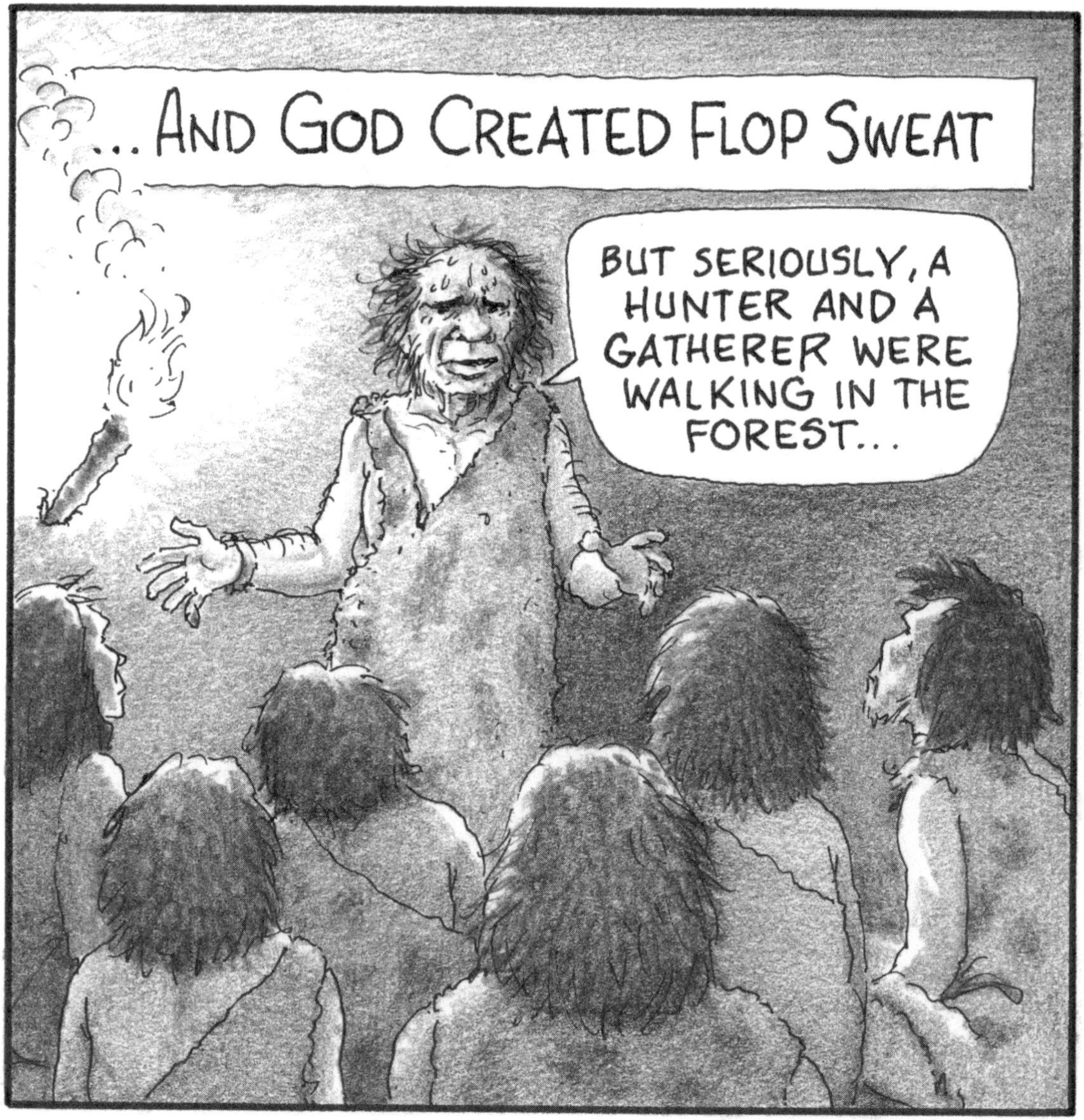
...AND GOD CREATED FLOP SWEAT
BUT SERIOUSLY, A HUNTER AND A GATHERER WERE WALKING IN THE FOREST...

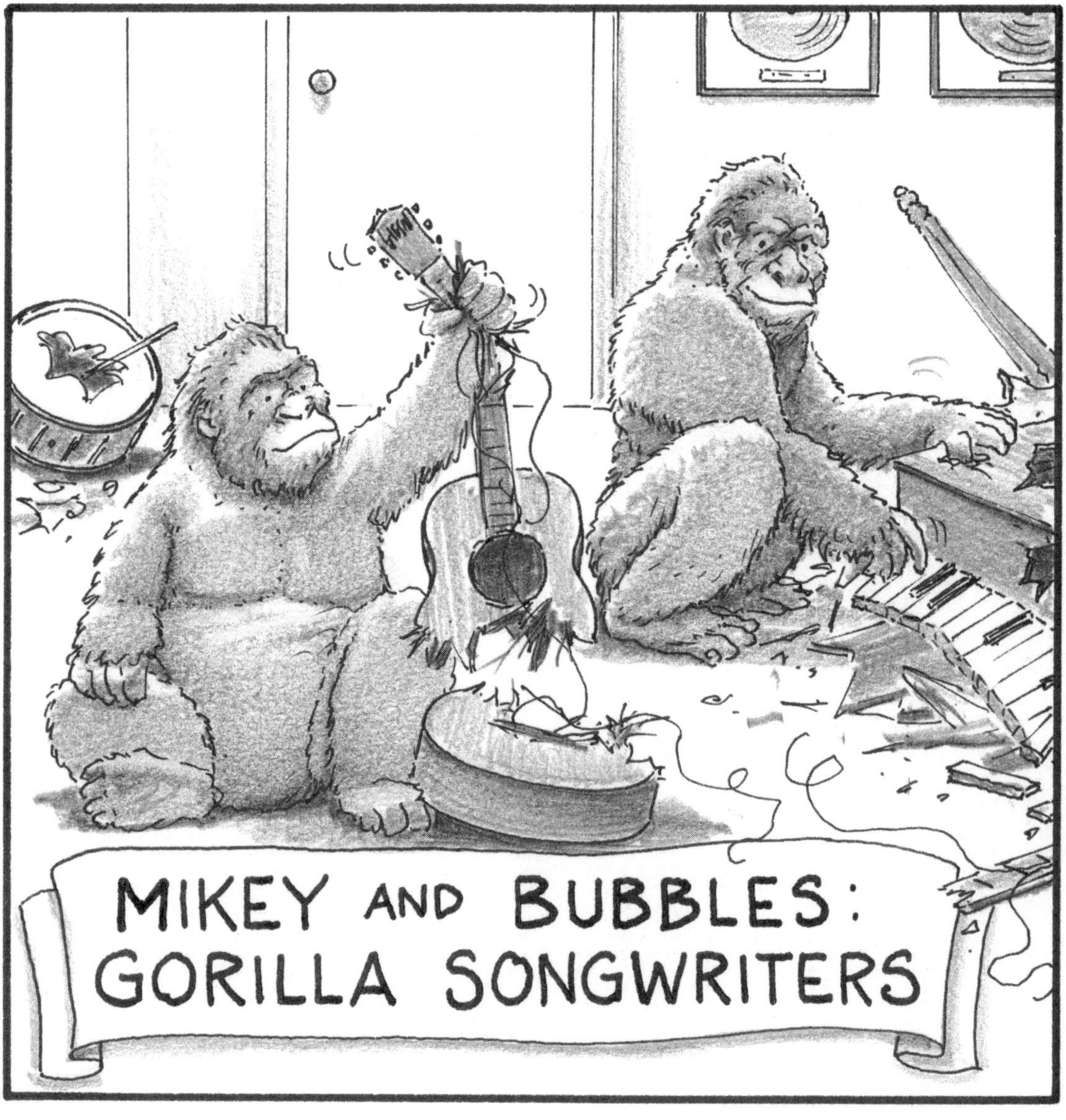
MIKEY AND BUBBLES:
GORILLA SONGWRITERS

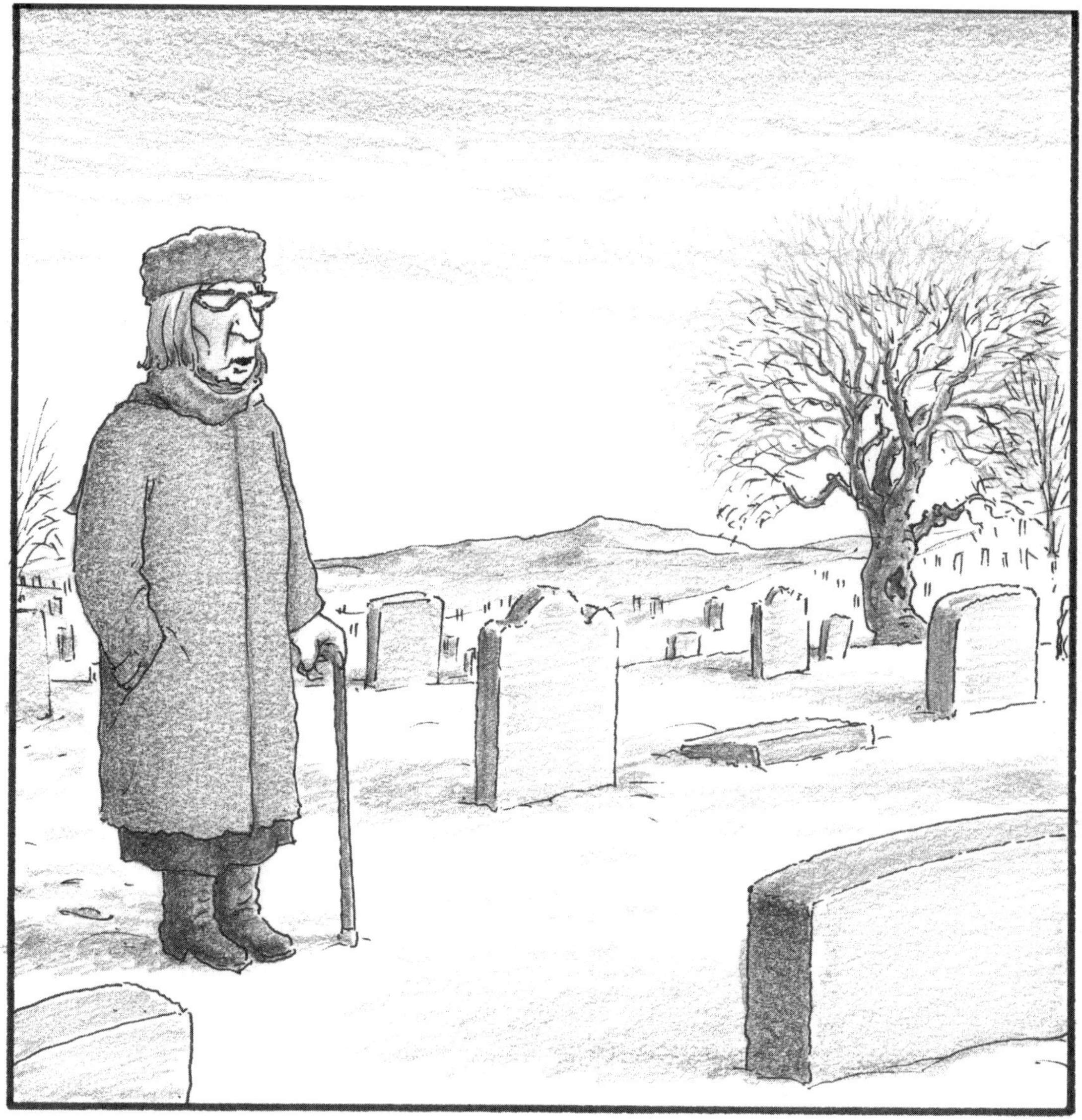

"AND NOW, DEAR, I'M GOING TO HUM ANNOYINGLY AND SEE HOW *YOU* LIKE IT."

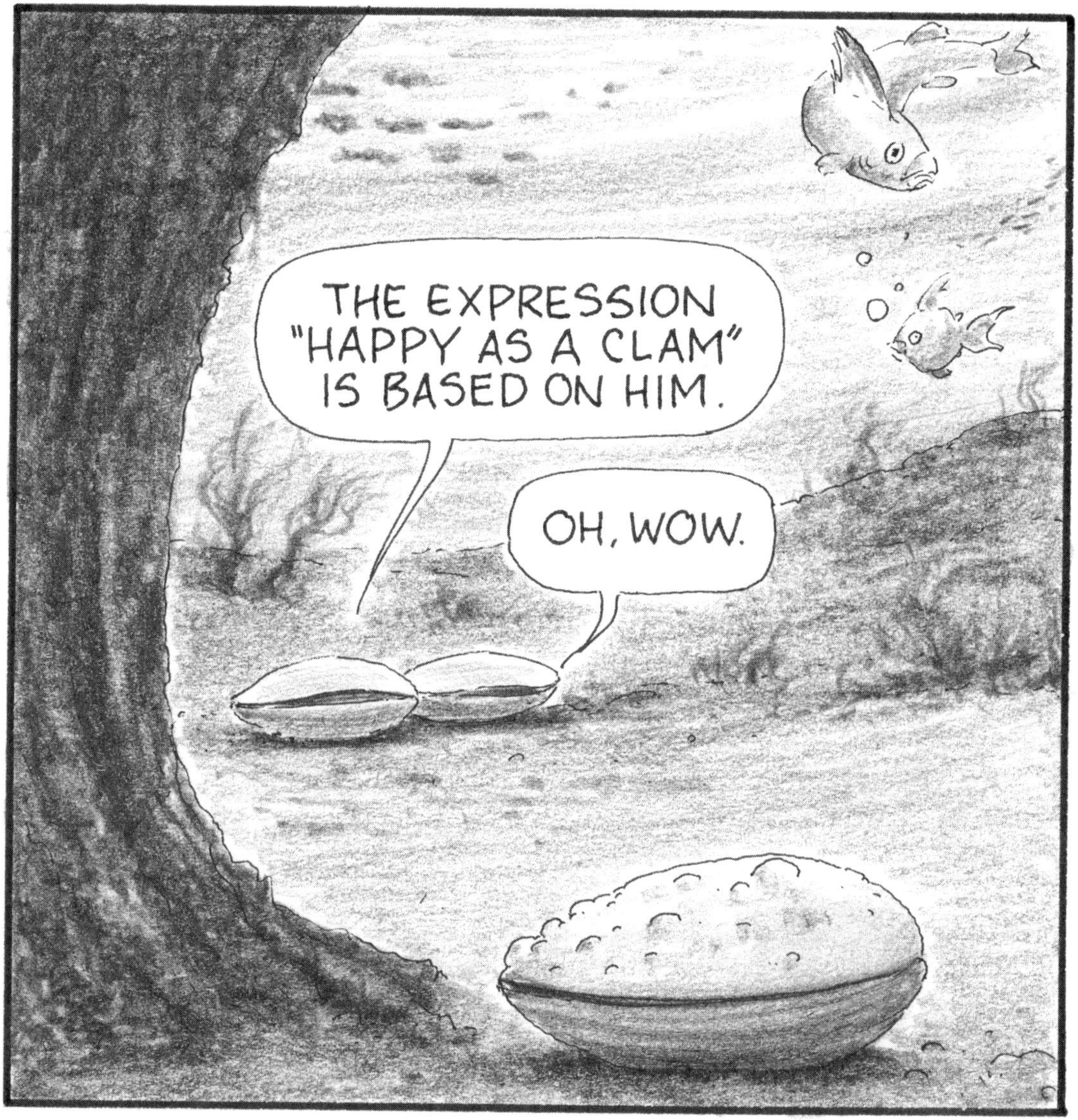
THE EXPRESSION "HAPPY AS A CLAM" IS BASED ON HIM.
OH, WOW.

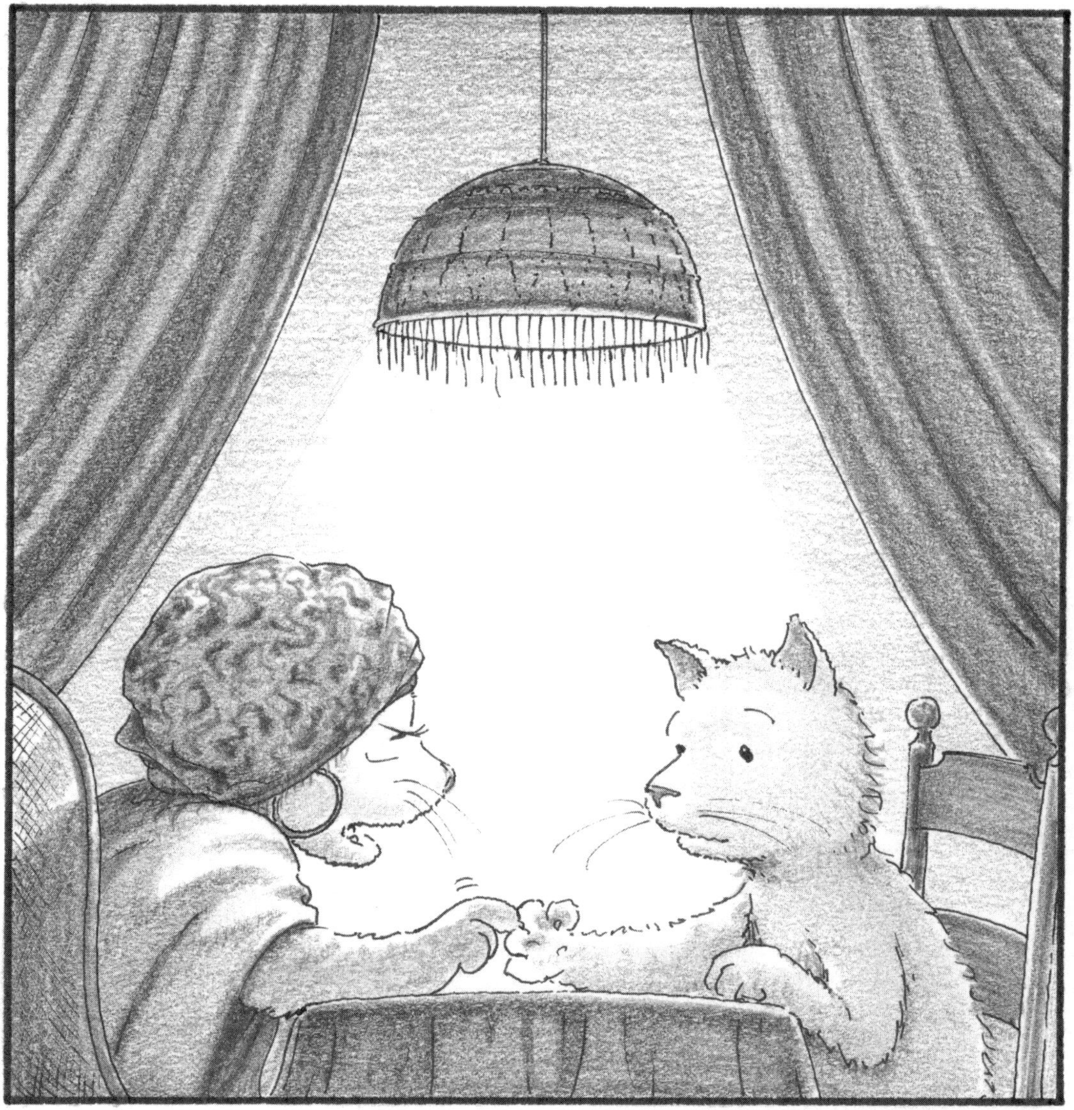

"YOU WILL MEET A TALL, MYSTERIOUS STRANGER—YOU WILL RUB FUR ON HIS PANT LEG."

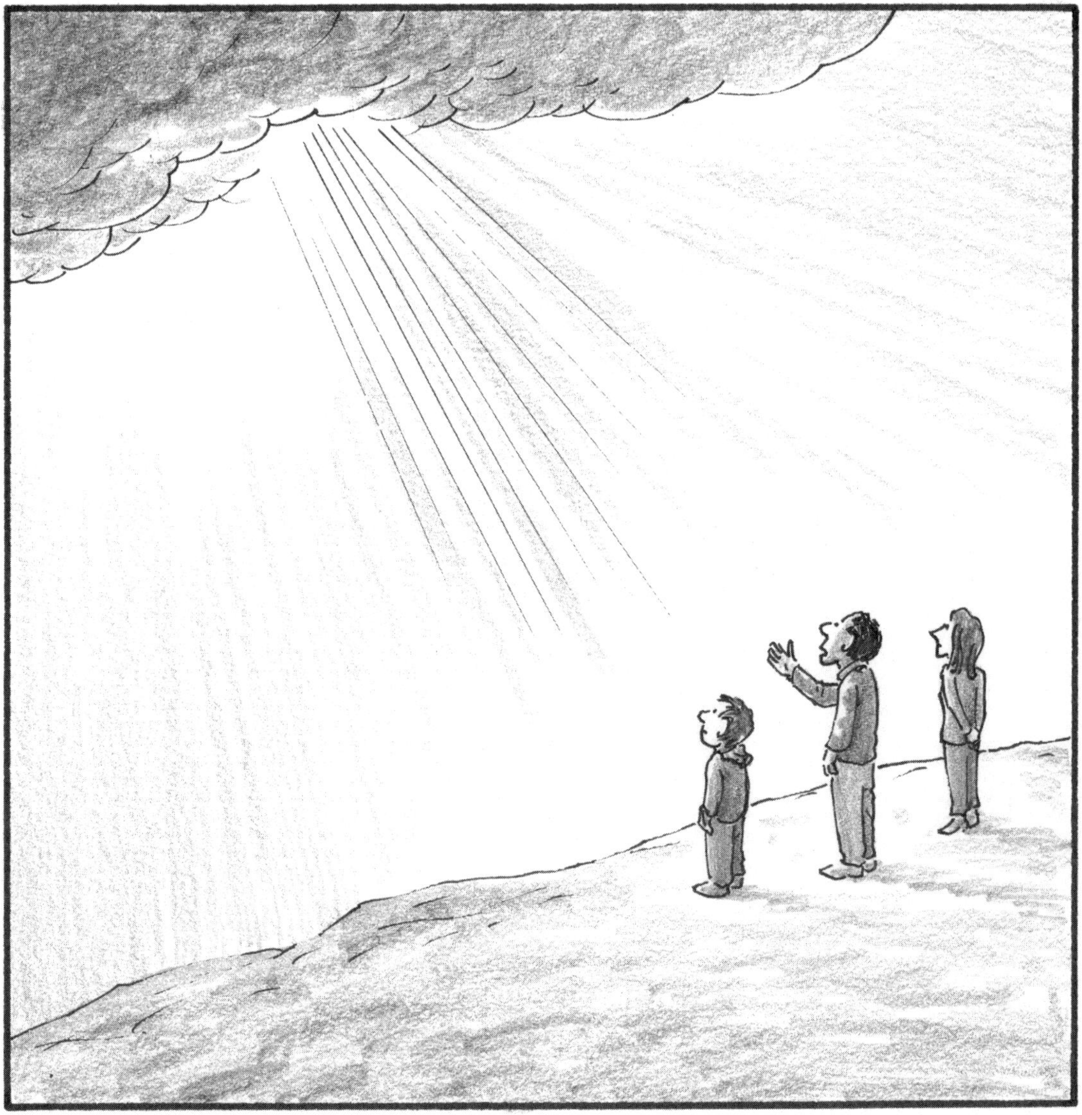

"WE'RE HAVING PRIVACY CONCERNS WITH YOUR OMNISCIENCE."

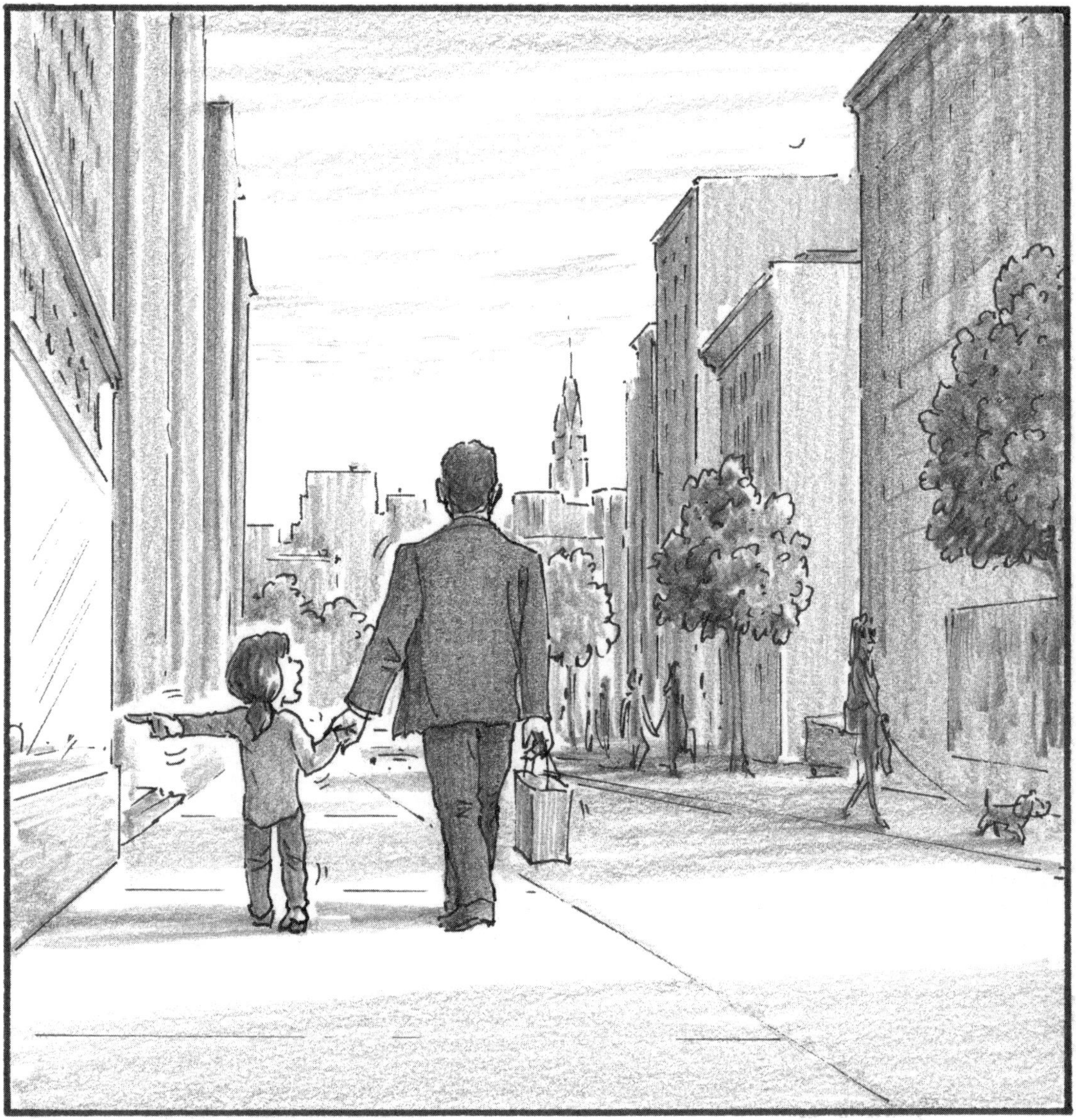

"WAIT, DADDY! I'M THAT WINDOW'S TARGET AUDIENCE!"

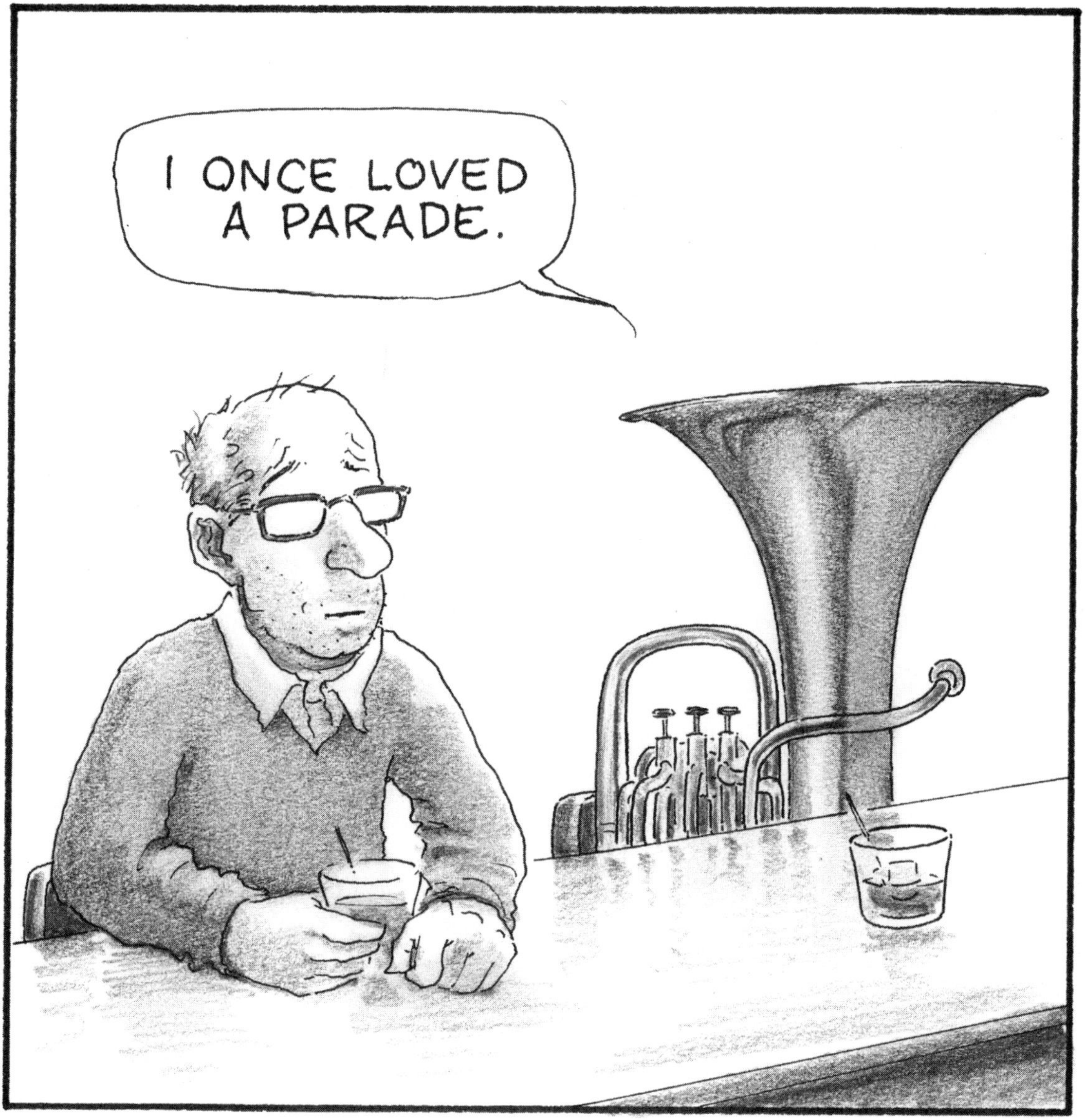
I ONCE LOVED A PARADE.

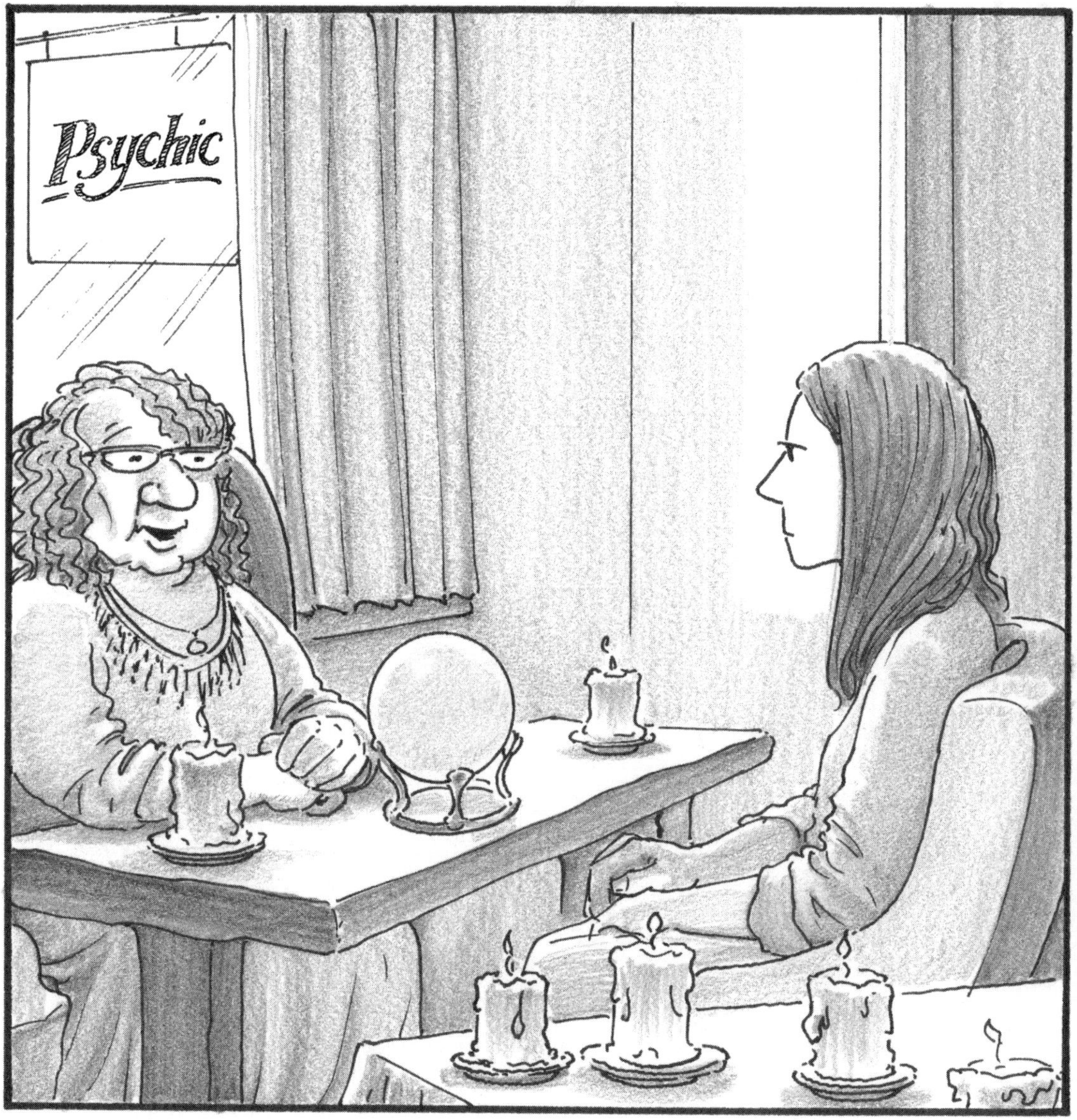
Psychic

"SO, WHAT BRINGS YOU HERE TODAY?"

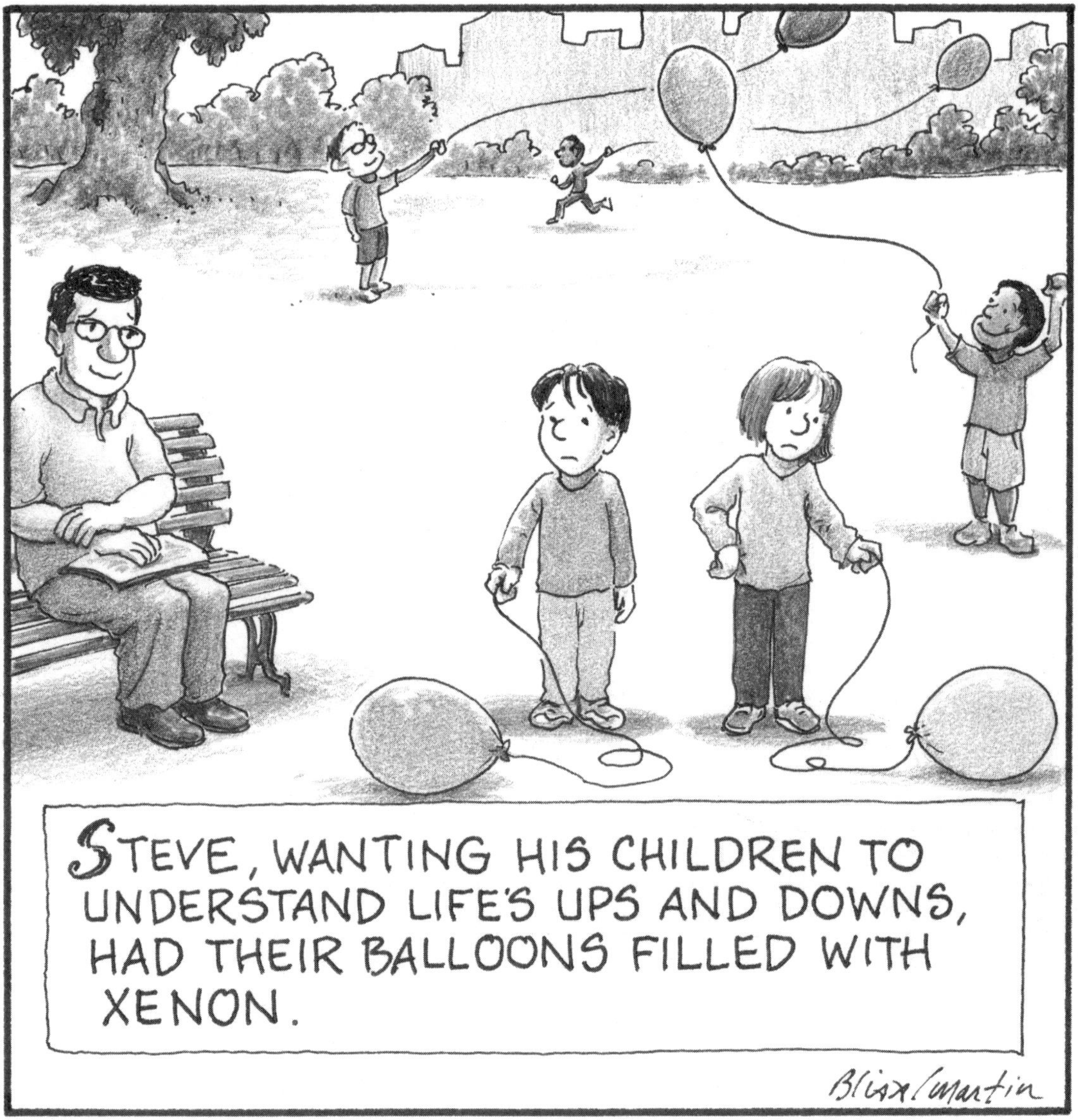
STEVE, WANTING HIS CHILDREN TO UNDERSTAND LIFE'S UPS AND DOWNS, HAD THEIR BALLOONS FILLED WITH XENON.
Bliss/Martin

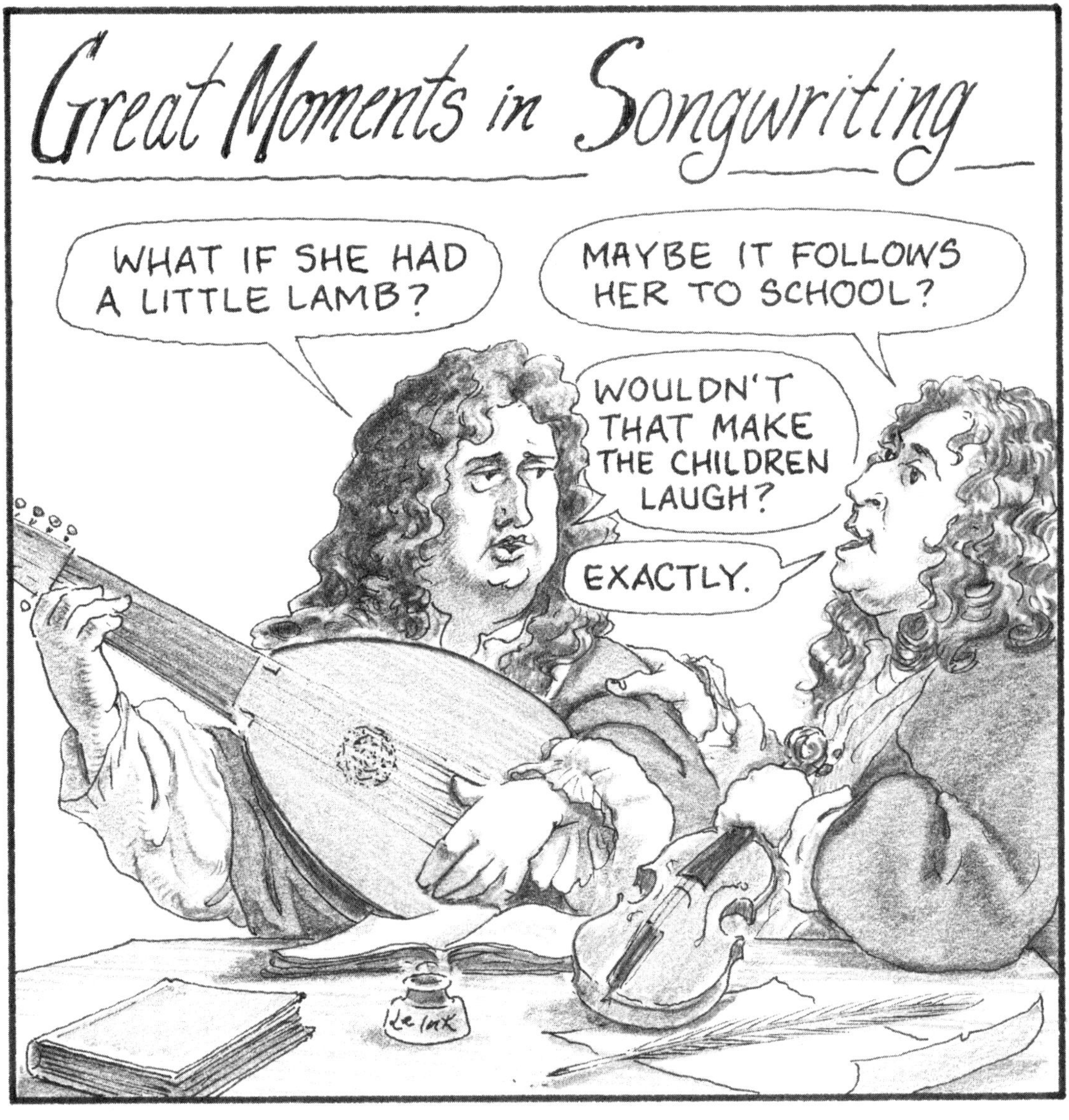
Great Moments in Songwriting
WHAT IF SHE HAD A LITTLE LAMB?
MAYBE IT FOLLOWS HER TO SCHOOL?
WOULDN'T THAT MAKE THE CHILDREN LAUGH?
EXACTLY.

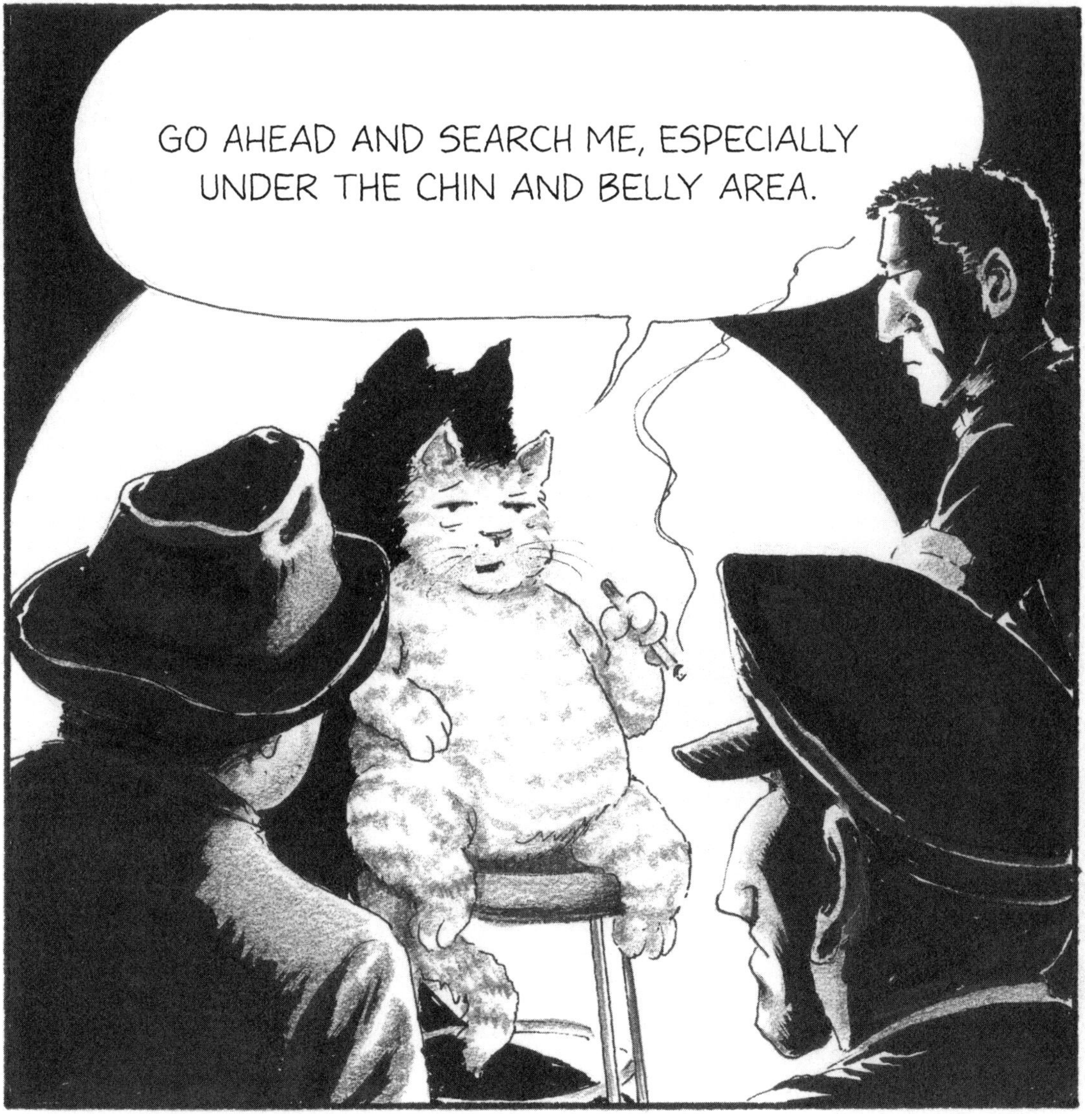
GO AHEAD AND SEARCH ME, ESPECIALLY UNDER THE CHIN AND BELLY AREA.

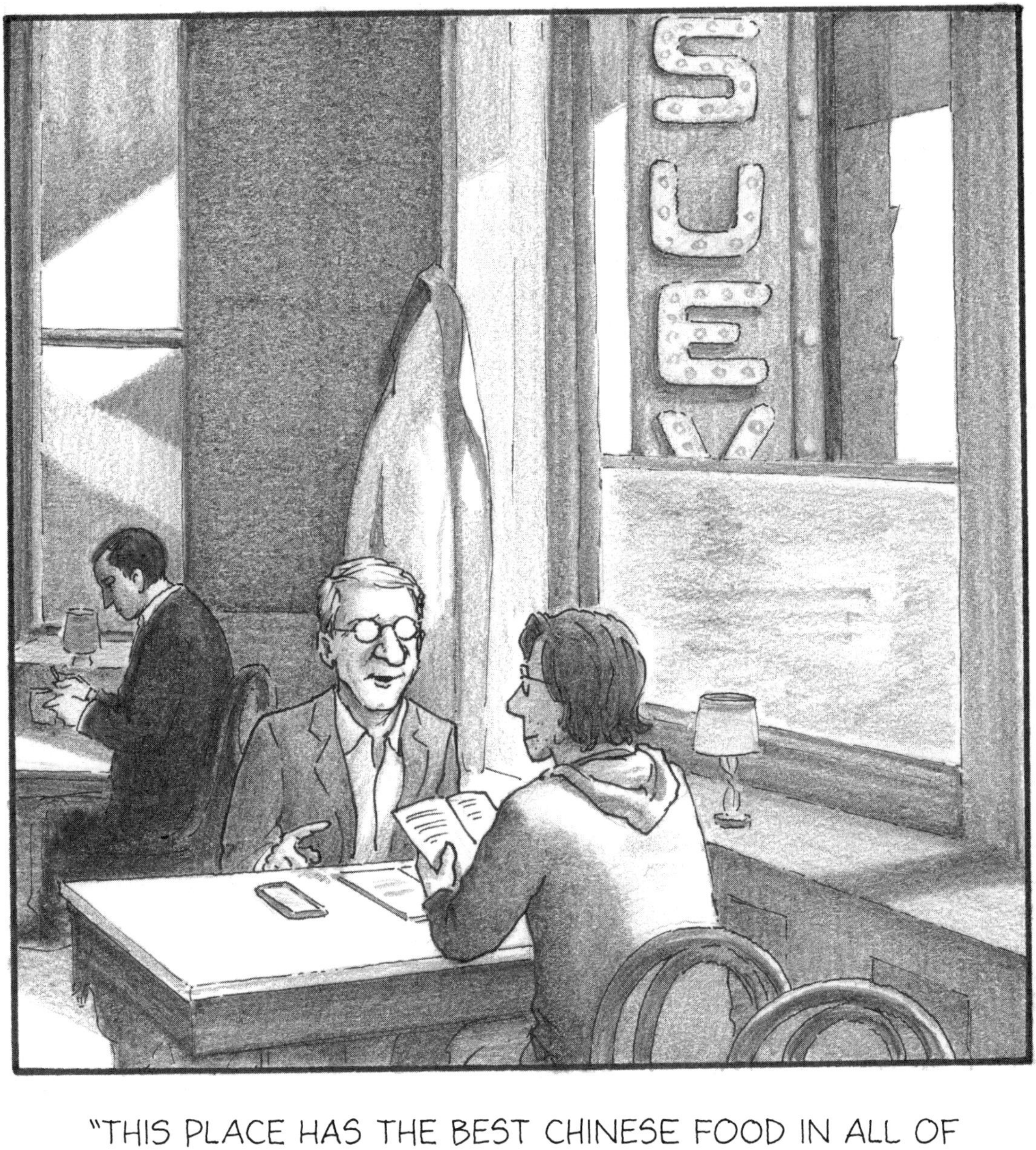
SUE

"THIS PLACE HAS THE BEST CHINESE FOOD IN ALL OF HOPPER'S PAINTINGS."

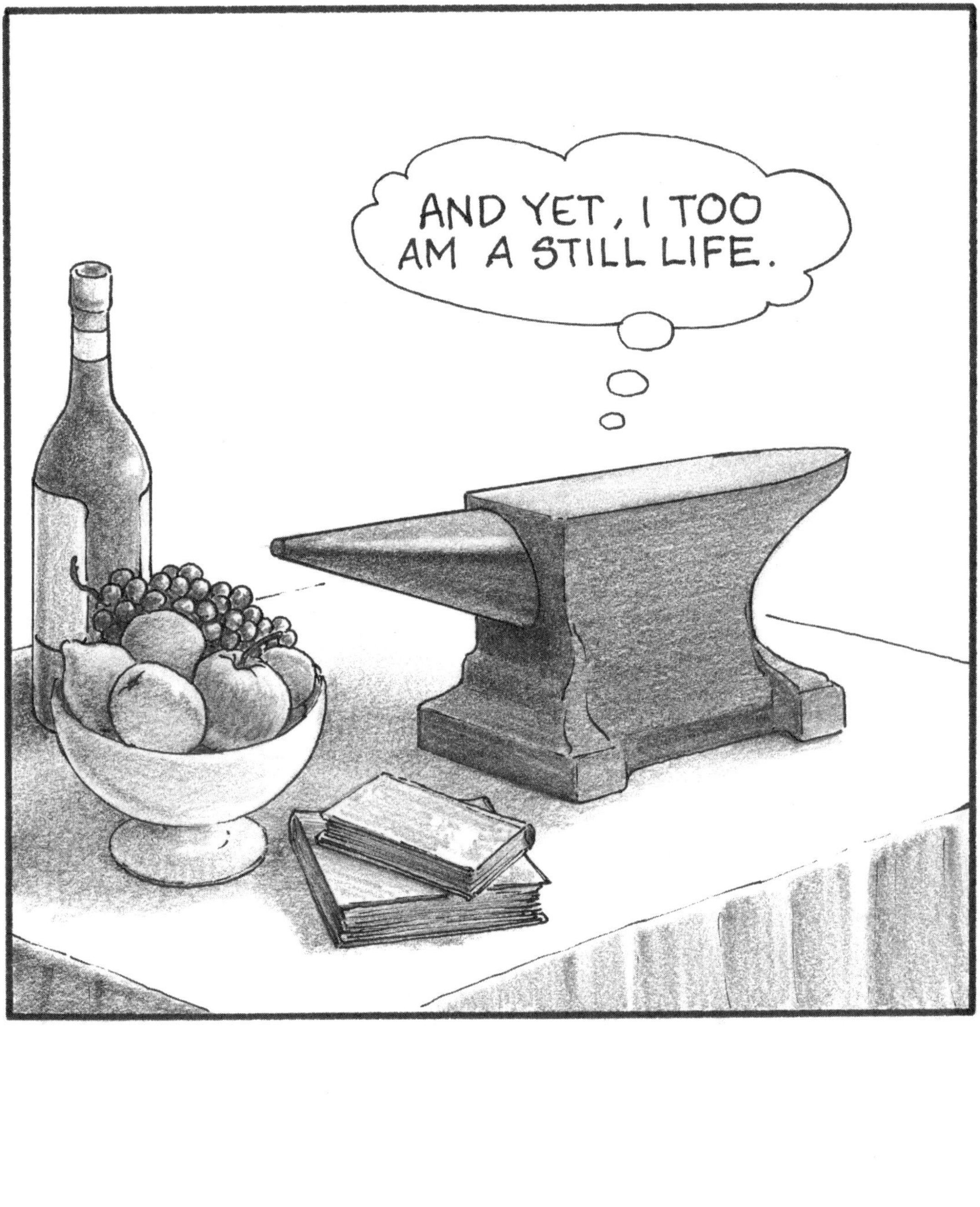
AND YET, I TOO
AM A STILL LIFE.

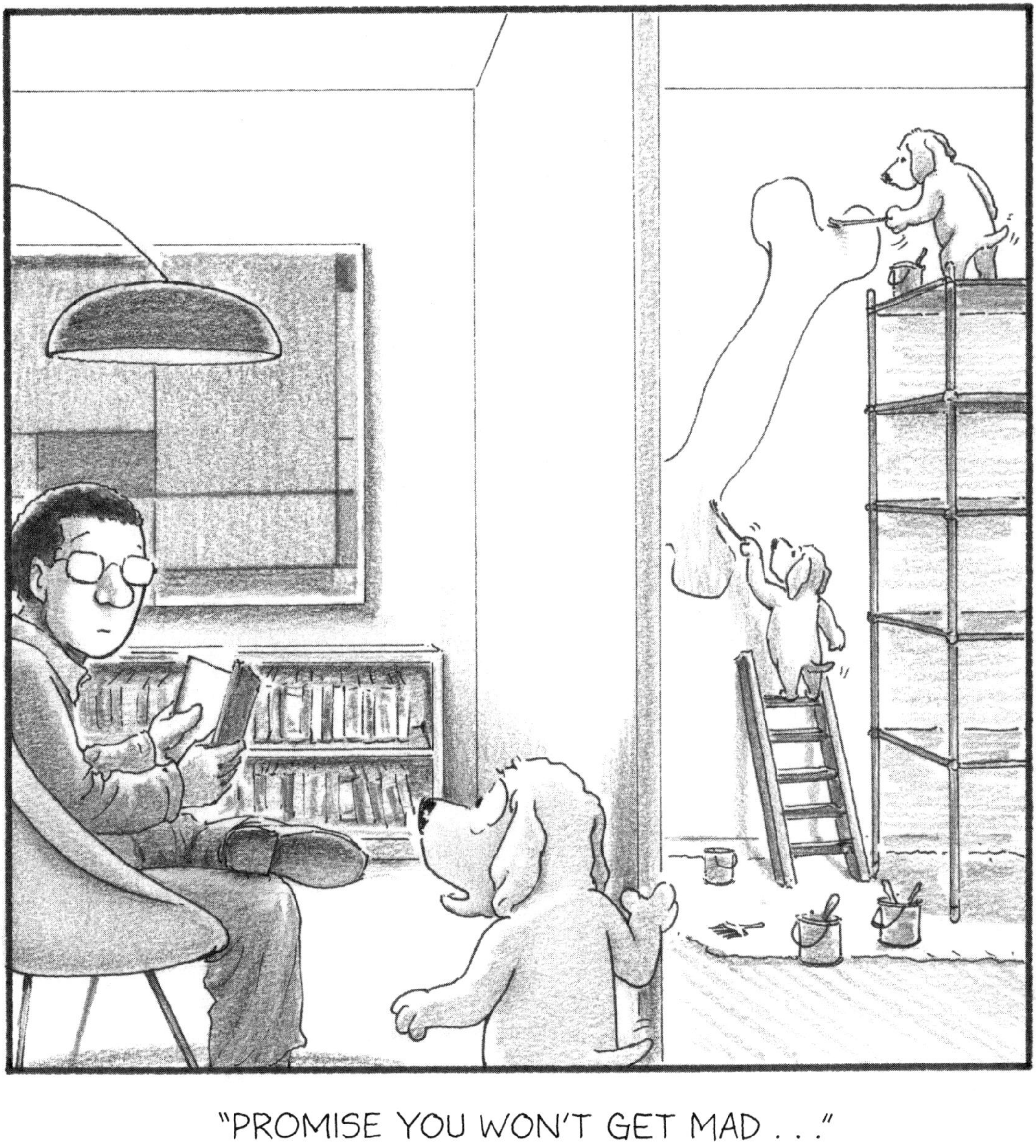

"PROMISE YOU WON'T GET MAD . . ."

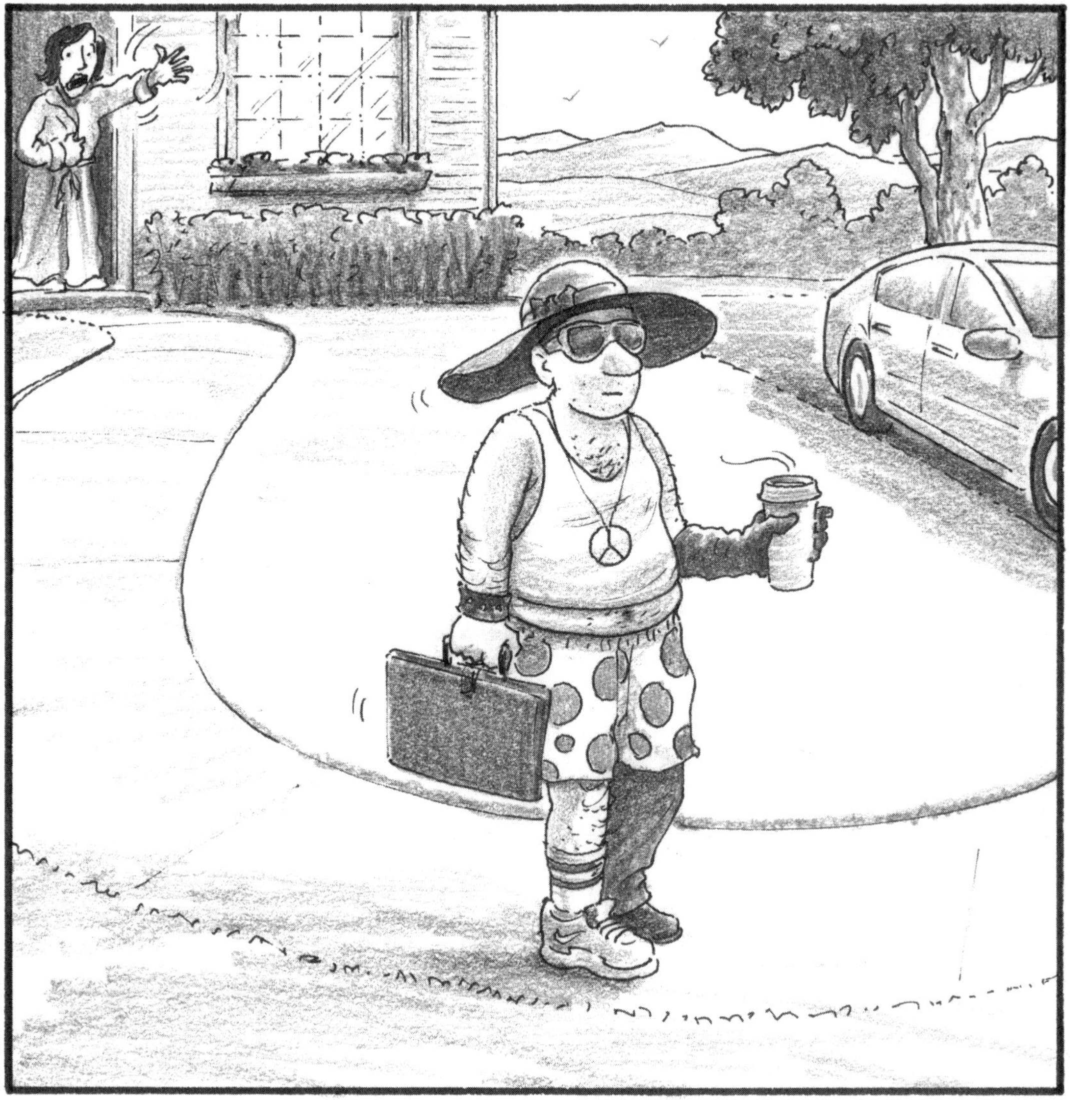

"HAROLD! CONSIDER YOUR OPTICS!"

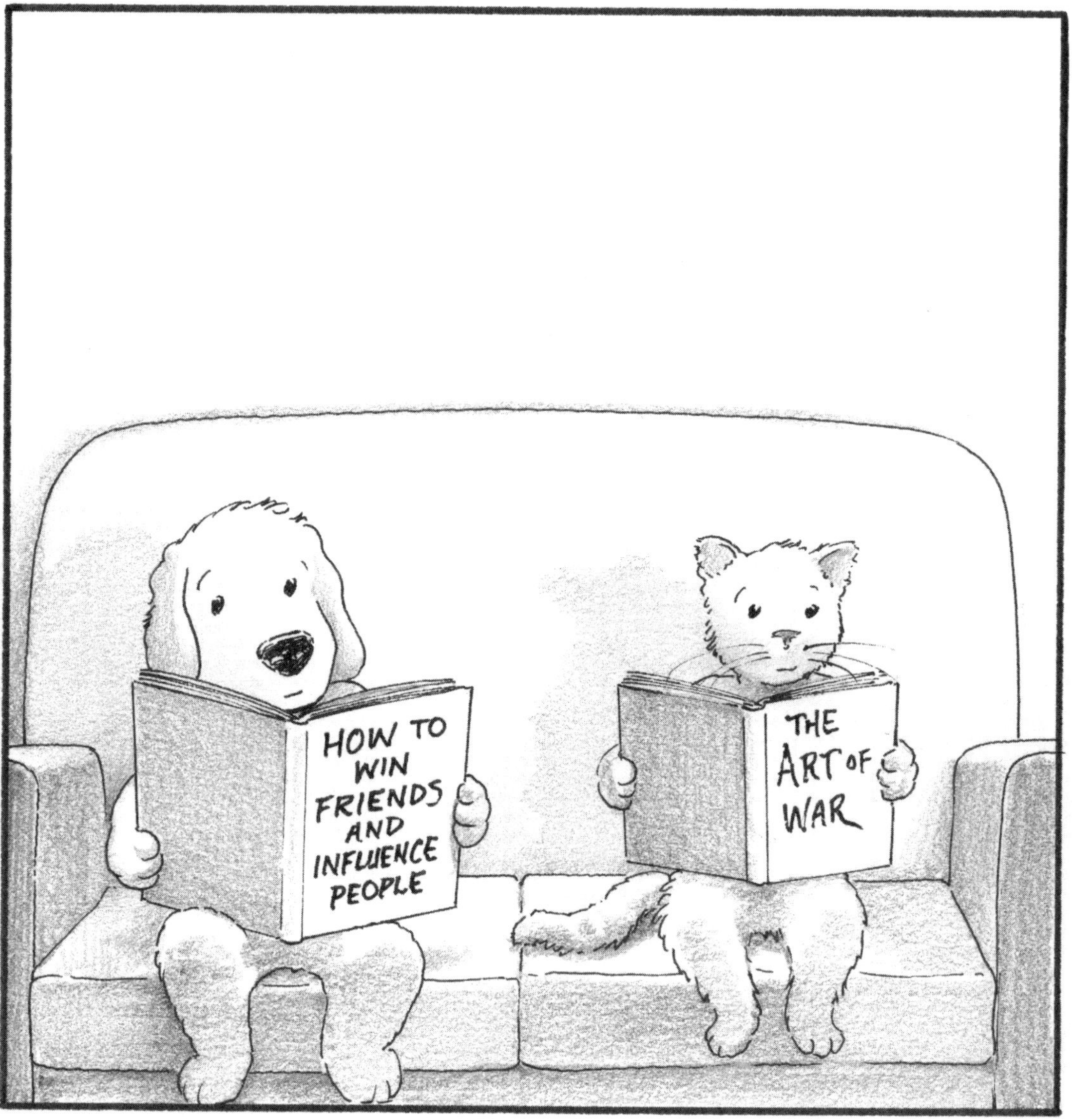
HOW TO WIN FRIENDS AND INFLUENCE PEOPLE
THE ART OF WAR

THE INVENTION OF FIRE

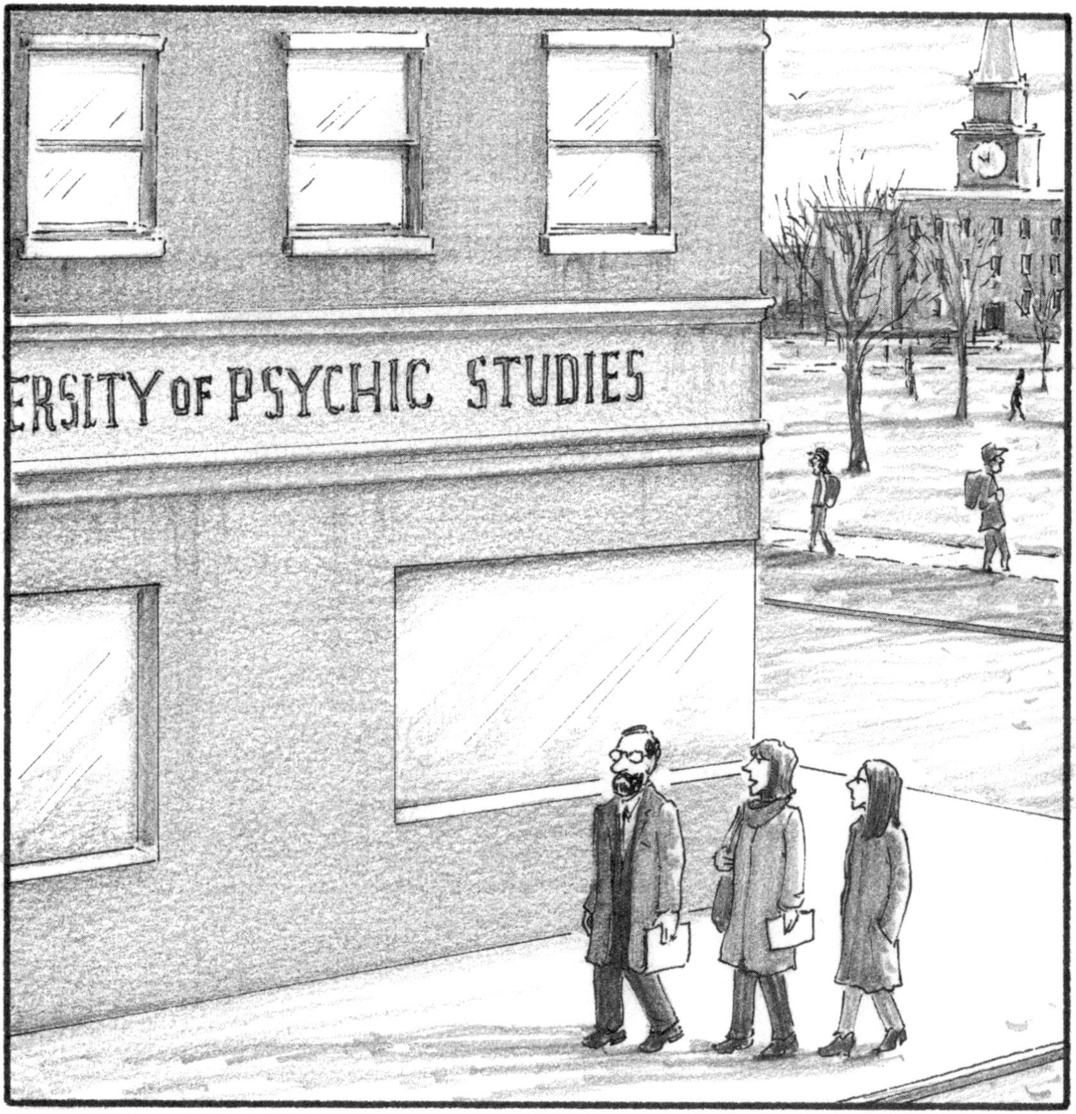
ERSITY OF PSYCHIC STUDIES

"HOW MUCH IS THE INTUITION TO GO HERE?"

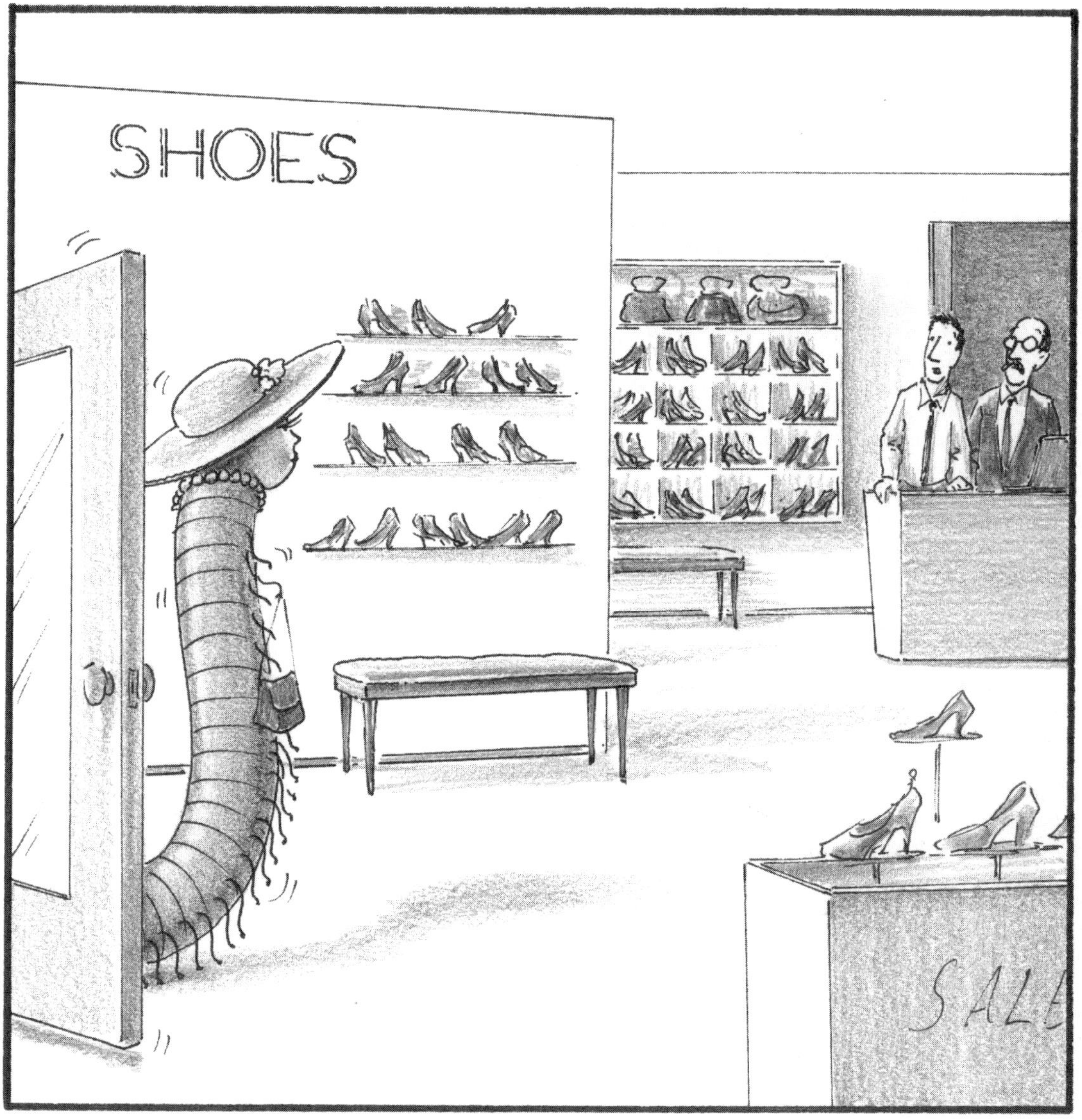
SHOES

"UH-OH . . ."

ROBERTA IS PRACTICED IN THE ART OF COQUETRY.

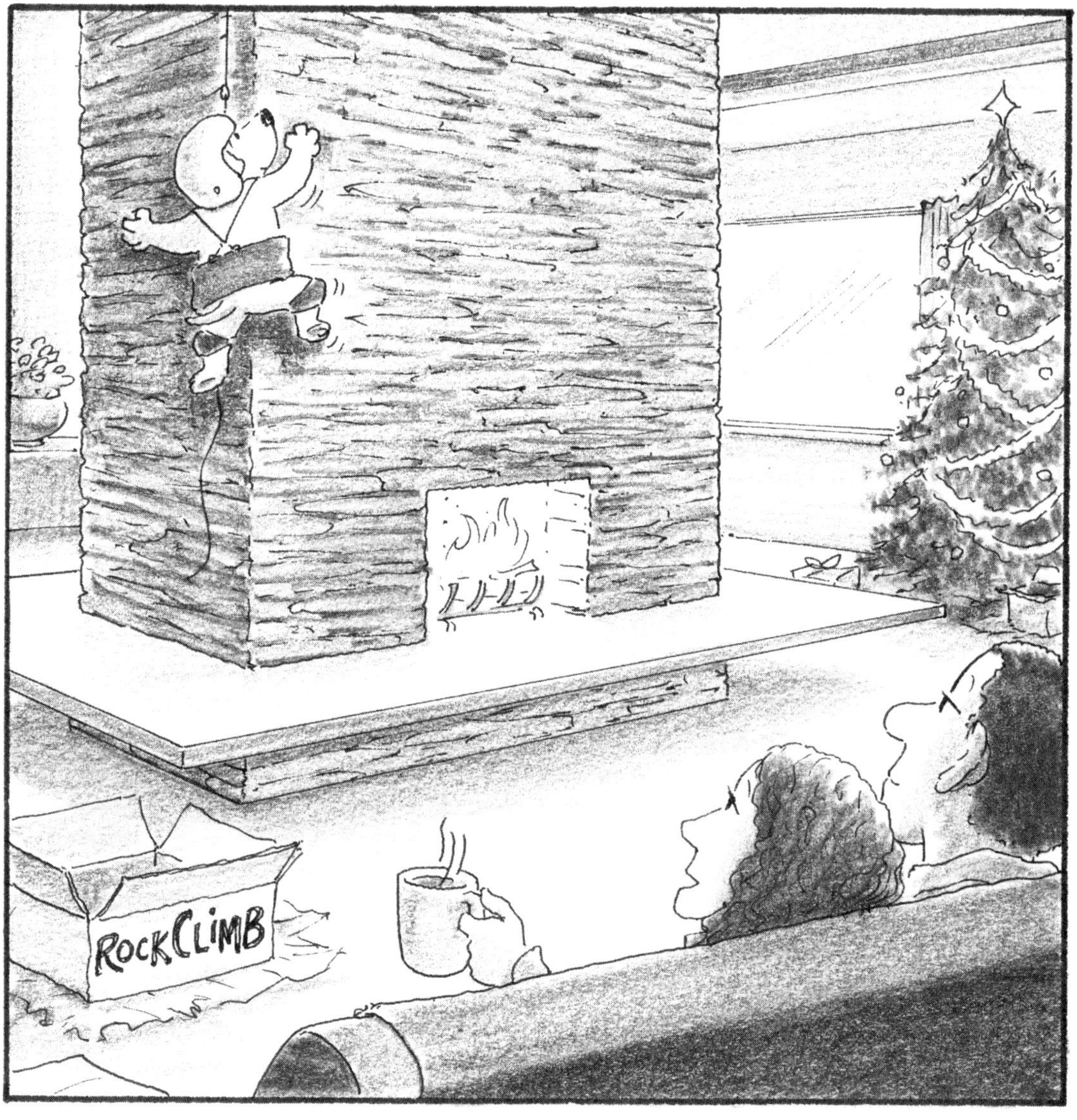
ROCK CLIMB

"YOU WERE RIGHT. HE LOVES IT."

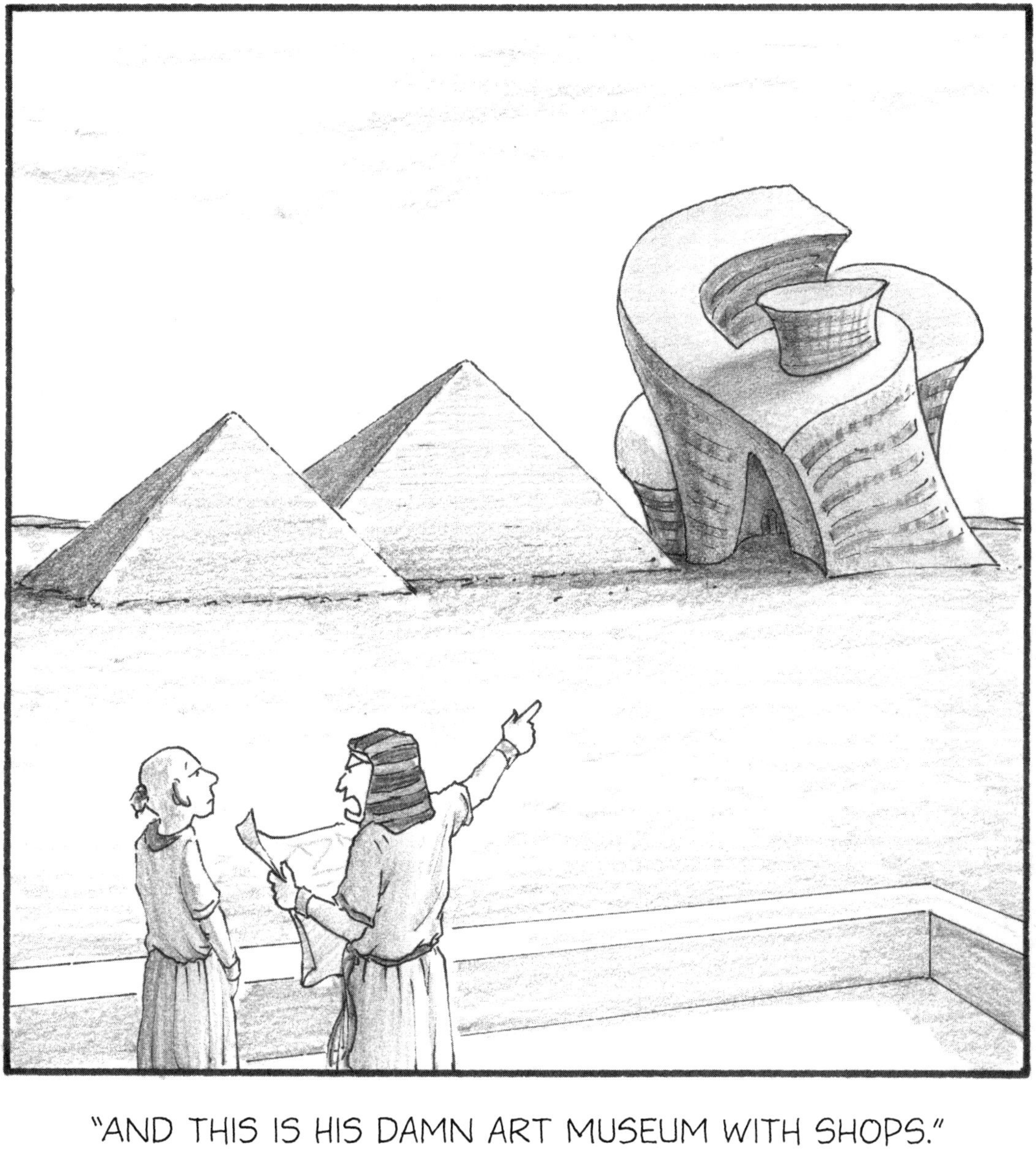

"AND THIS IS HIS DAMN ART MUSEUM WITH SHOPS."

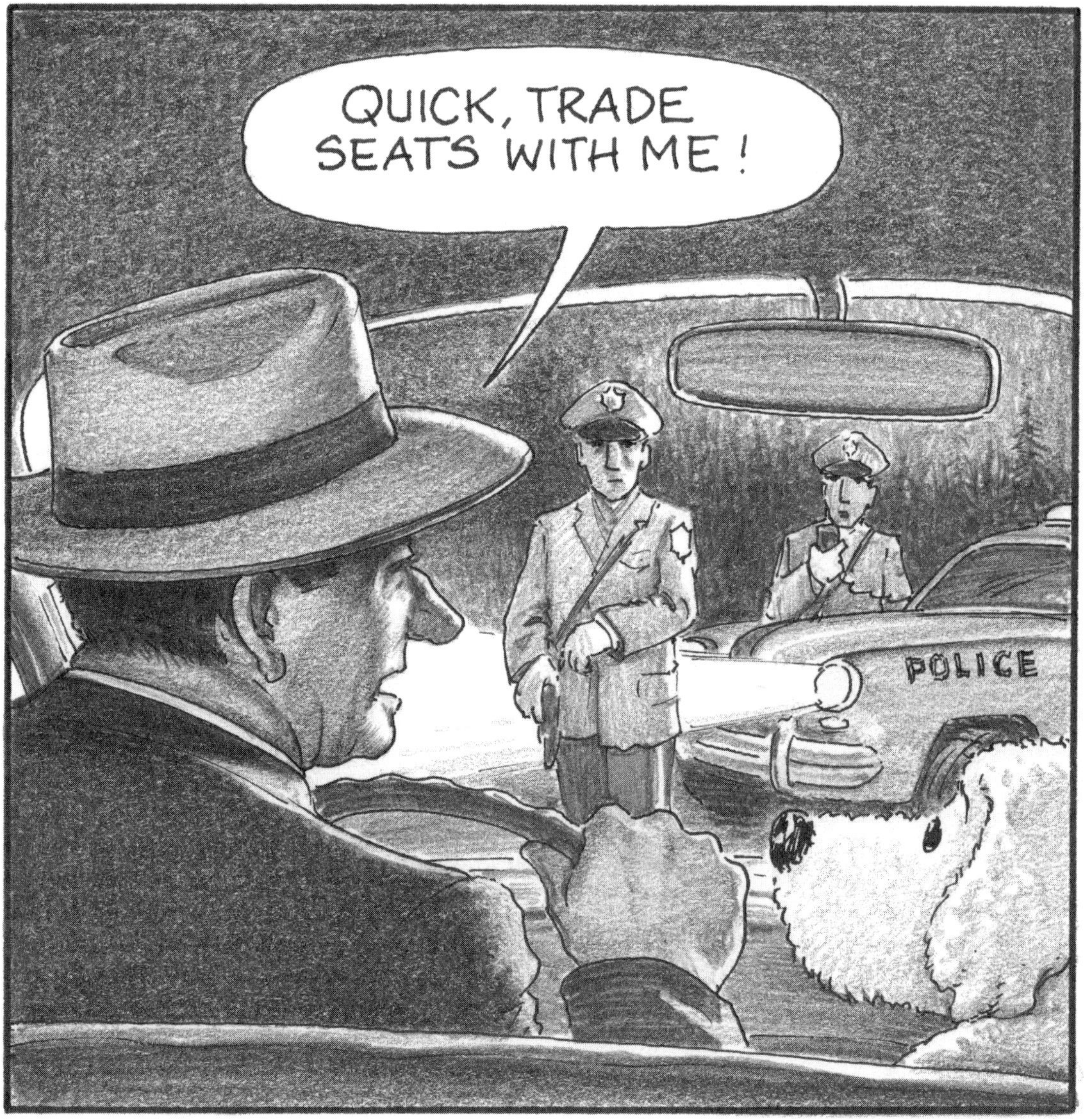
QUICK, TRADE SEATS WITH ME!
POLICE

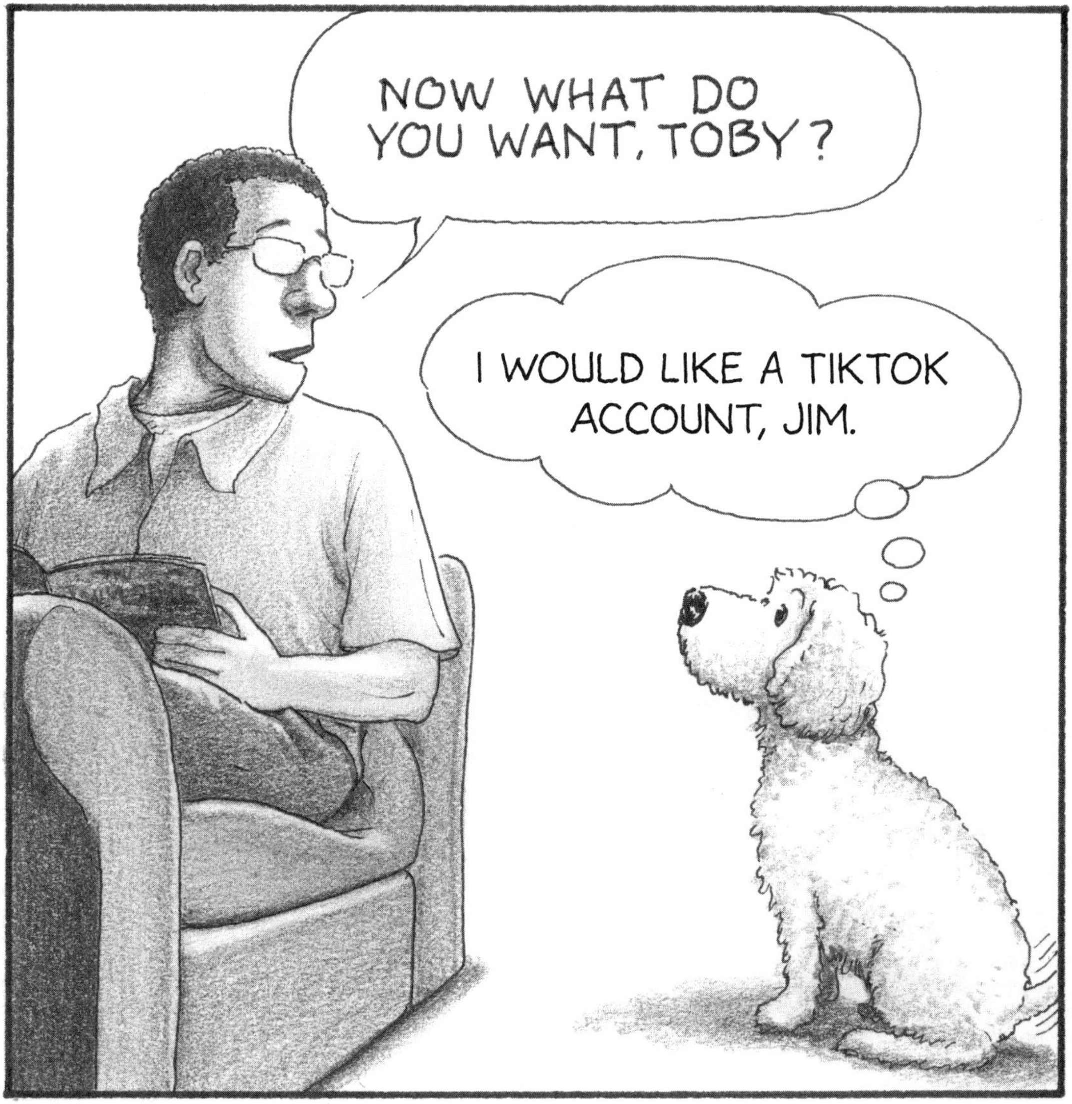
NOW WHAT DO YOU WANT, TOBY?
I WOULD LIKE A TIKTOK ACCOUNT, JIM.

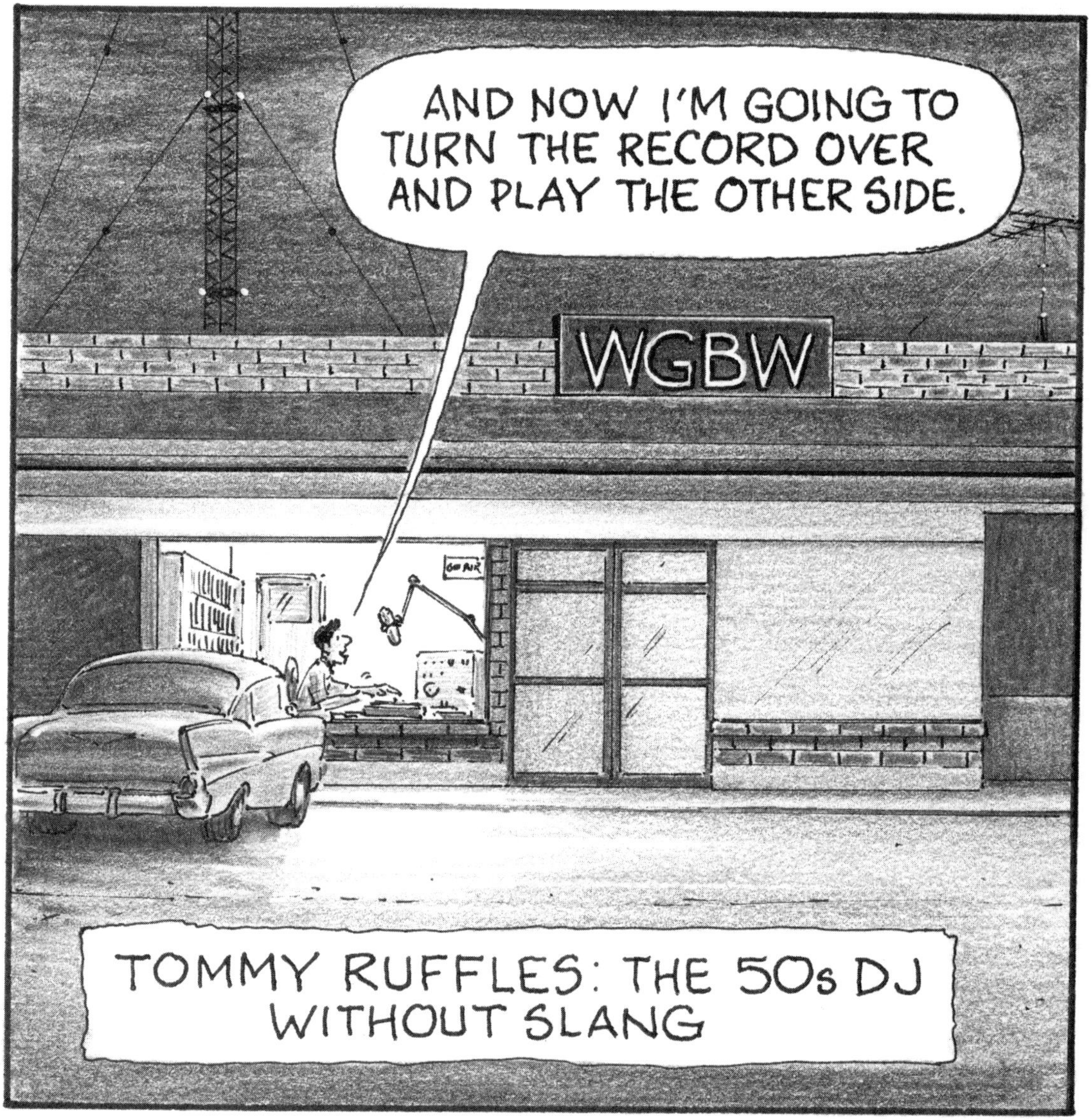
AND NOW I'M GOING TO TURN THE RECORD OVER AND PLAY THE OTHER SIDE.
WGBW
TOMMY RUFFLES: THE 50s DJ WITHOUT SLANG

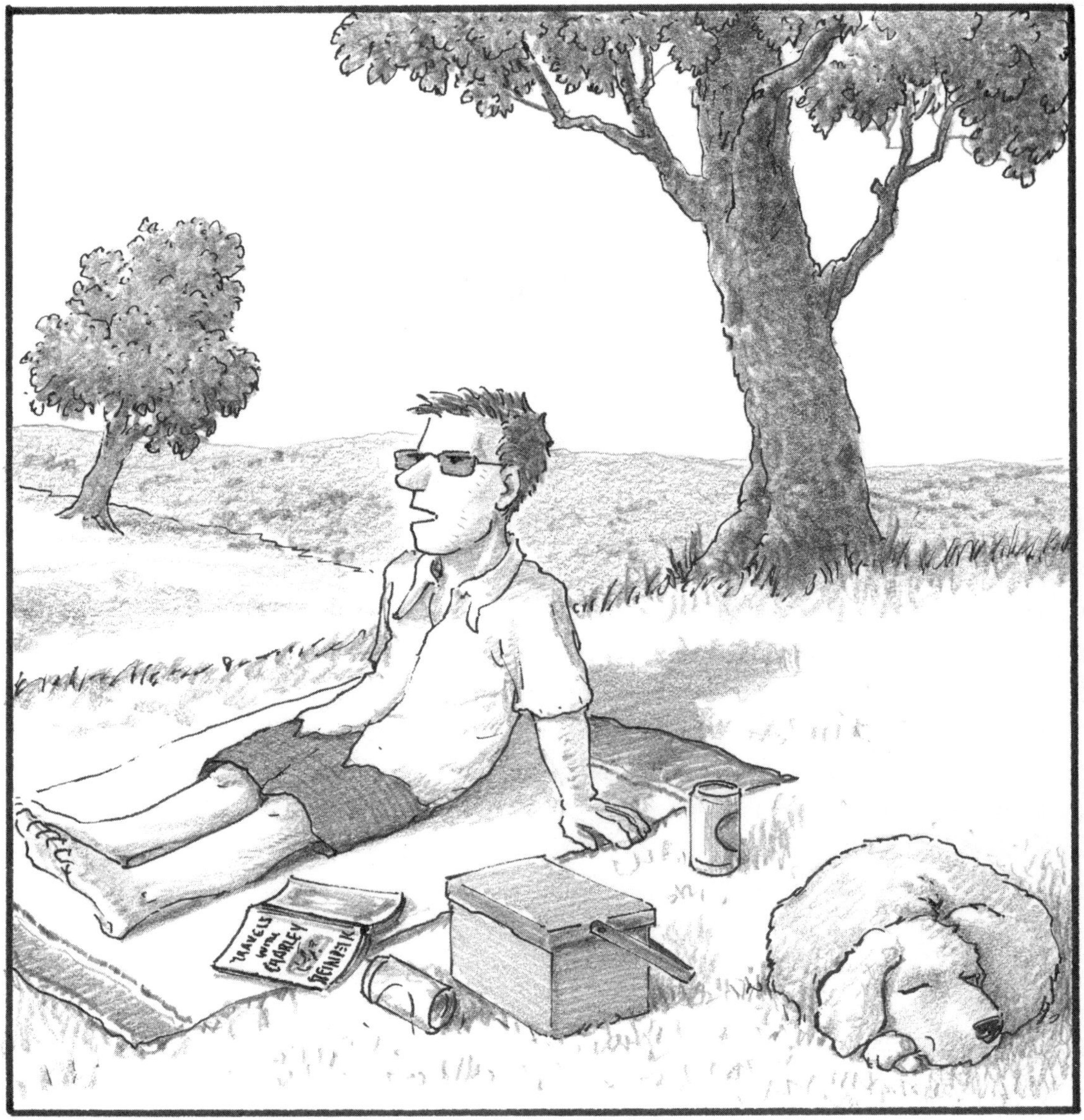
TRAVELS
WITH
CHARLEY
STEINBECK

"IT'S DAYS LIKE THIS THAT MAKE ME LONG FOR DAYS LIKE THIS."

Penny and Me

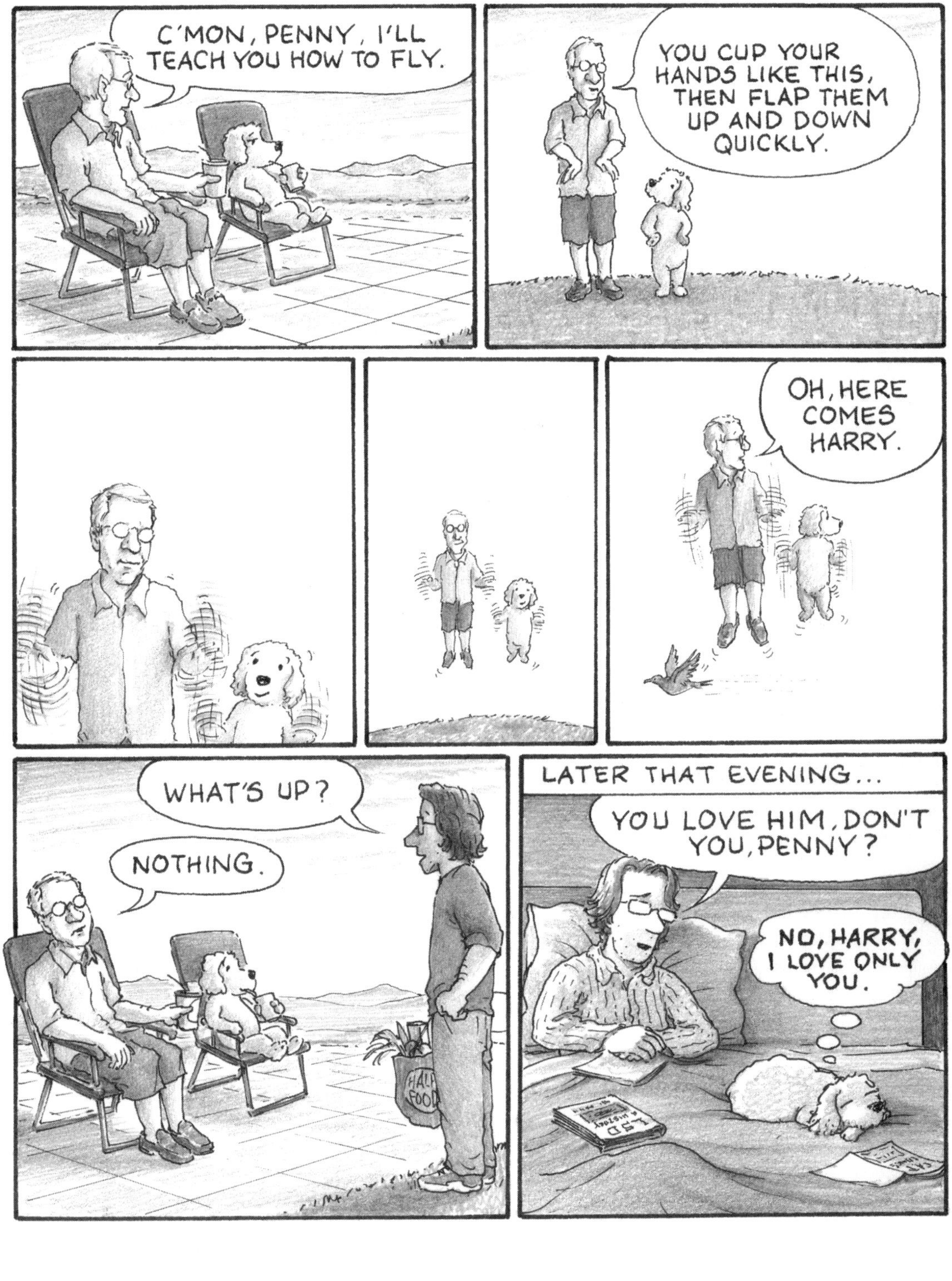
C'MON, PENNY, I'LL TEACH YOU HOW TO FLY.
YOU CUP YOUR HANDS LIKE THIS, THEN FLAP THEM UP AND DOWN QUICKLY.
OH, HERE COMES HARRY.
WHAT'S UP?
NOTHING.
LATER THAT EVENING...
YOU LOVE HIM, DON'T YOU, PENNY?
NO, HARRY, I LOVE ONLY YOU.

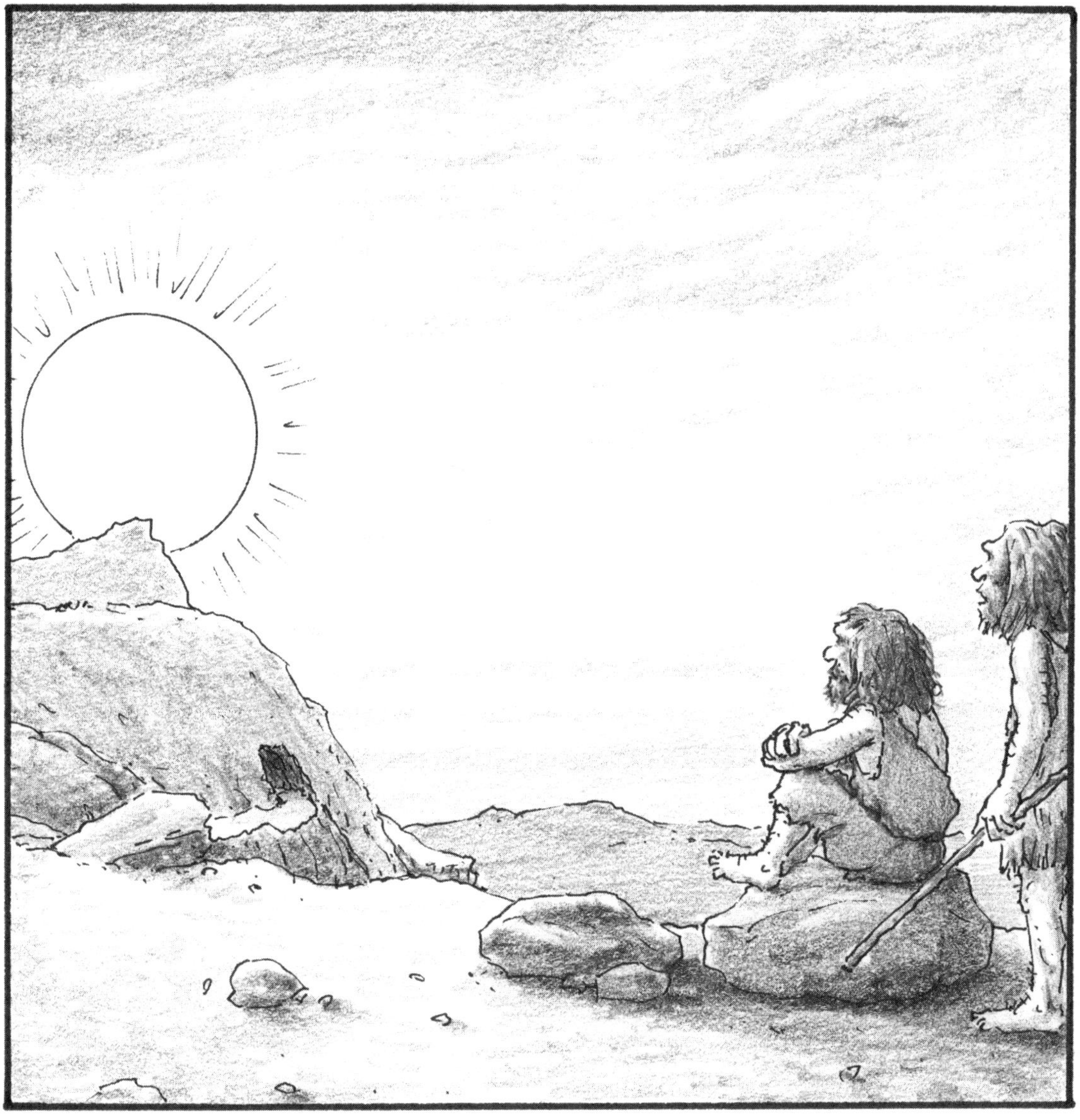

"IS ANYTHING GOOD ON?"

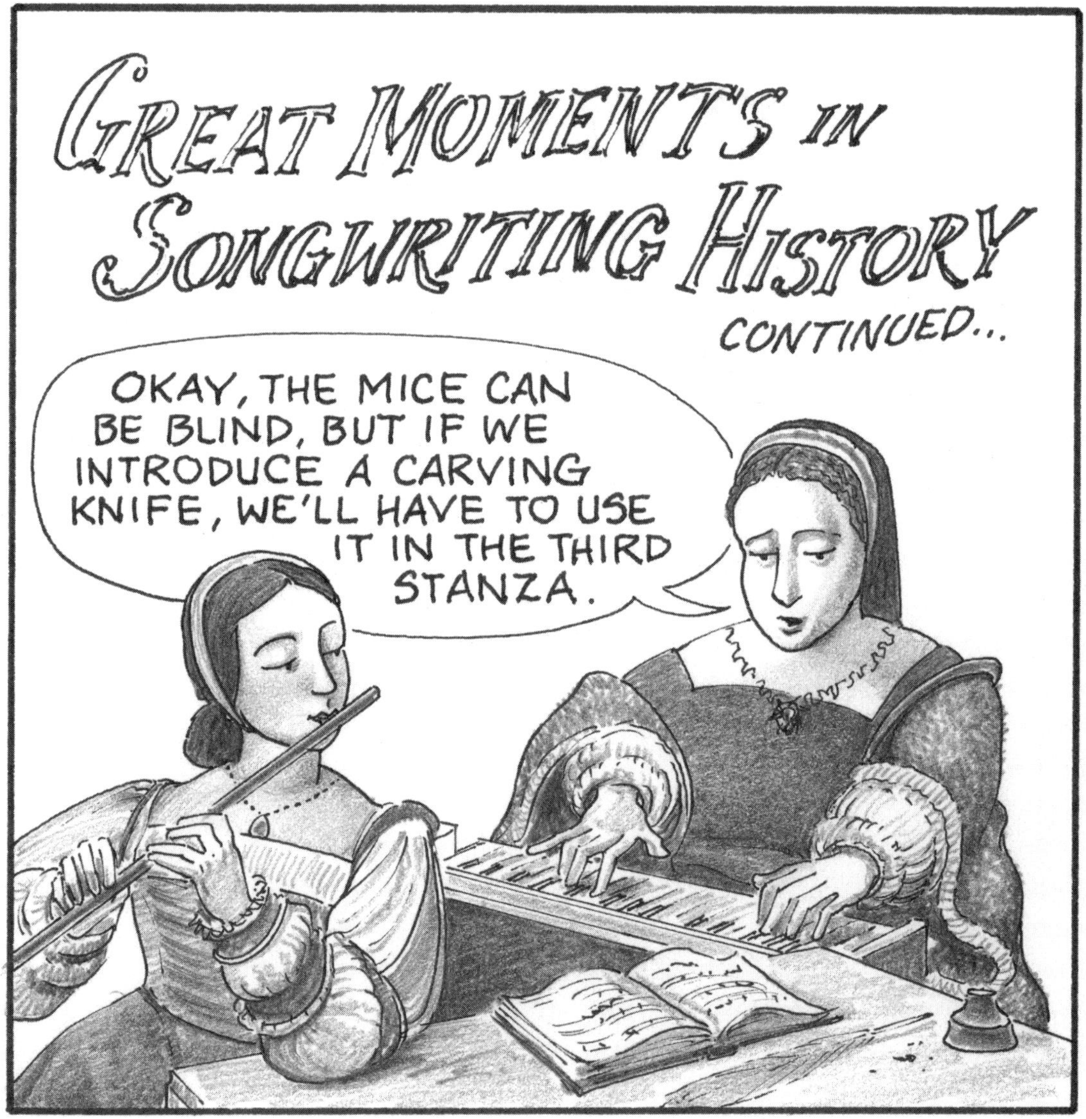
GREAT MOMENTS IN SONGWRITING HISTORY
CONTINUED...
OKAY, THE MICE CAN BE BLIND, BUT IF WE INTRODUCE A CARVING KNIFE, WE'LL HAVE TO USE IT IN THE THIRD STANZA.

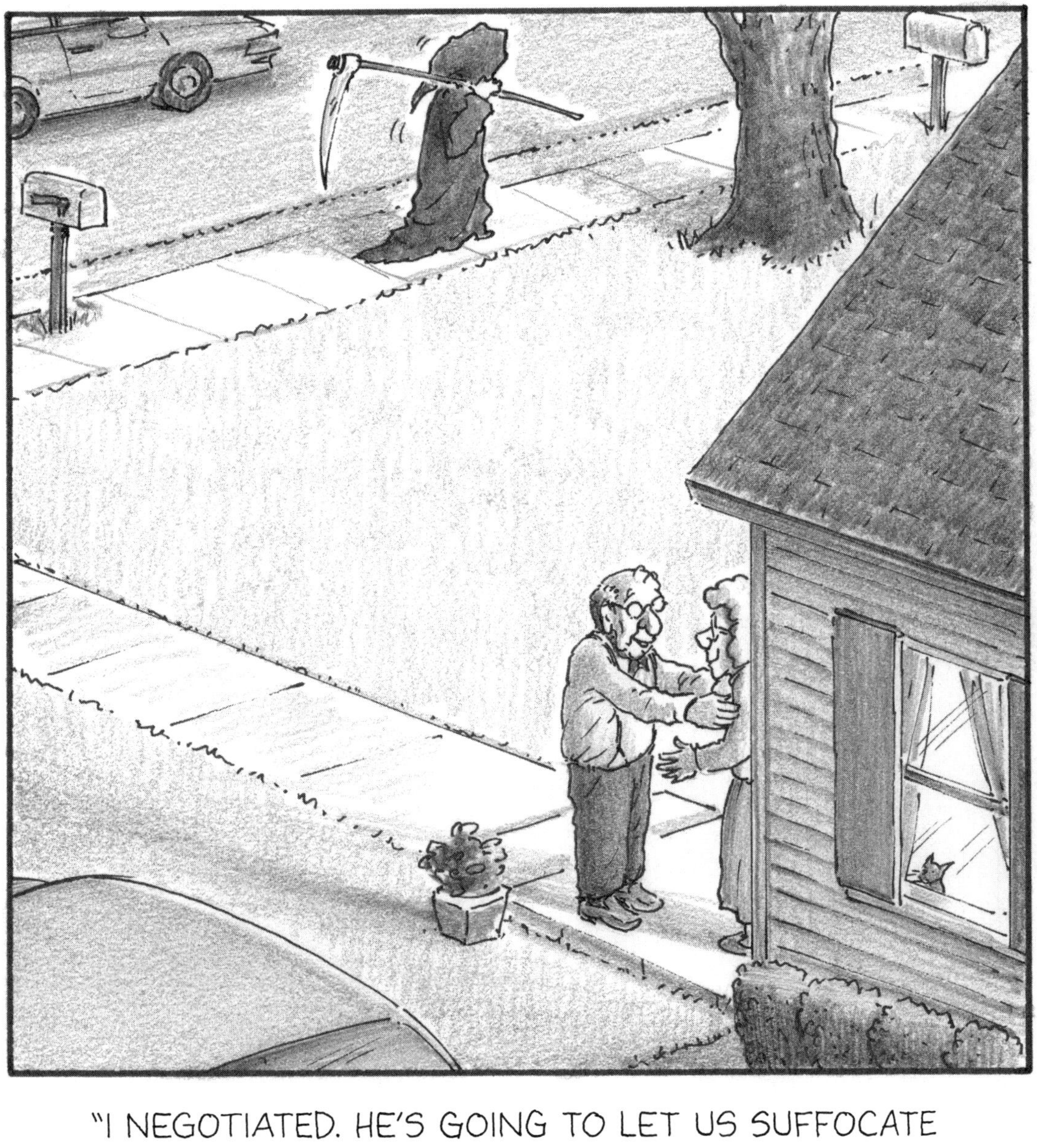

"I NEGOTIATED. HE'S GOING TO LET US SUFFOCATE IN OUR OWN ENNUI!"

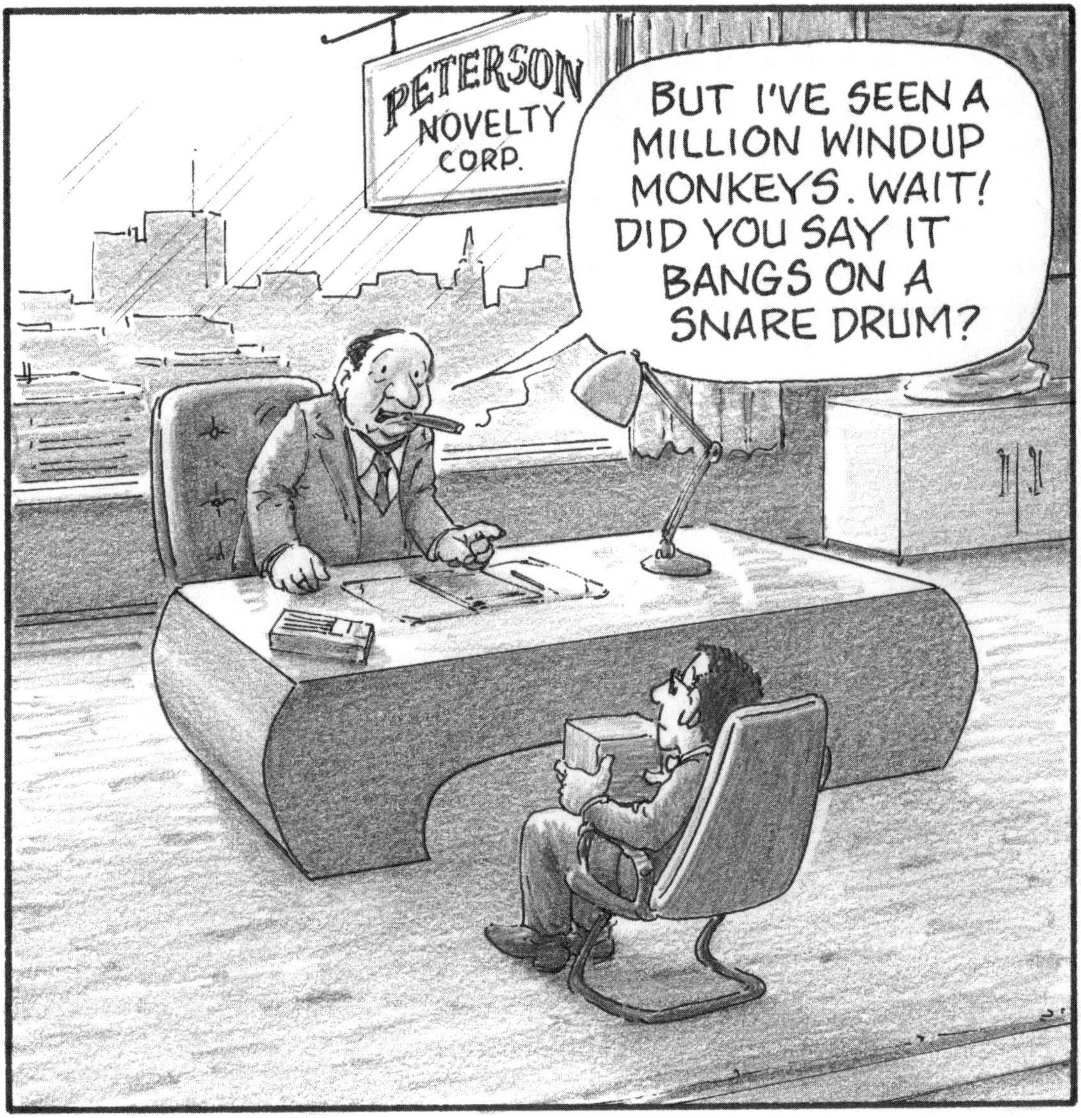
PETERSON
NOVELTY
CORP.
BUT I'VE SEEN A
MILLION WINDUP
MONKEYS. WAIT!
DID YOU SAY IT
BANGS ON A
SNARE DRUM?

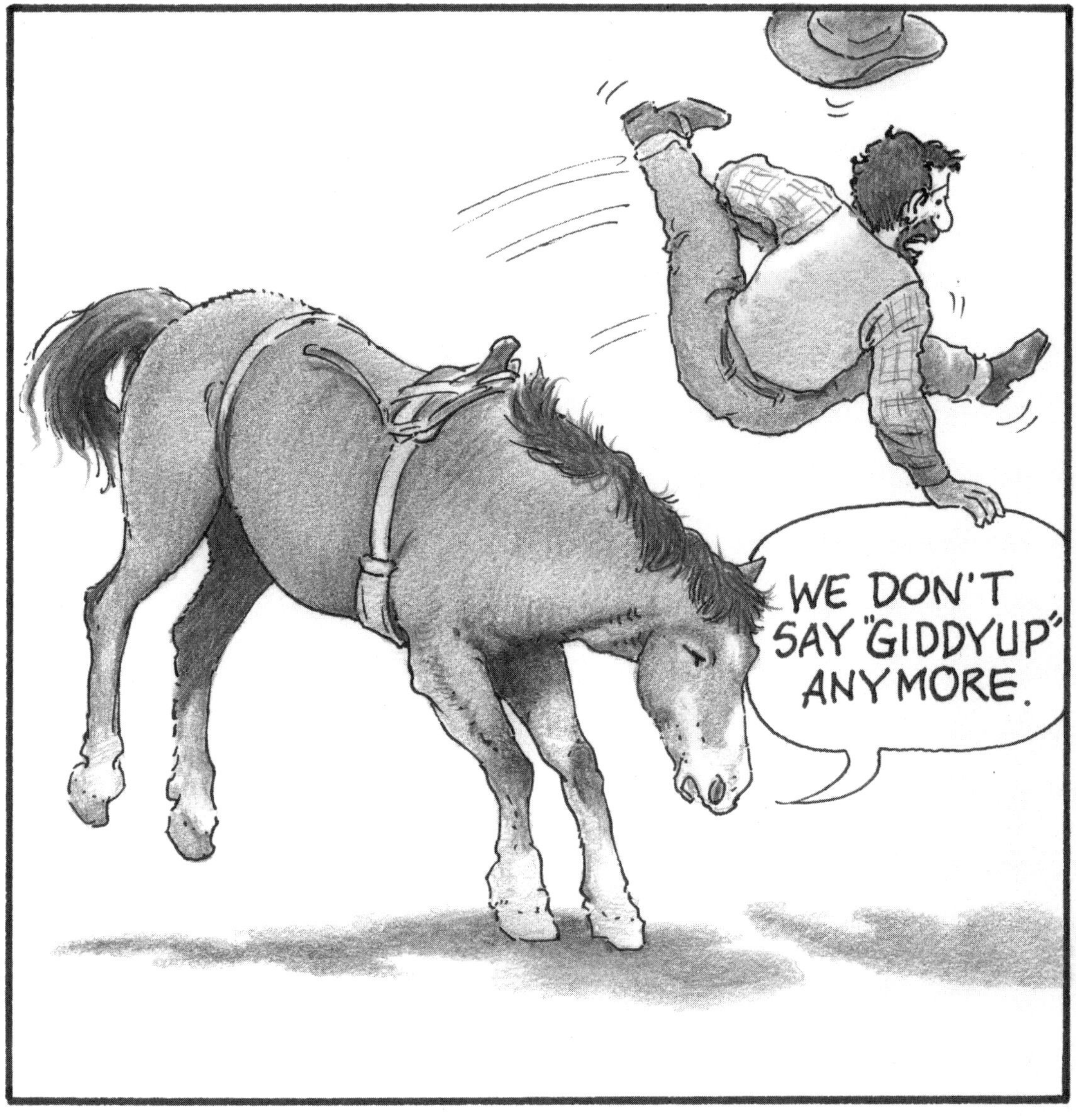
WE DON'T SAY "GIDDYUP" ANYMORE.

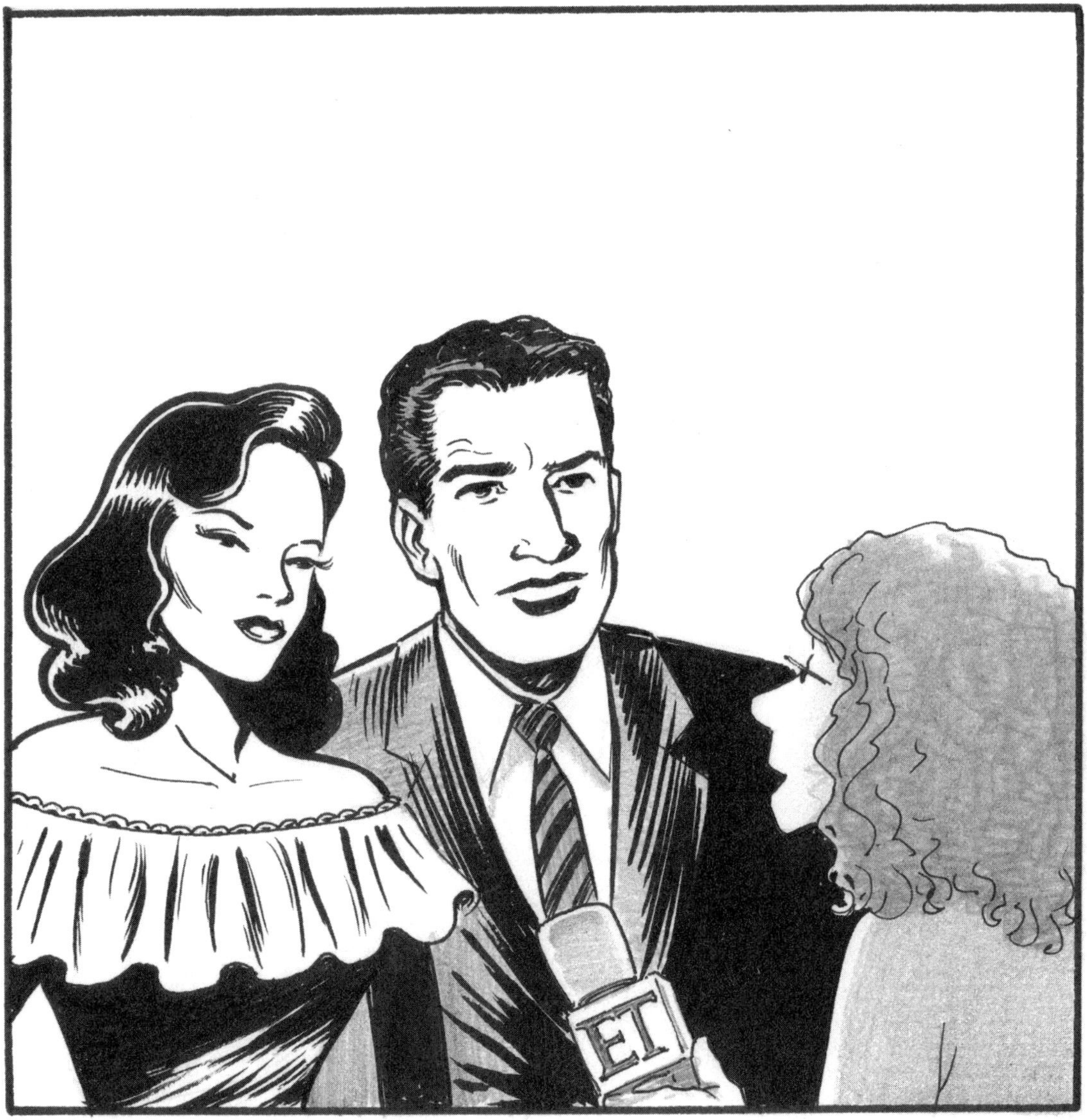
ET

"AND WHAT ATTRACTED YOU TWO TO EACH OTHER?"

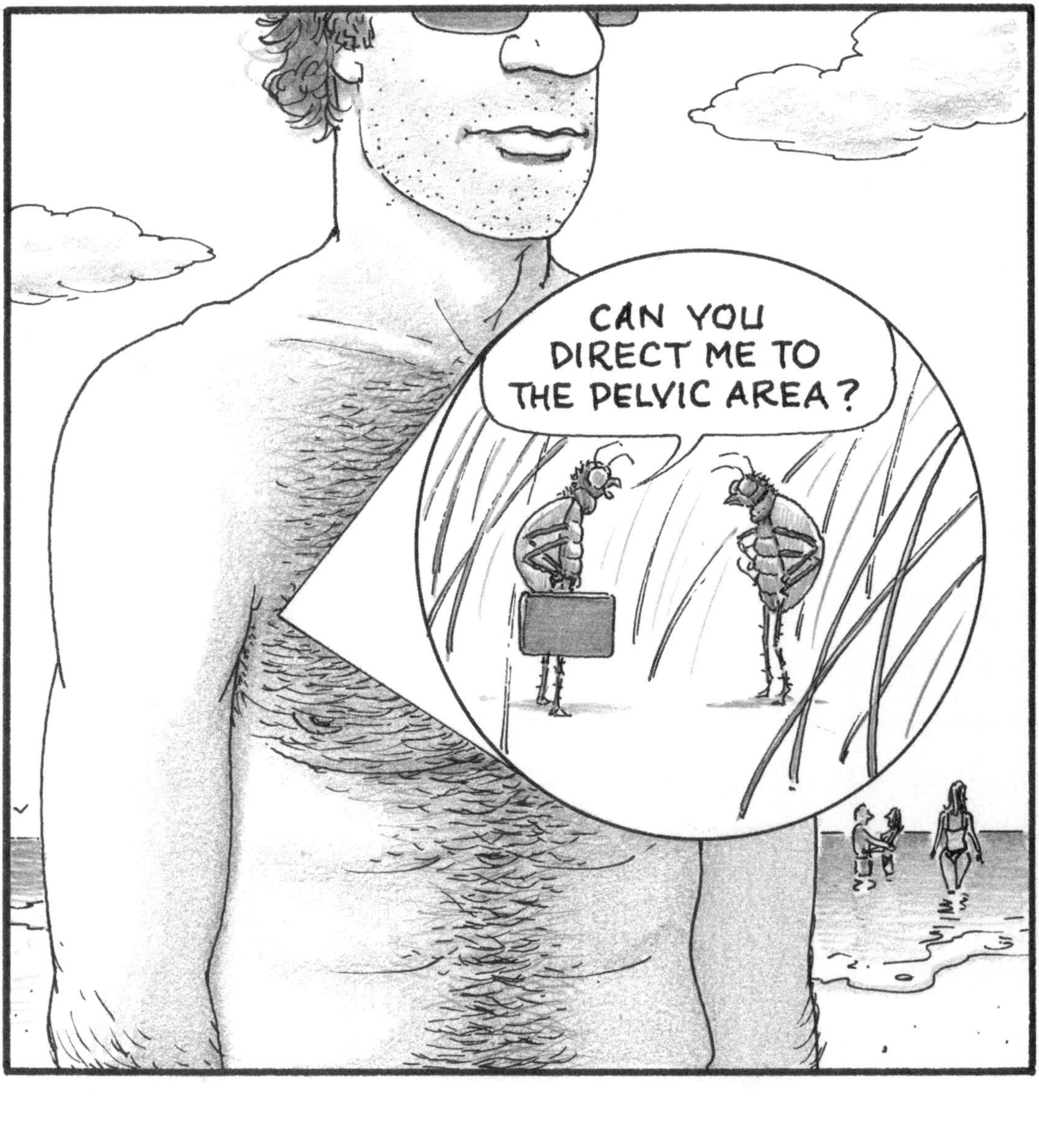
CAN YOU DIRECT ME TO THE PELVIC AREA?

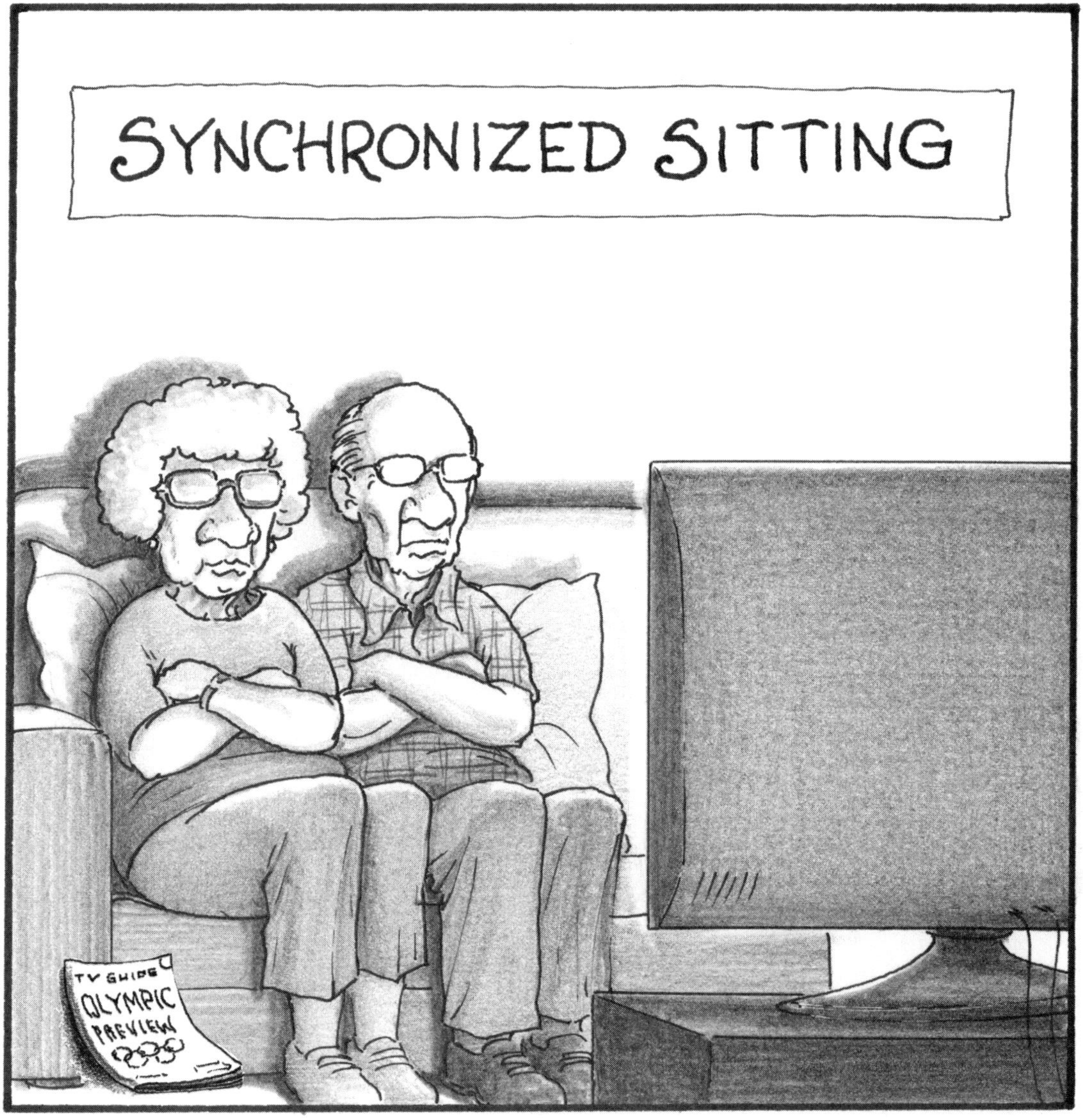
SYNCHRONIZED SITTING
TV GUIDE
OLYMPIC
PREVIEW

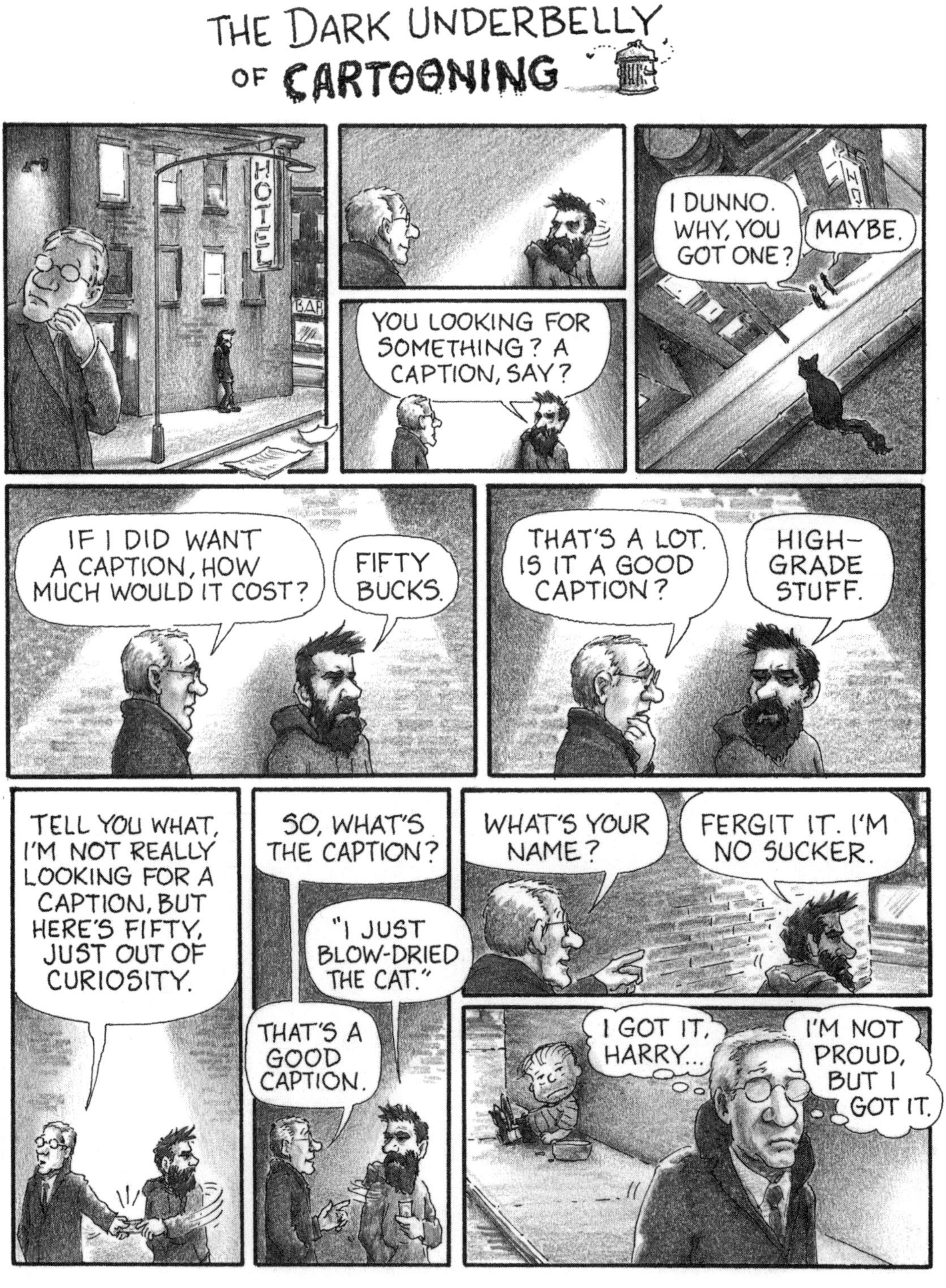
THE DARK UNDERBELLY OF CARTOONING
HOTEL
BAR
YOU LOOKING FOR SOMETHING? A CAPTION, SAY?
I DUNNO. WHY, YOU GOT ONE?
MAYBE.
IF I DID WANT A CAPTION, HOW MUCH WOULD IT COST?
FIFTY BUCKS.
THAT'S A LOT. IS IT A GOOD CAPTION?
HIGH-GRADE STUFF.
TELL YOU WHAT, I'M NOT REALLY LOOKING FOR A CAPTION, BUT HERE'S FIFTY, JUST OUT OF CURIOSITY.
SO, WHAT'S THE CAPTION?
"I JUST BLOW-DRIED THE CAT."
THAT'S A GOOD CAPTION.
WHAT'S YOUR NAME?
FERGIT IT. I'M NO SUCKER.
I GOT IT, HARRY...
I'M NOT PROUD, BUT I GOT IT.

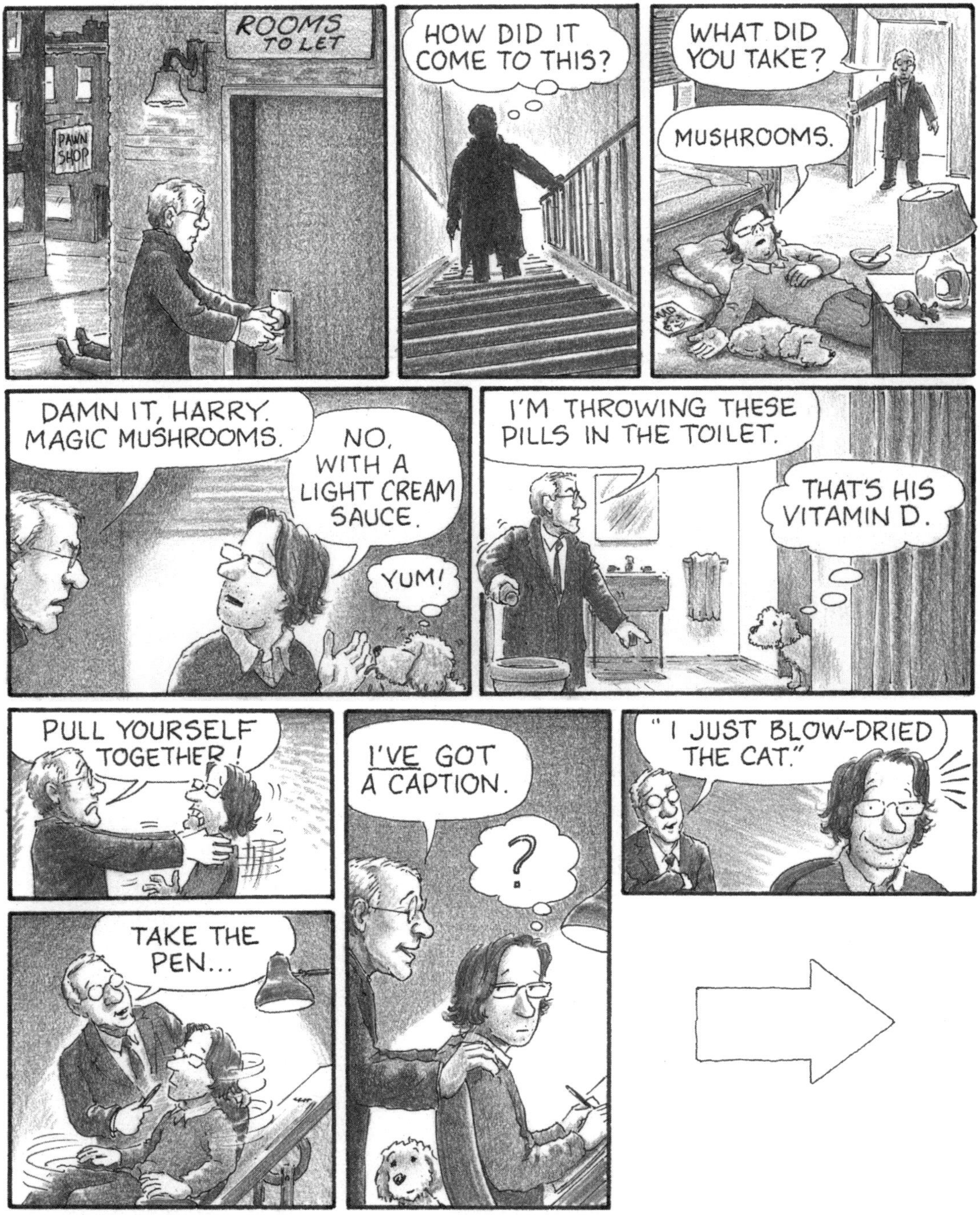
ROOMS TO LET
PAWN SHOP
HOW DID IT COME TO THIS?
WHAT DID YOU TAKE?
MUSHROOMS.
DAMN IT, HARRY. MAGIC MUSHROOMS.
NO, WITH A LIGHT CREAM SAUCE.
YUM!
I'M THROWING THESE PILLS IN THE TOILET.
THAT'S HIS VITAMIN D.
PULL YOURSELF TOGETHER!
TAKE THE PEN...
I'VE GOT A CAPTION.
?
"I JUST BLOW-DRIED THE CAT."

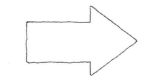

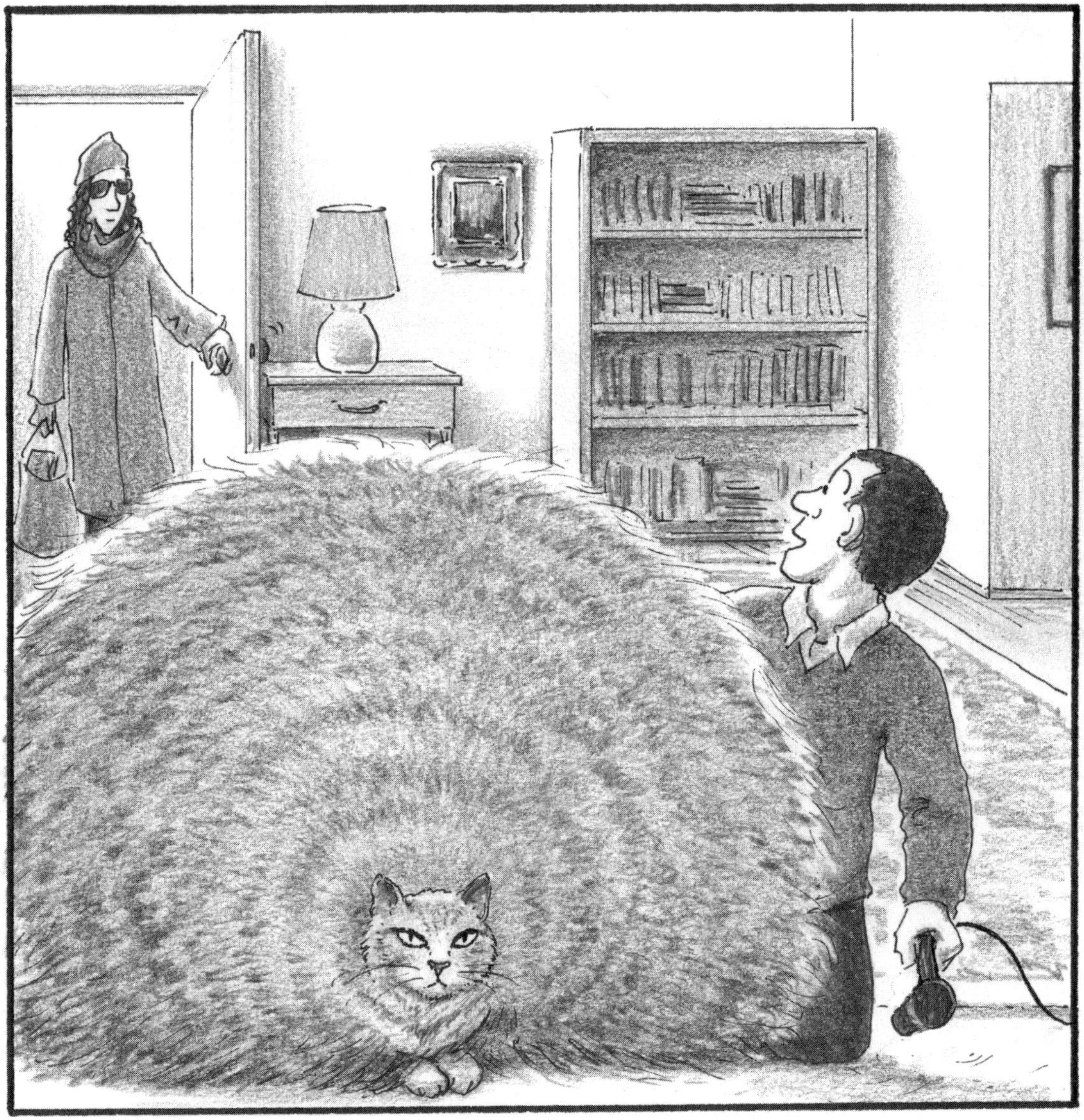

"I JUST BLOW-DRIED THE CAT."

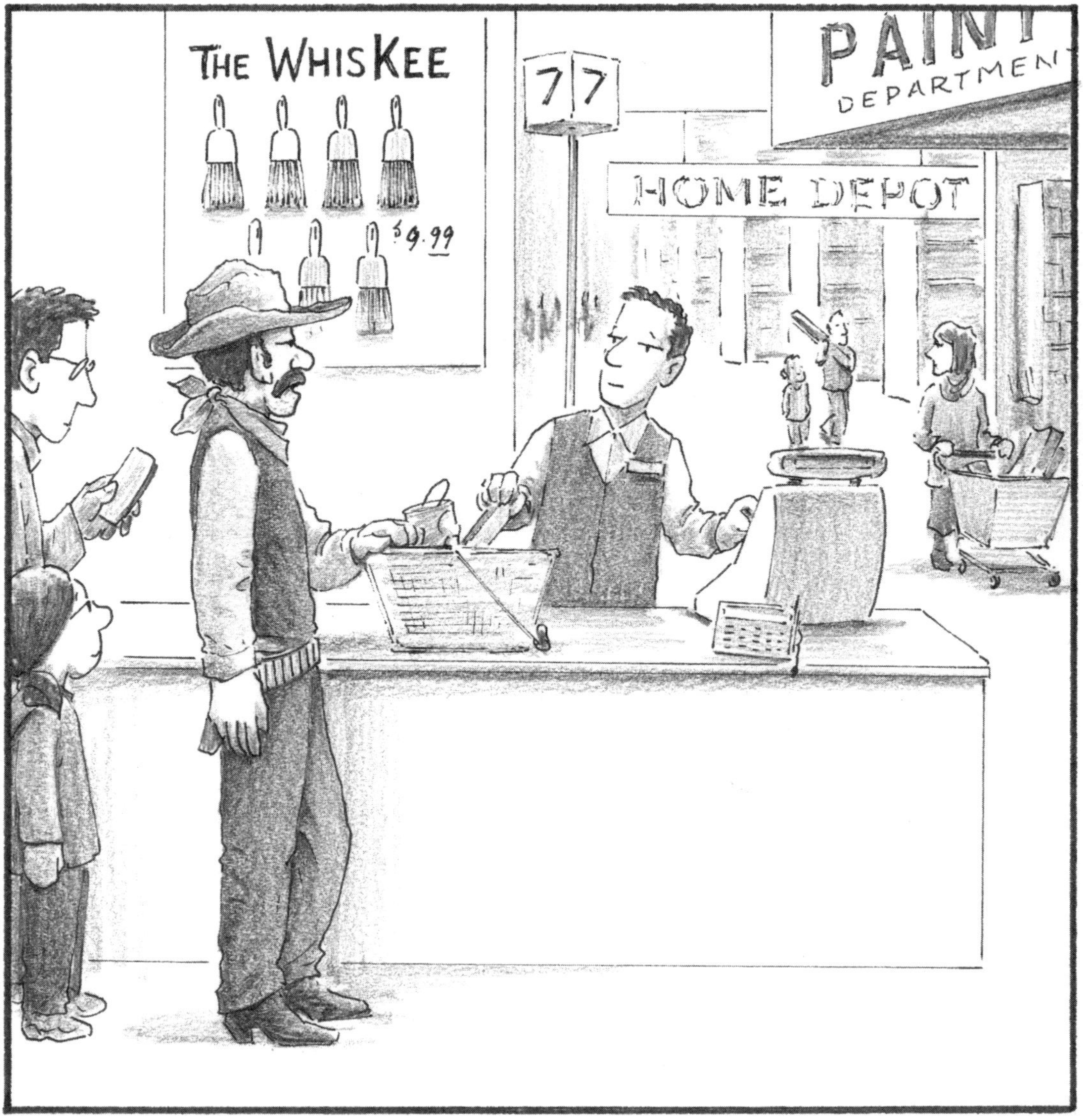
THE WHISKEE
$9.99
77
PAINT
DEPARTMENT
HOME DEPOT

"GIMME A WHISKEE."

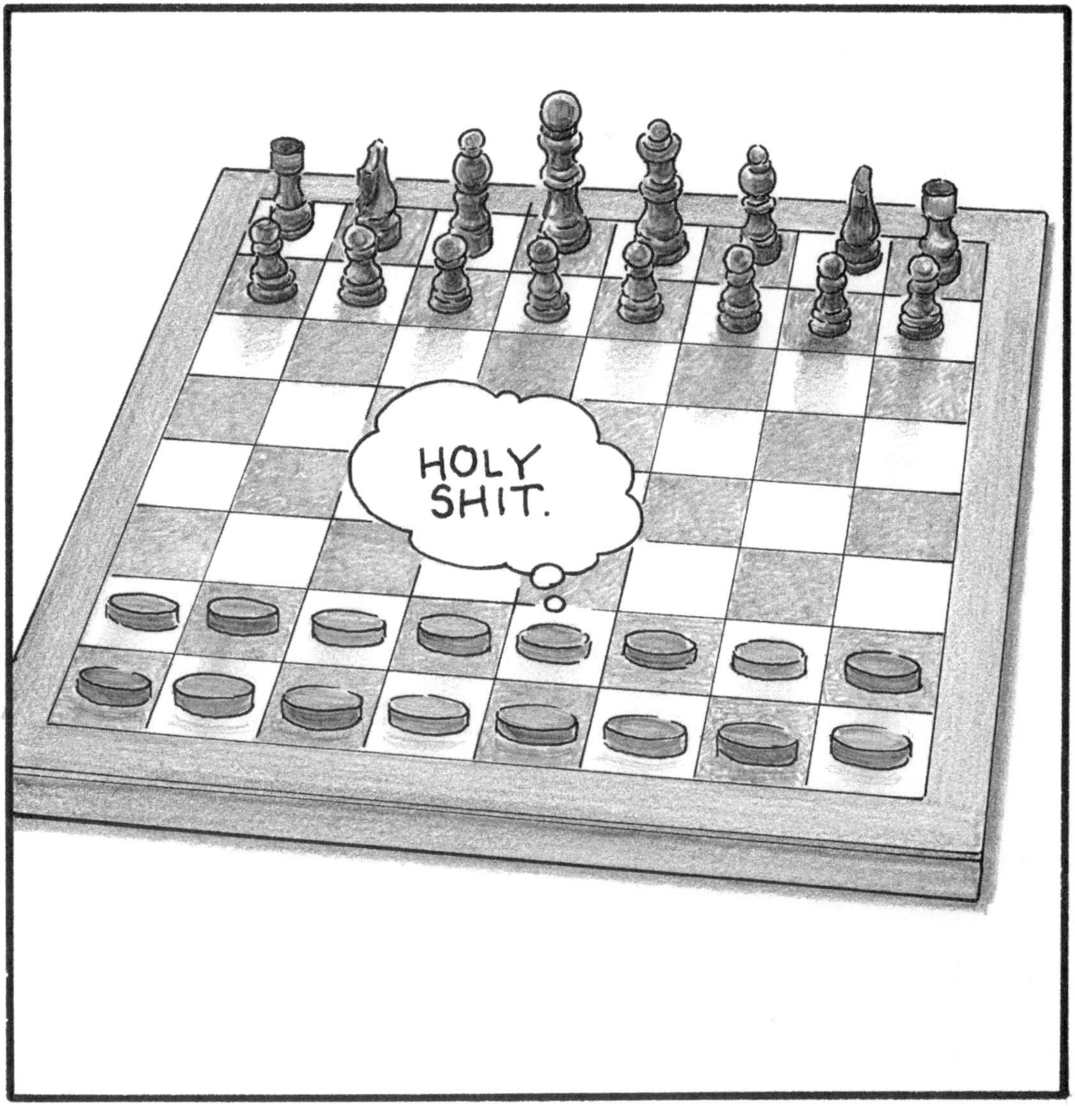
HOLY SHIT.

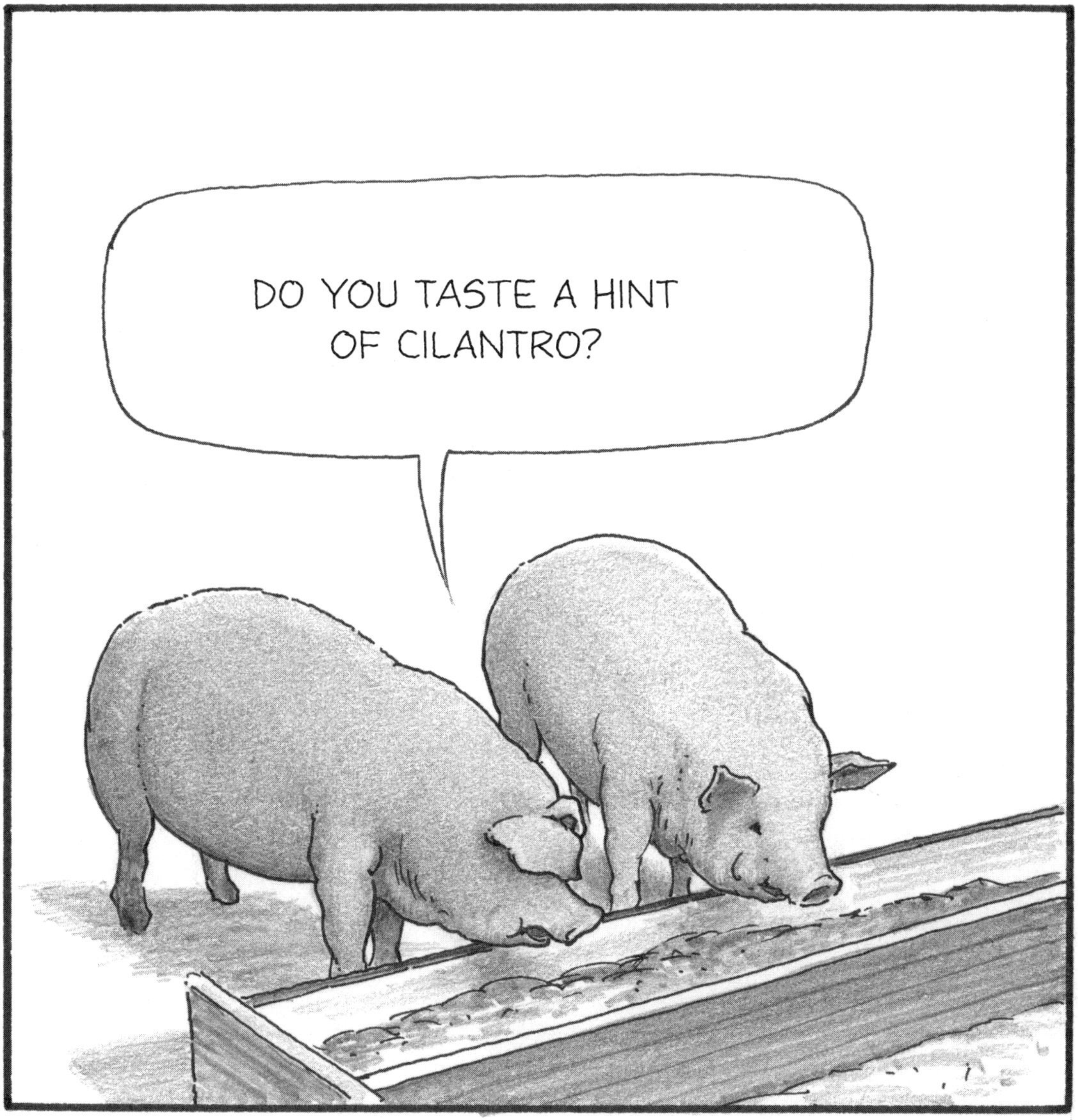
DO YOU TASTE A HINT OF CILANTRO?

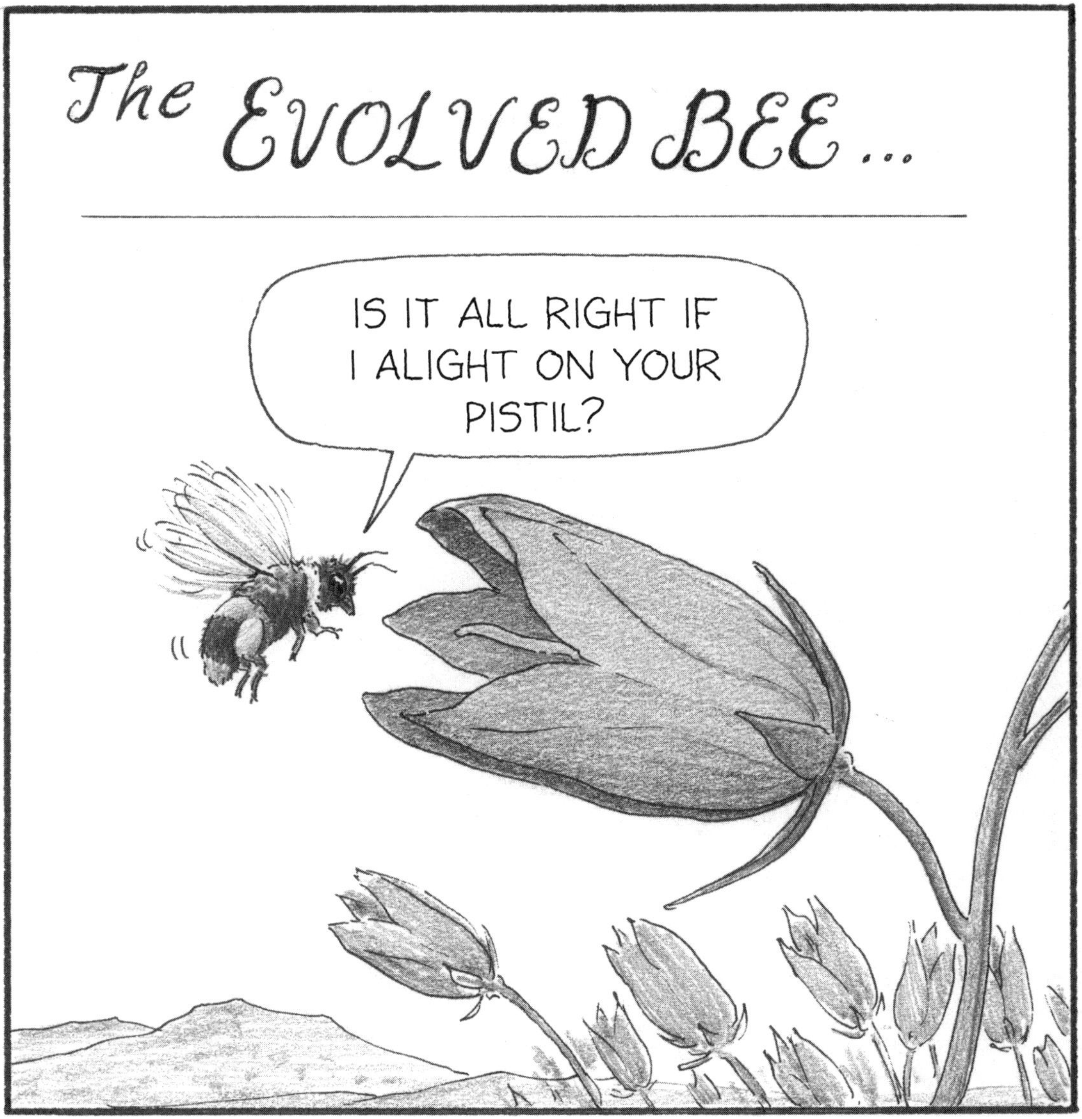
The EVOLVED BEE...
IS IT ALL RIGHT IF I ALIGHT ON YOUR PISTIL?

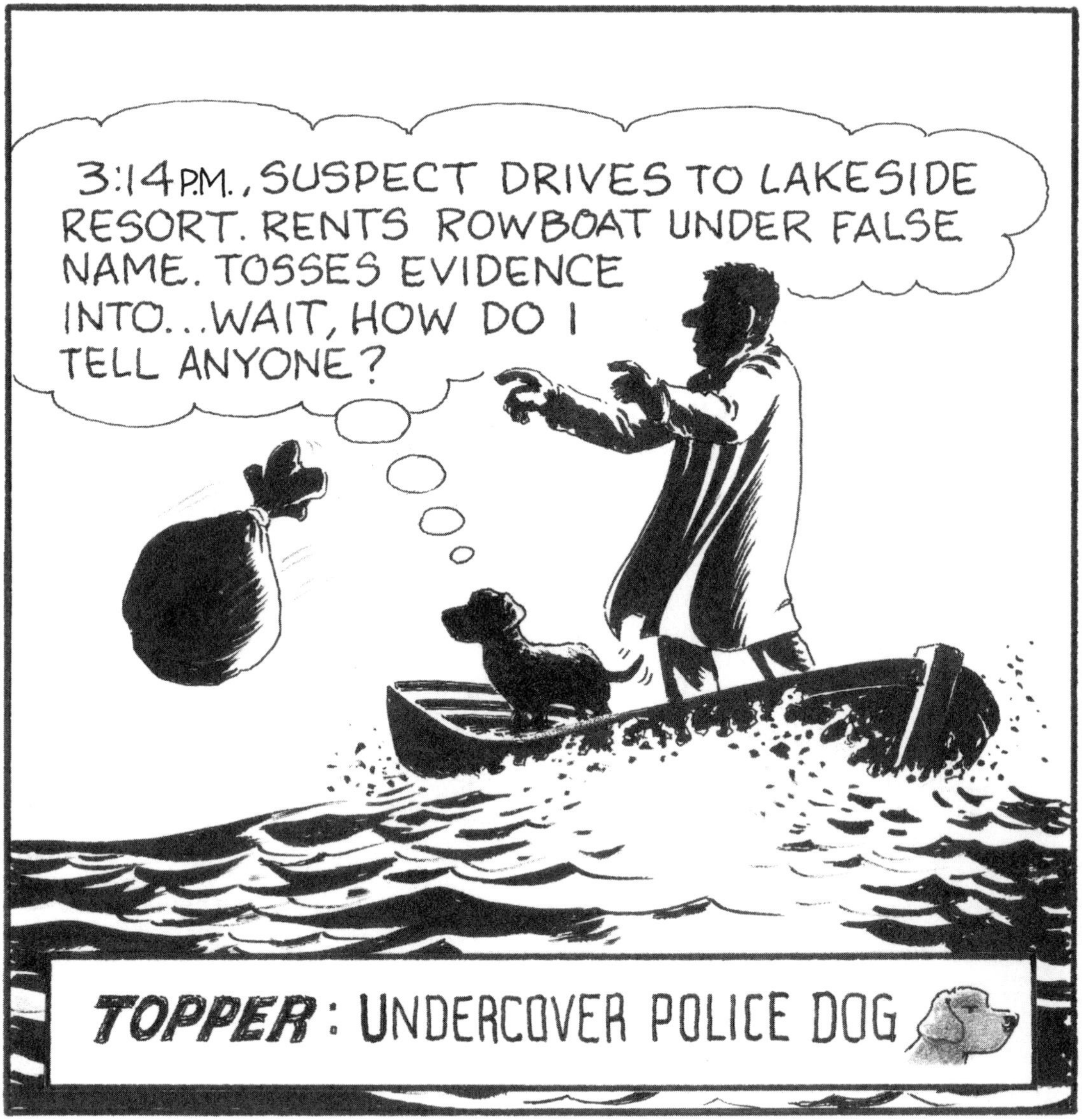
3:14 P.M., SUSPECT DRIVES TO LAKESIDE RESORT. RENTS ROWBOAT UNDER FALSE NAME. TOSSES EVIDENCE INTO...WAIT, HOW DO I TELL ANYONE?
TOPPER: UNDERCOVER POLICE DOG

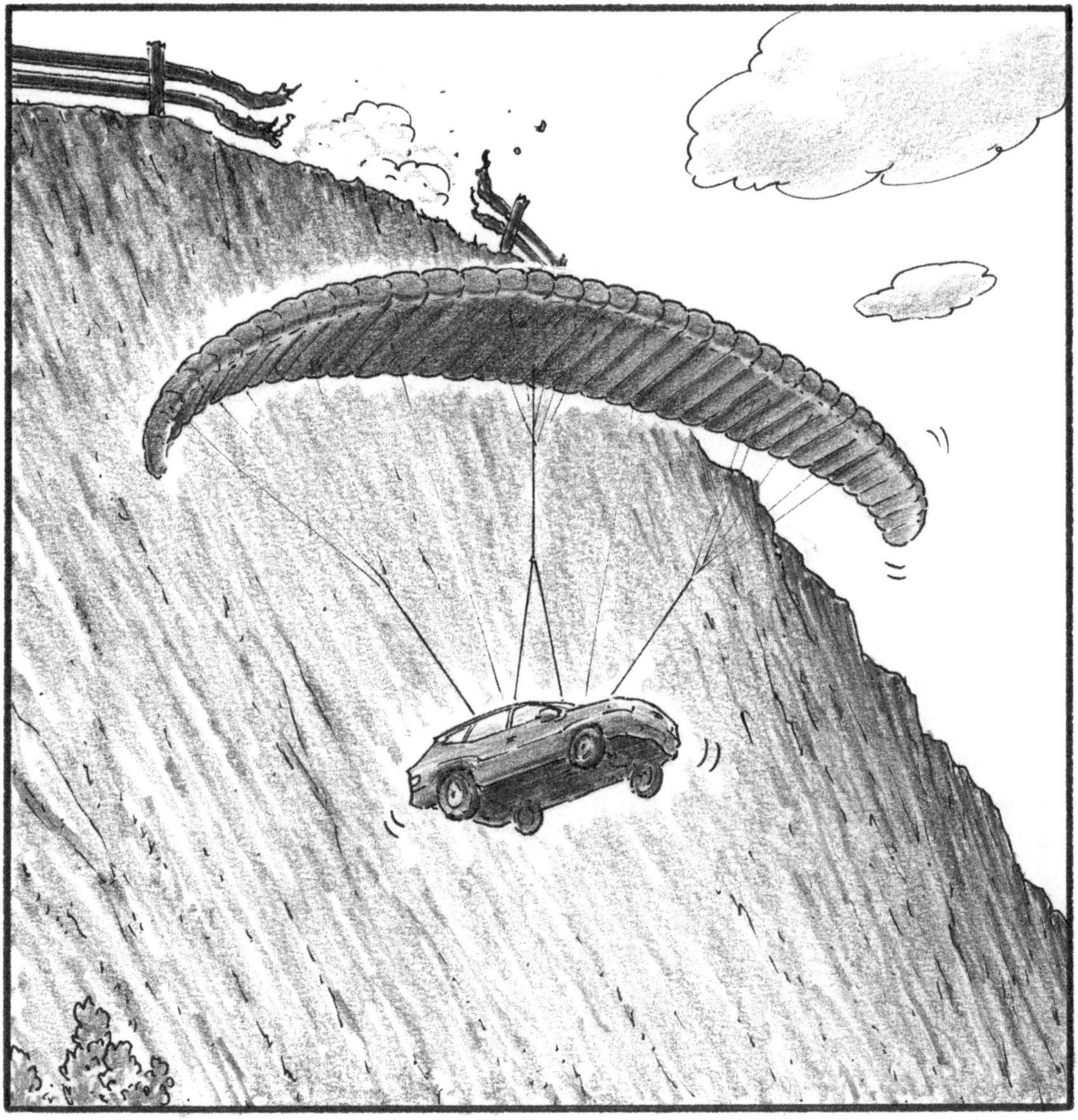

"AREN'T YOU GLAD I BOUGHT IT FULLY LOADED?"

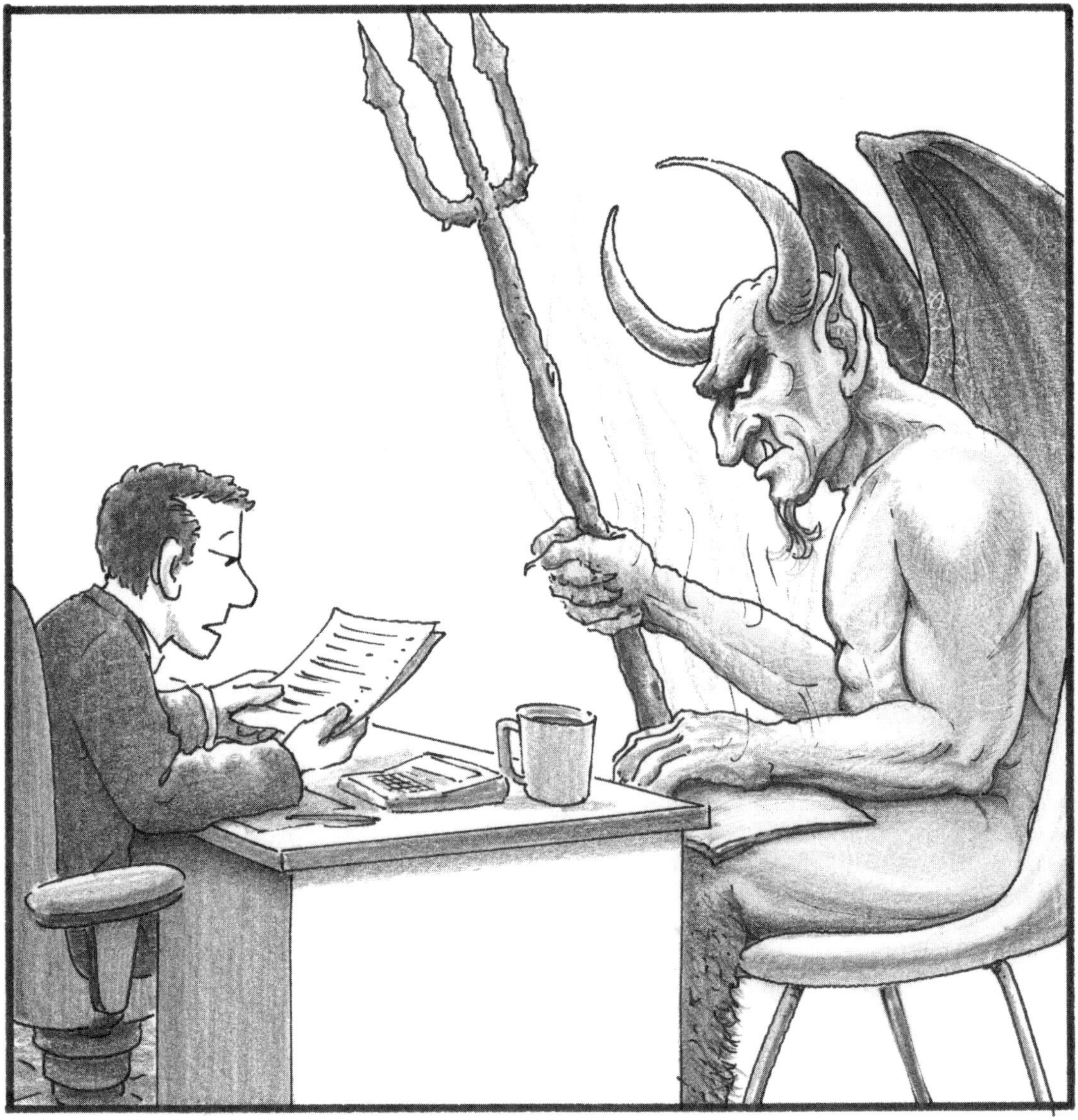

"NOW, THESE 'FLAMING SPIKES'—ARE THESE WORK RELATED?"

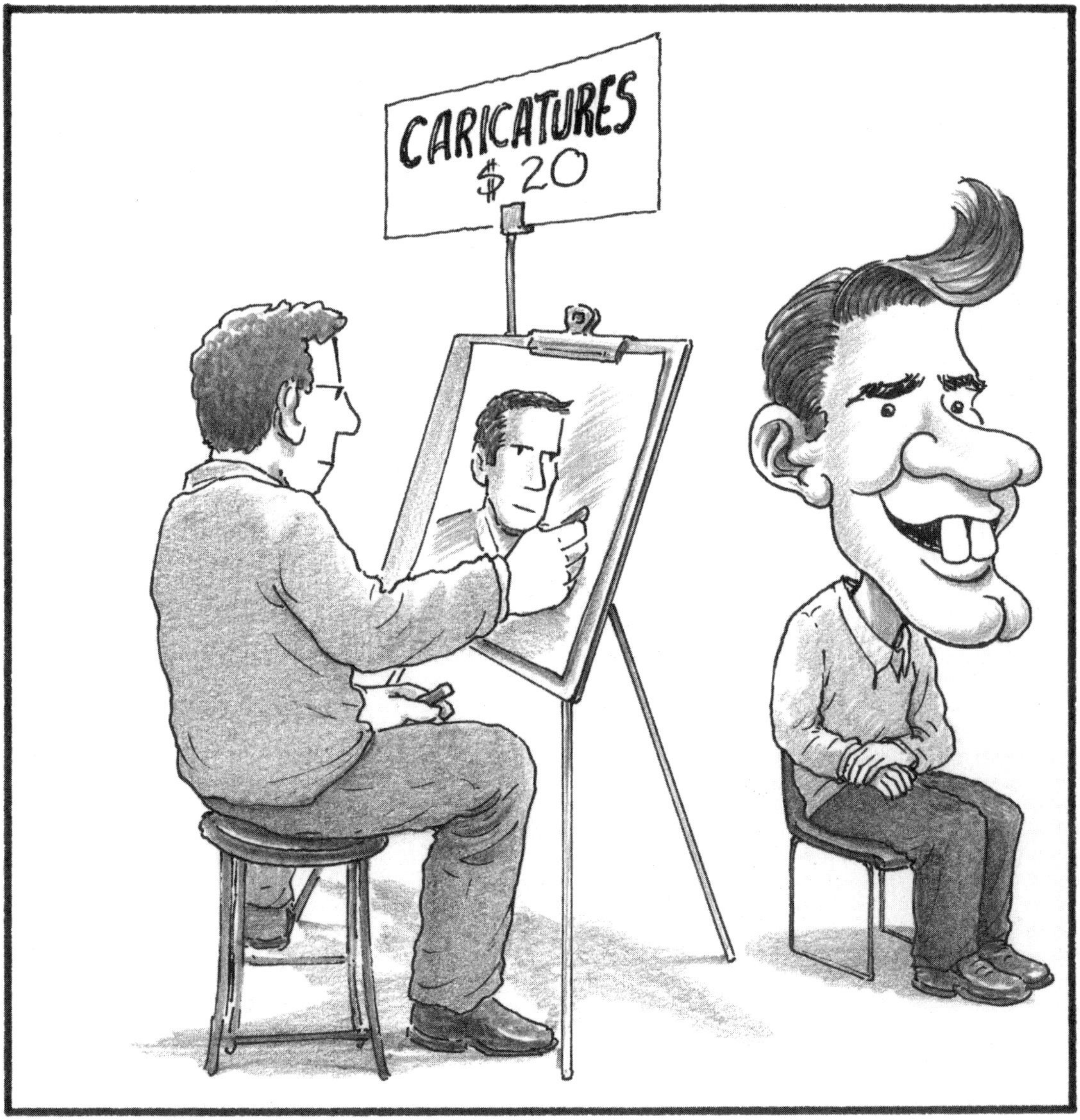
CARICATURES
$20

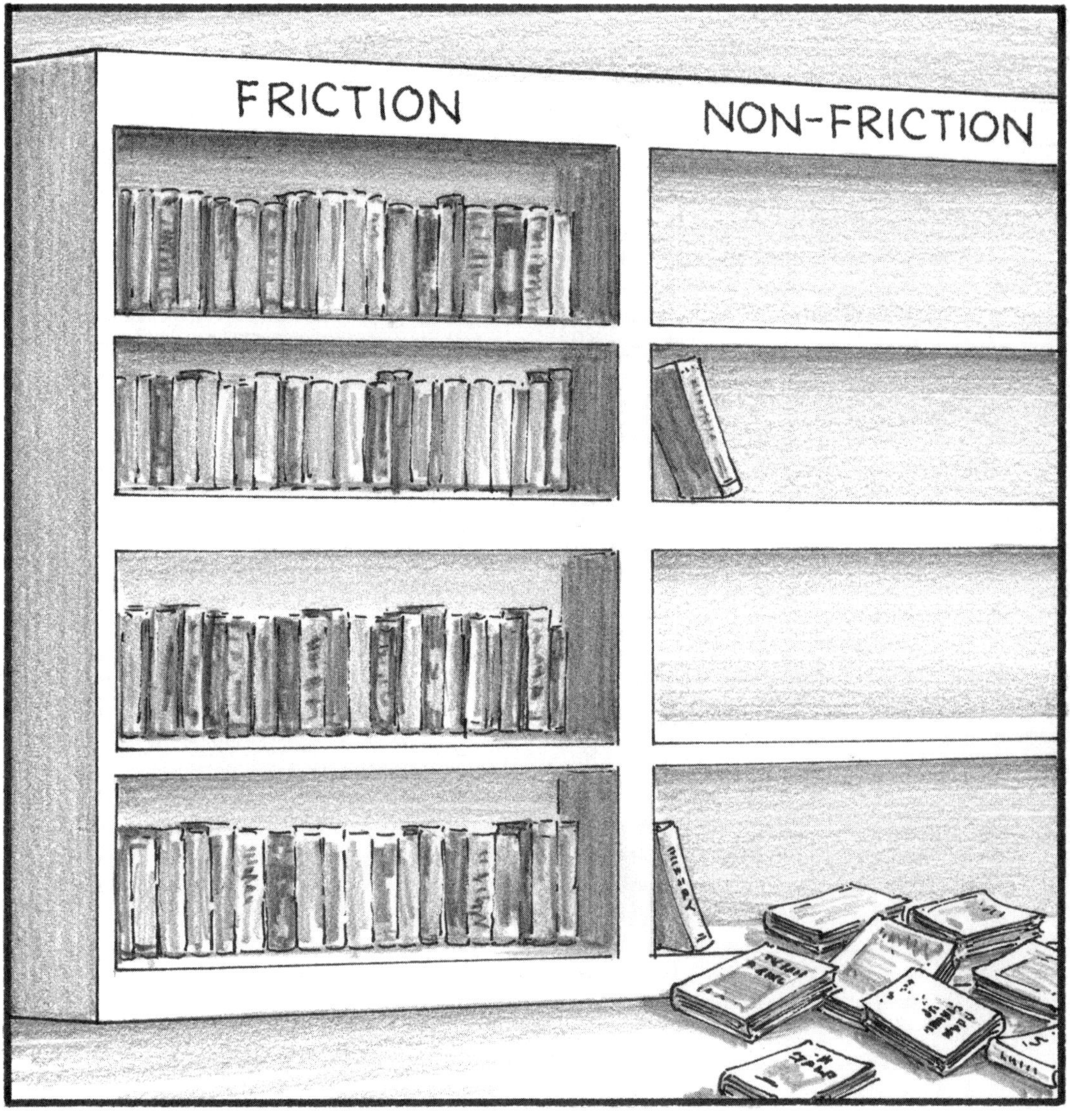
FRICTION
NON-FRICTION

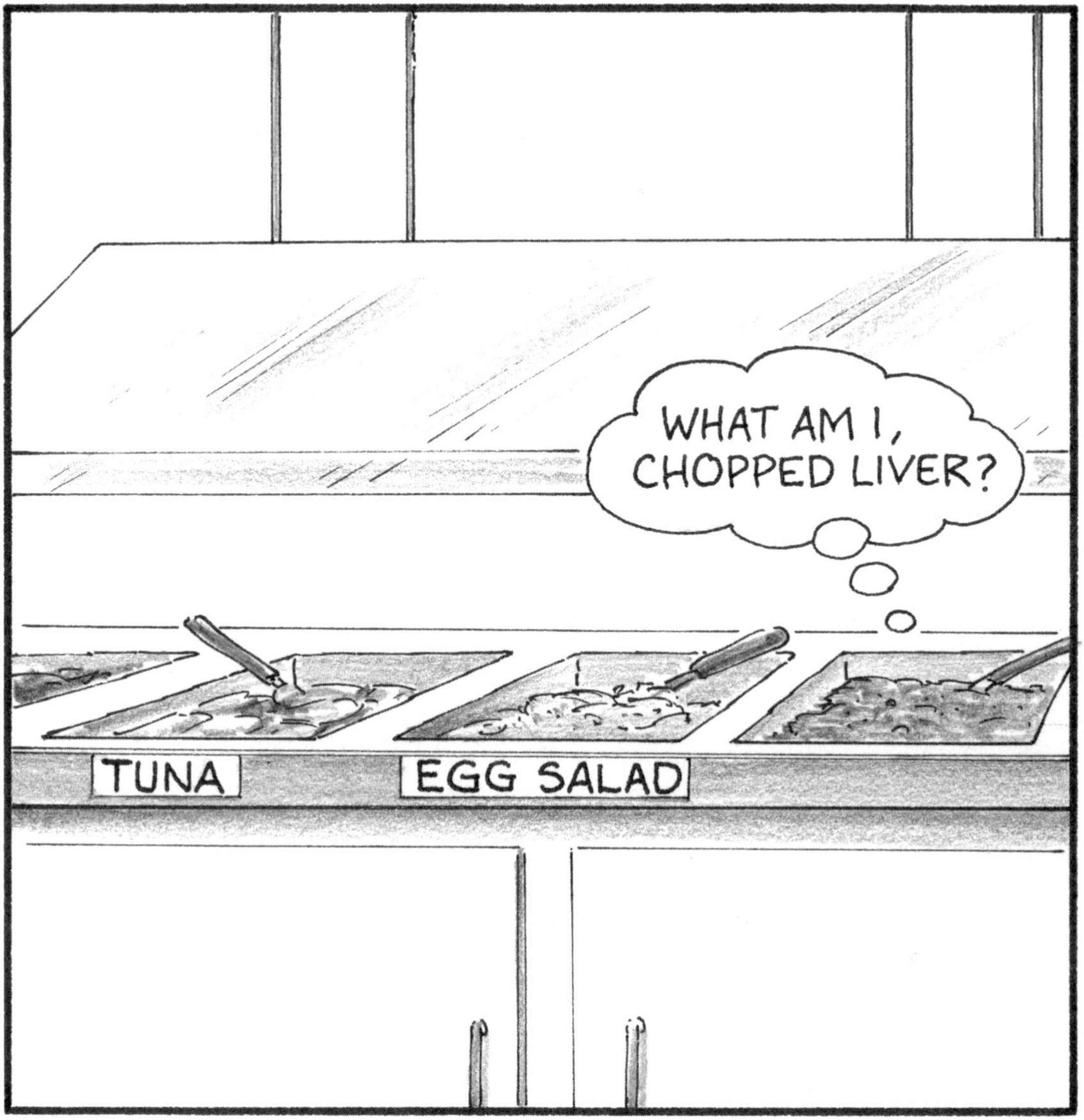
WHAT AM I, CHOPPED LIVER?
TUNA
EGG SALAD

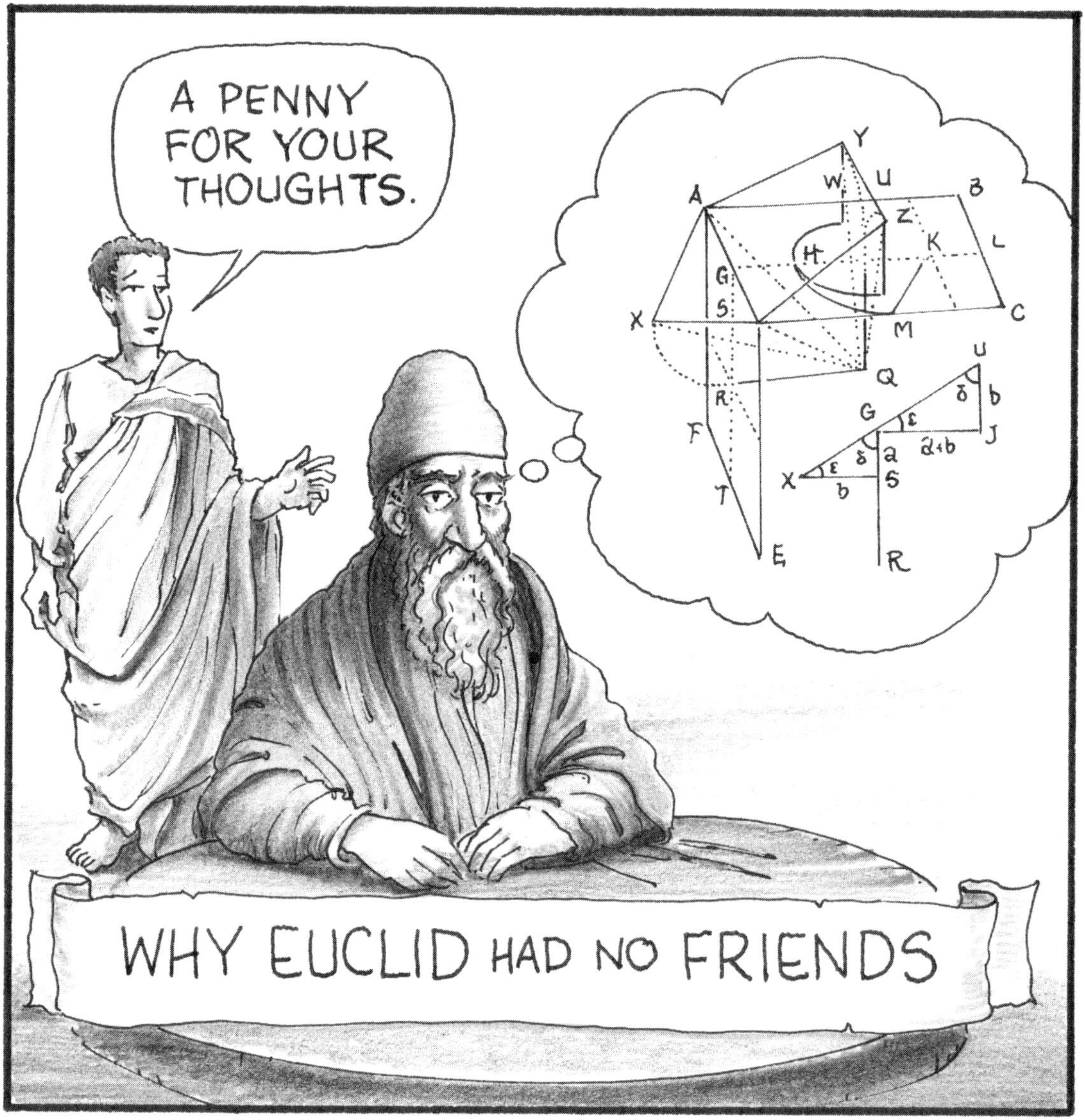
A PENNY FOR YOUR THOUGHTS.
WHY EUCLID HAD NO FRIENDS

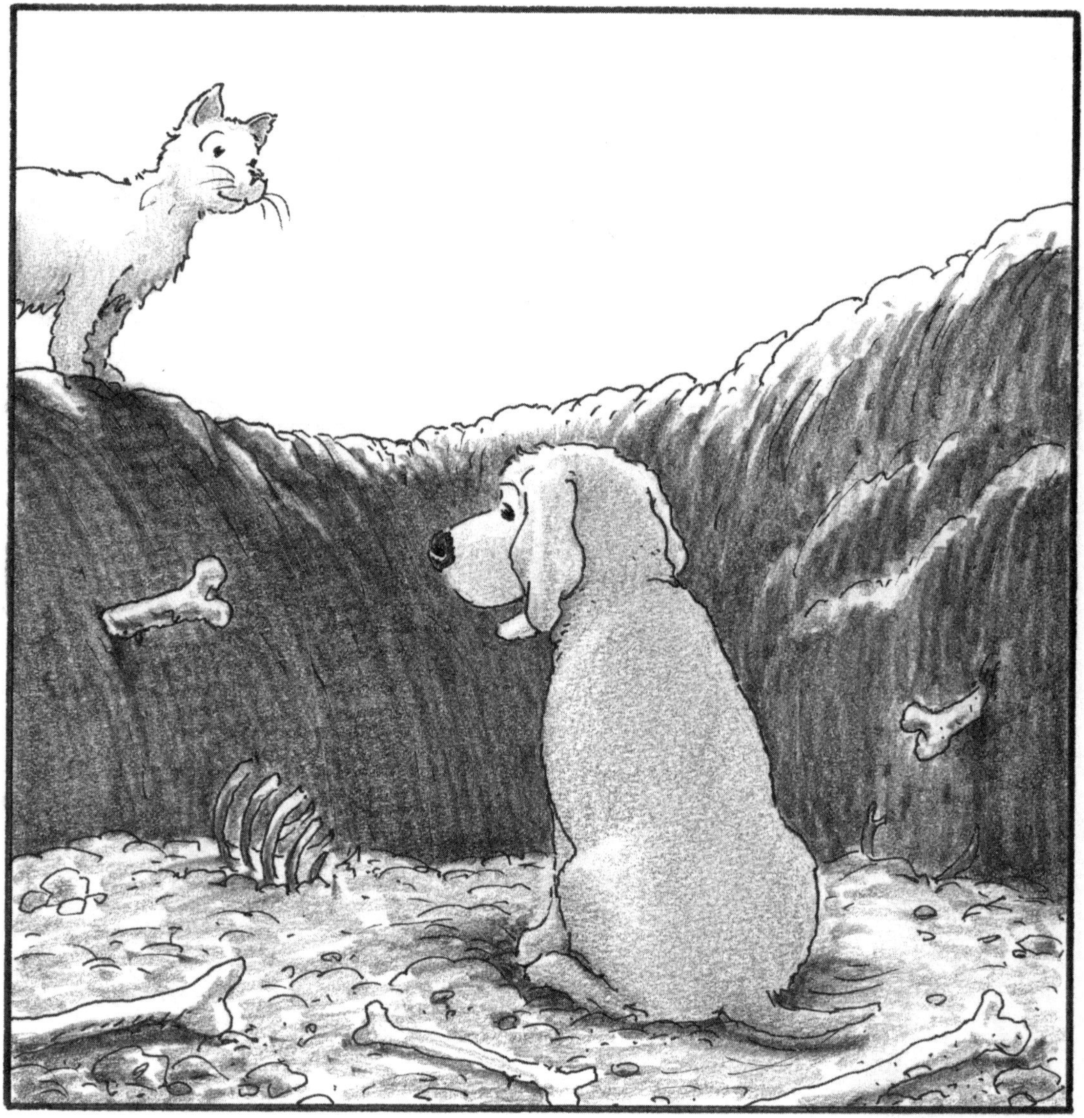

"IT'S LIKE GOING TO THE BANK TO VISIT YOUR MONEY."

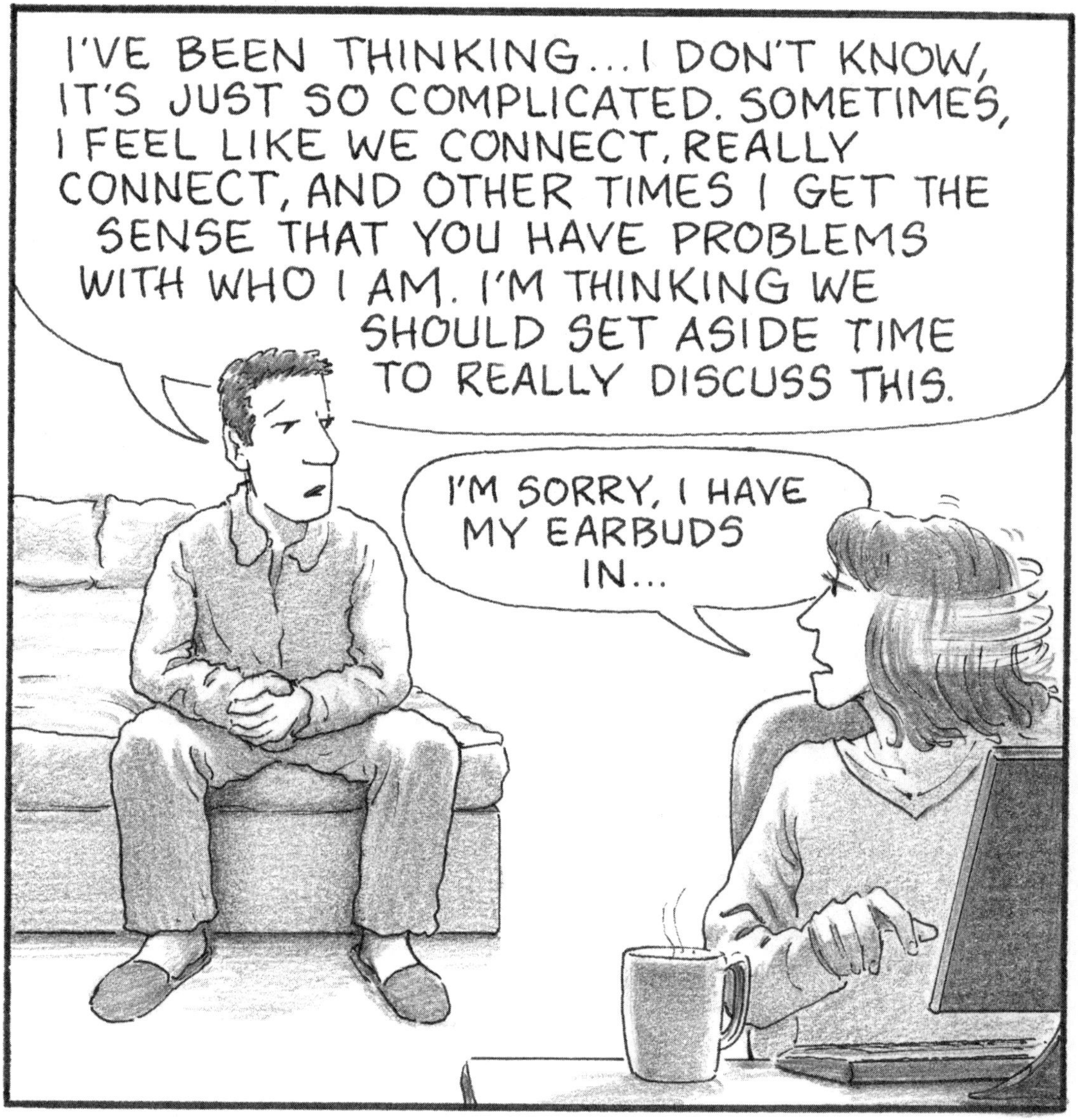
I'VE BEEN THINKING... I DON'T KNOW, IT'S JUST SO COMPLICATED. SOMETIMES, I FEEL LIKE WE CONNECT, REALLY CONNECT, AND OTHER TIMES I GET THE SENSE THAT YOU HAVE PROBLEMS WITH WHO I AM. I'M THINKING WE SHOULD SET ASIDE TIME TO REALLY DISCUSS THIS.
I'M SORRY, I HAVE MY EARBUDS IN...

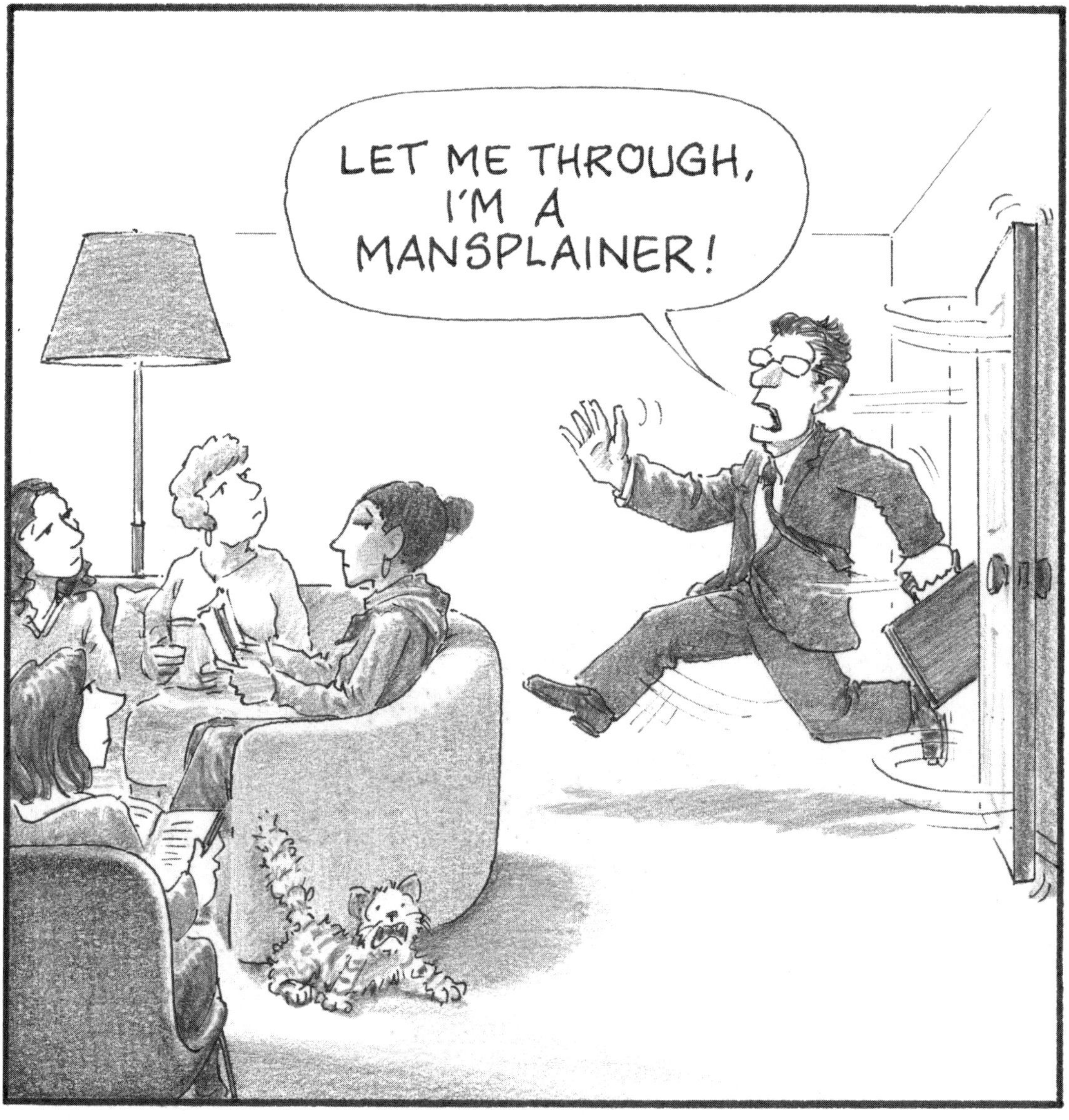
LET ME THROUGH, I'M A MANSPLAINER!

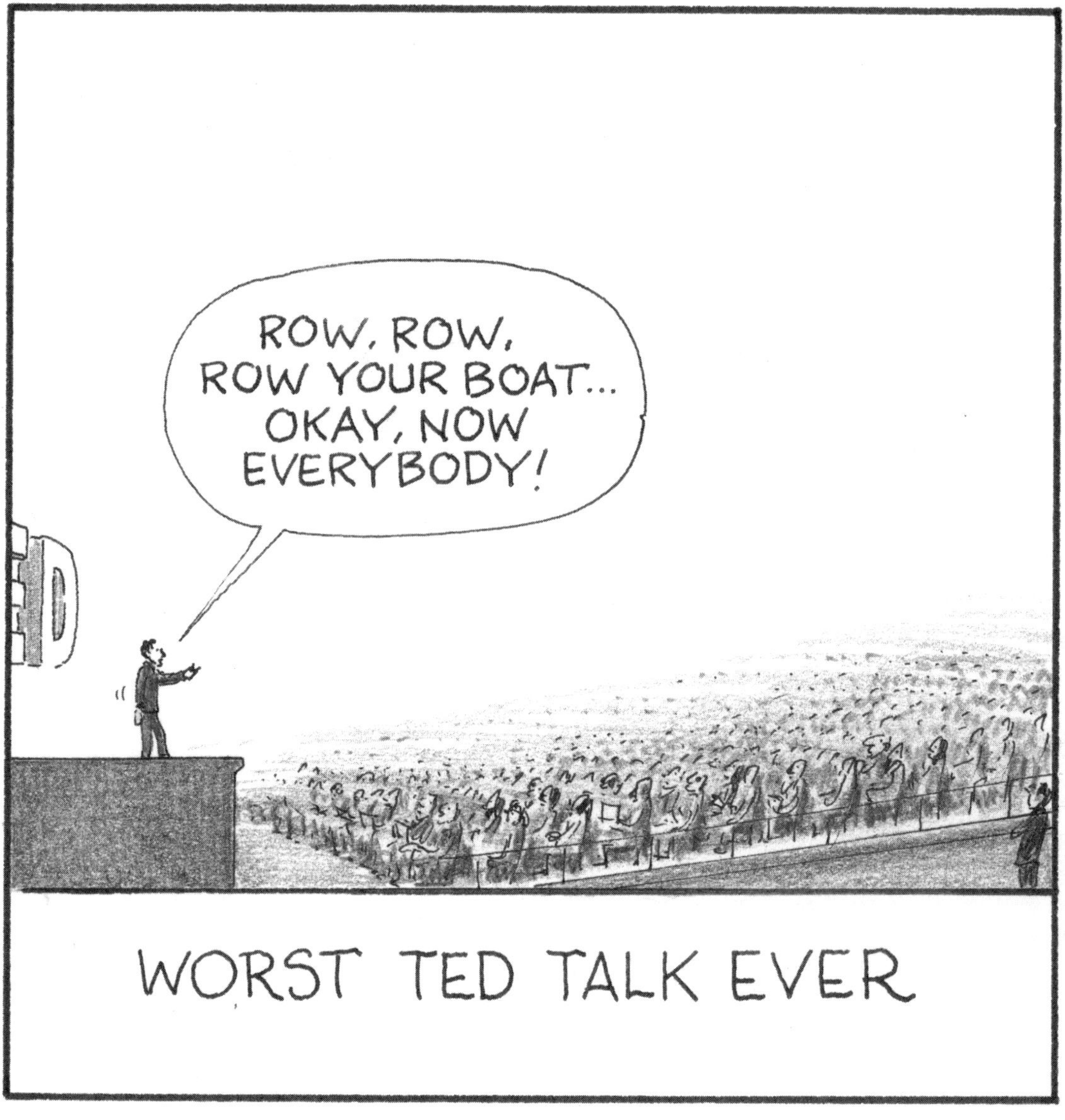
ROW, ROW, ROW YOUR BOAT... OKAY, NOW EVERYBODY!

WORST TED TALK EVER

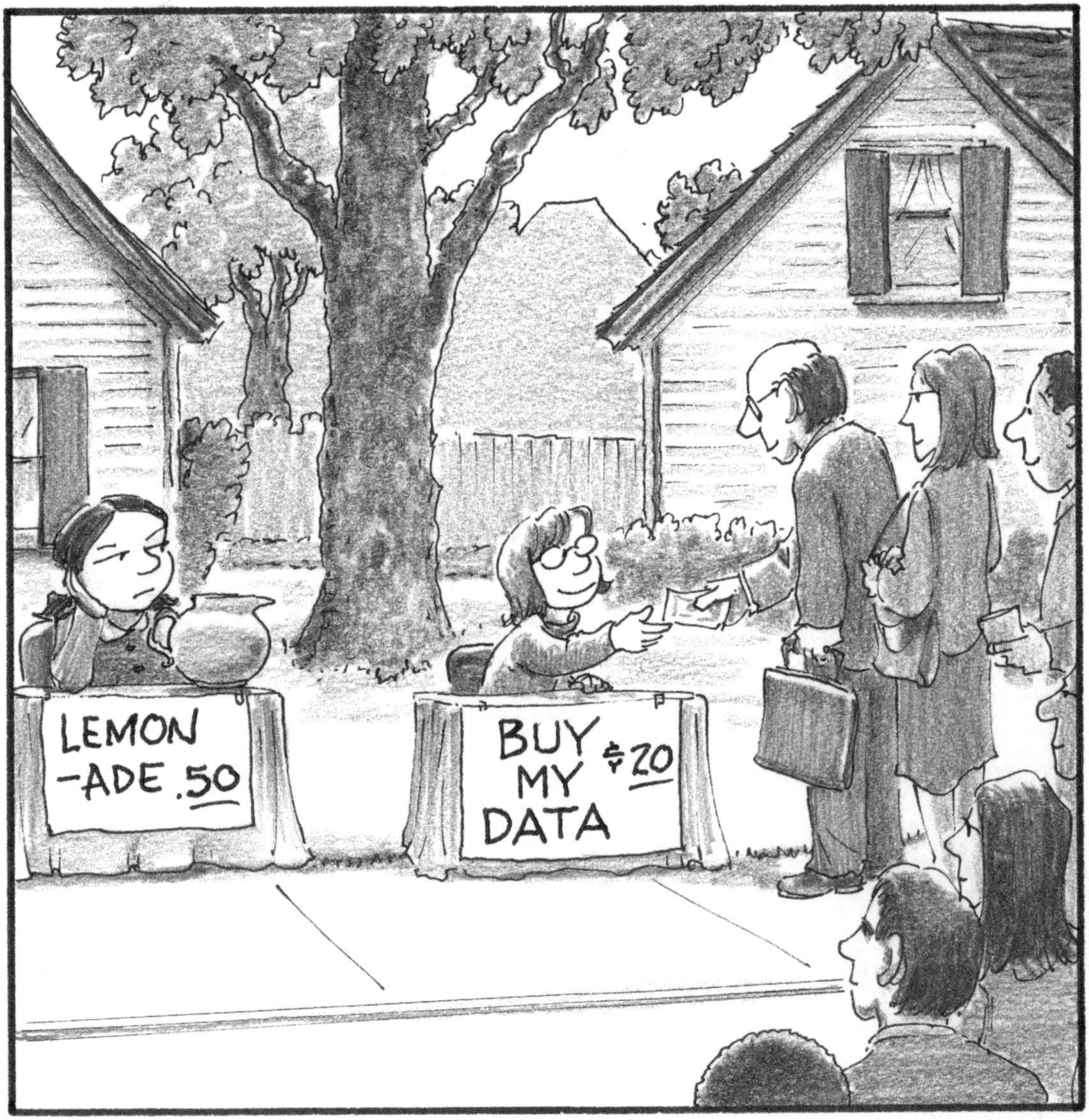
LEMON
-ADE .50
BUY
MY
DATA
$20

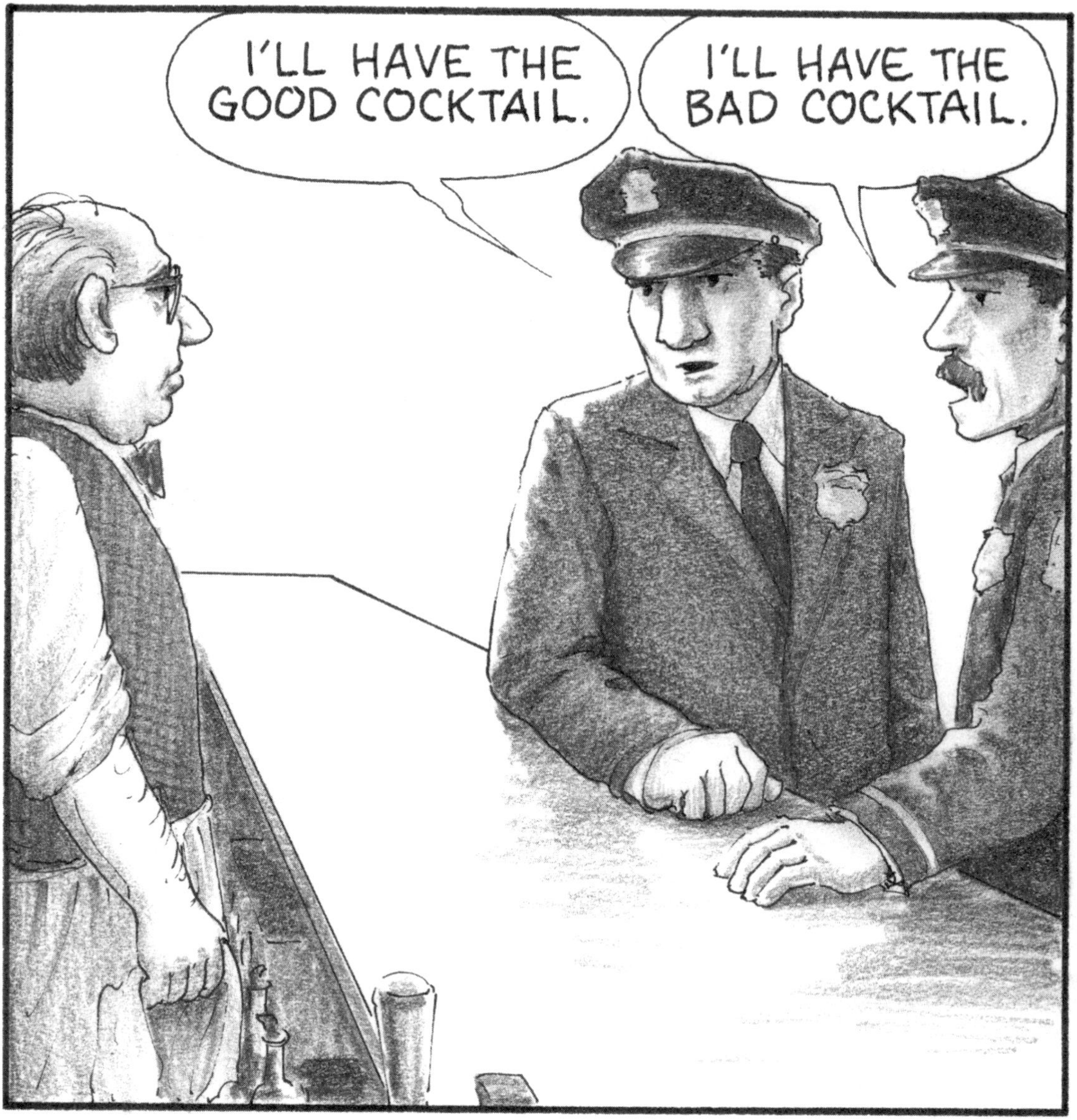
I'LL HAVE THE GOOD COCKTAIL.
I'LL HAVE THE BAD COCKTAIL.

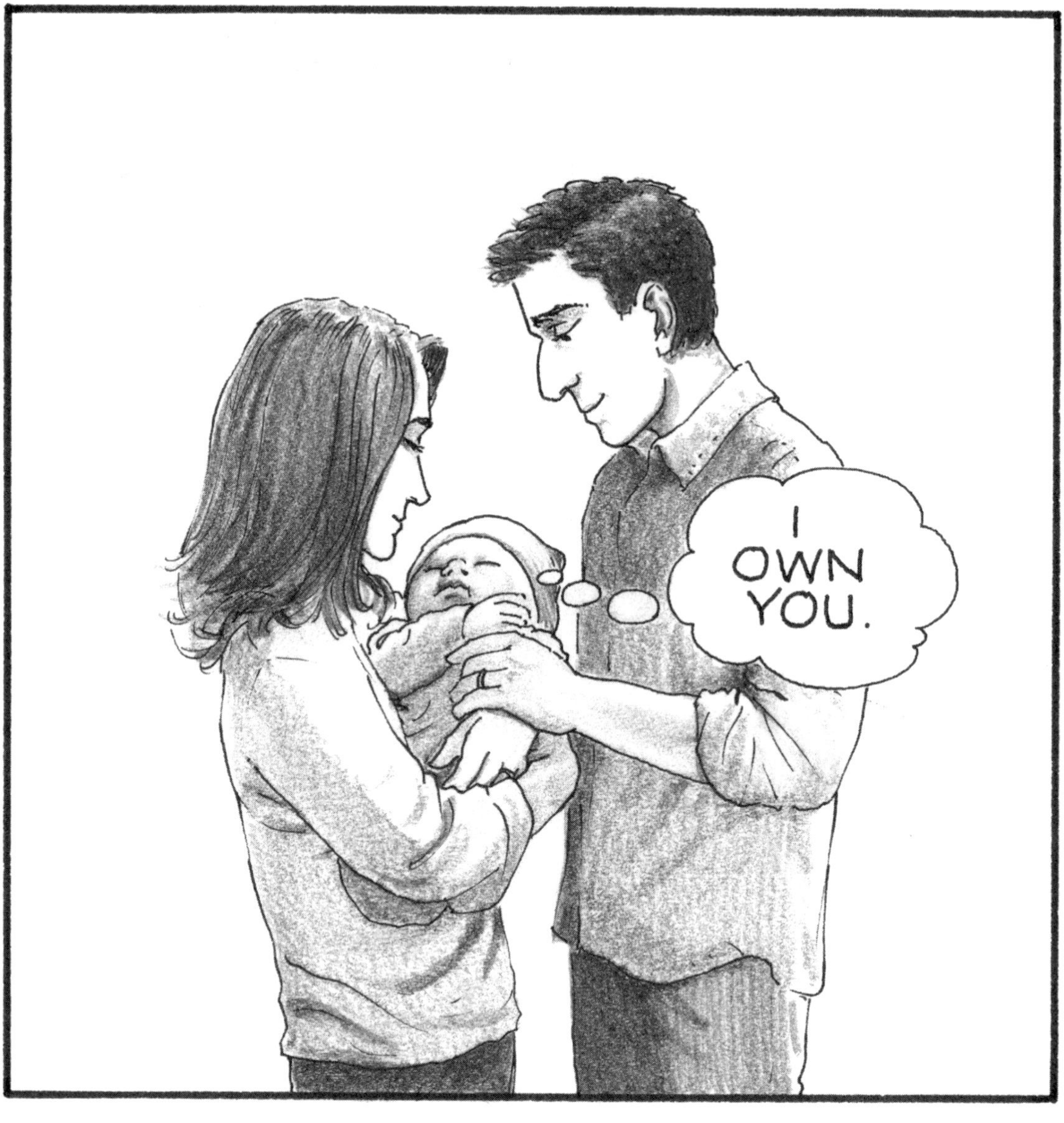
I OWN YOU.

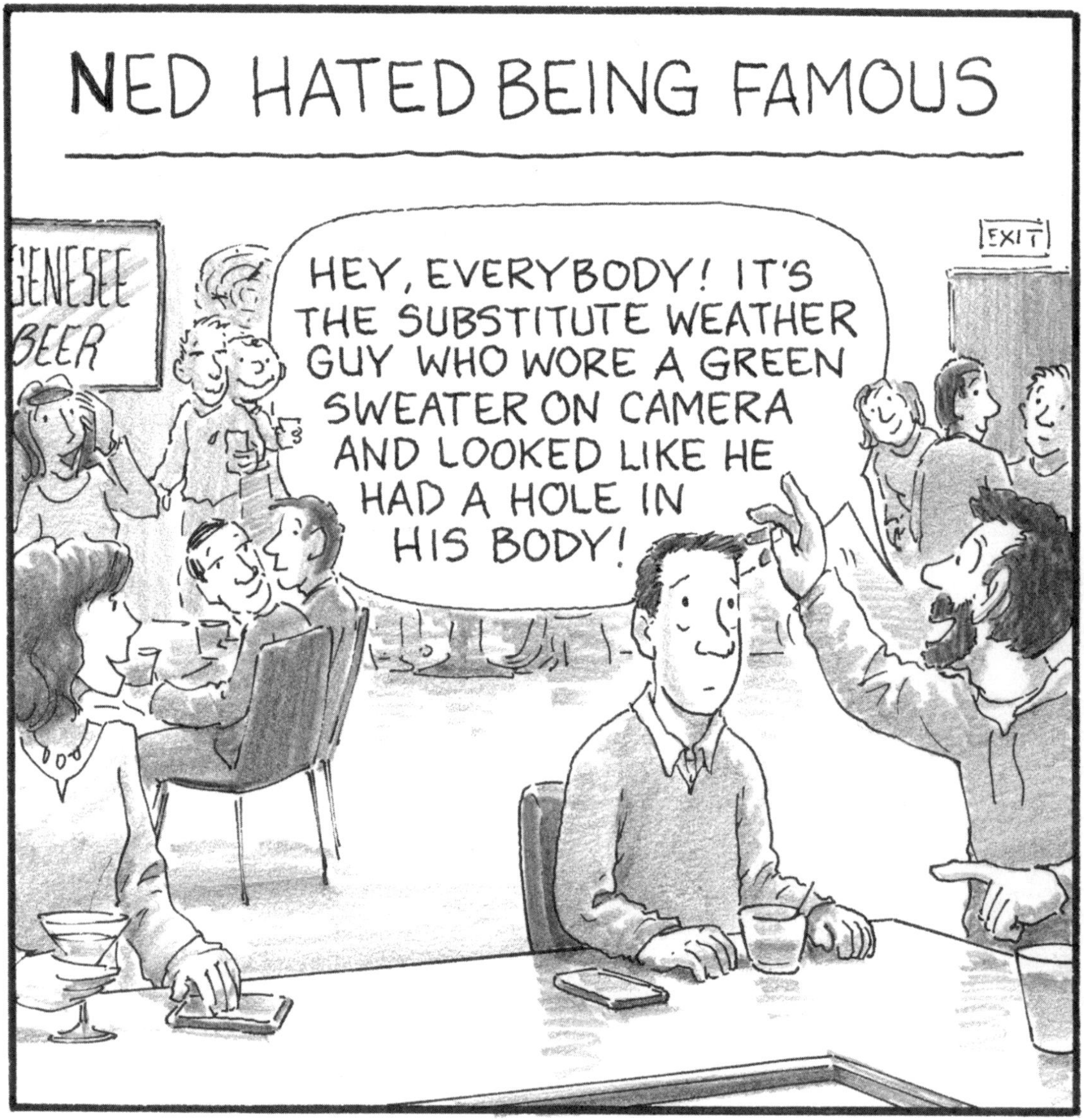
NED HATED BEING FAMOUS
GENESEE BEER
EXIT
HEY, EVERYBODY! IT'S THE SUBSTITUTE WEATHER GUY WHO WORE A GREEN SWEATER ON CAMERA AND LOOKED LIKE HE HAD A HOLE IN HIS BODY!

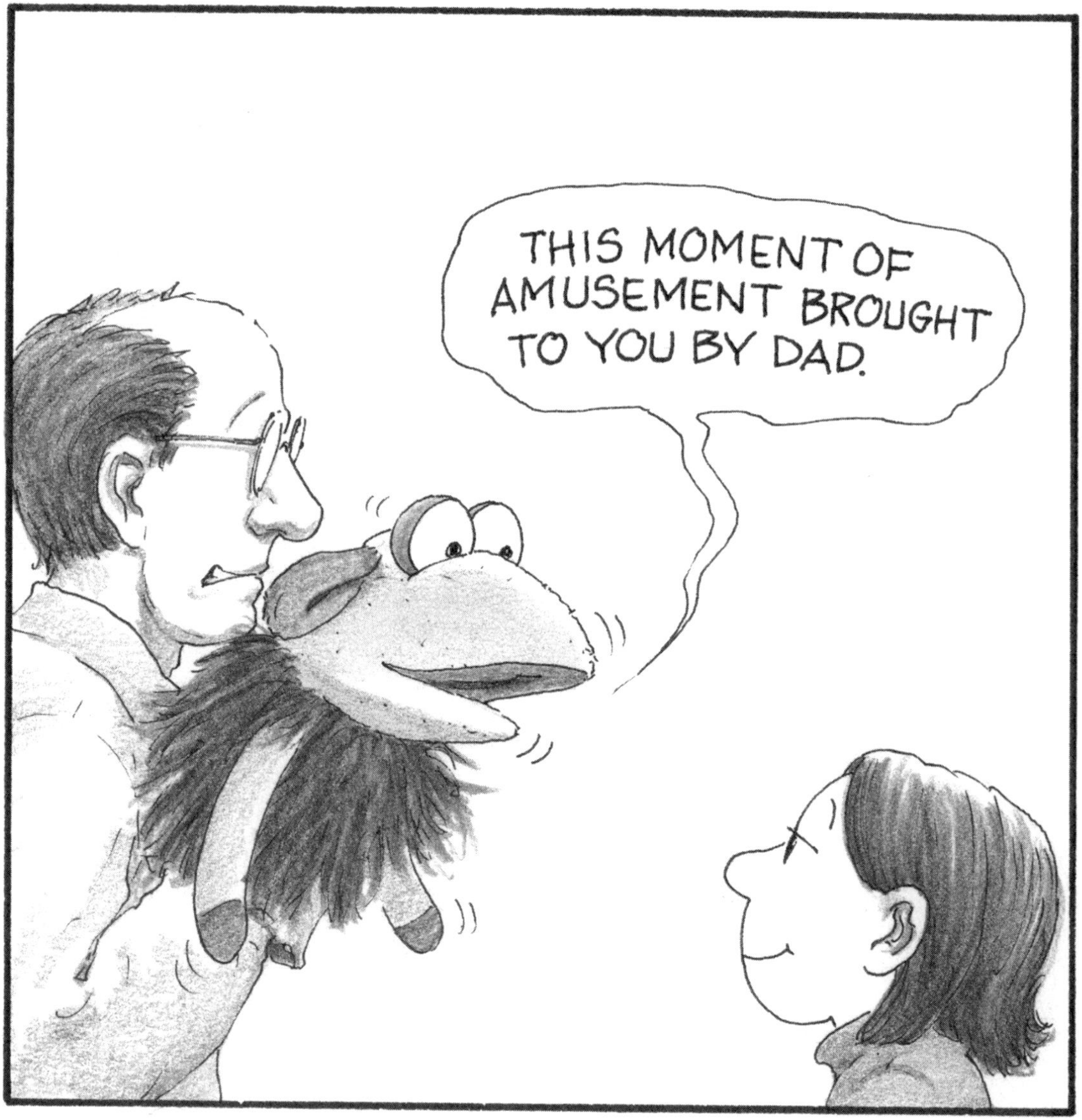
THIS MOMENT OF AMUSEMENT BROUGHT TO YOU BY DAD.

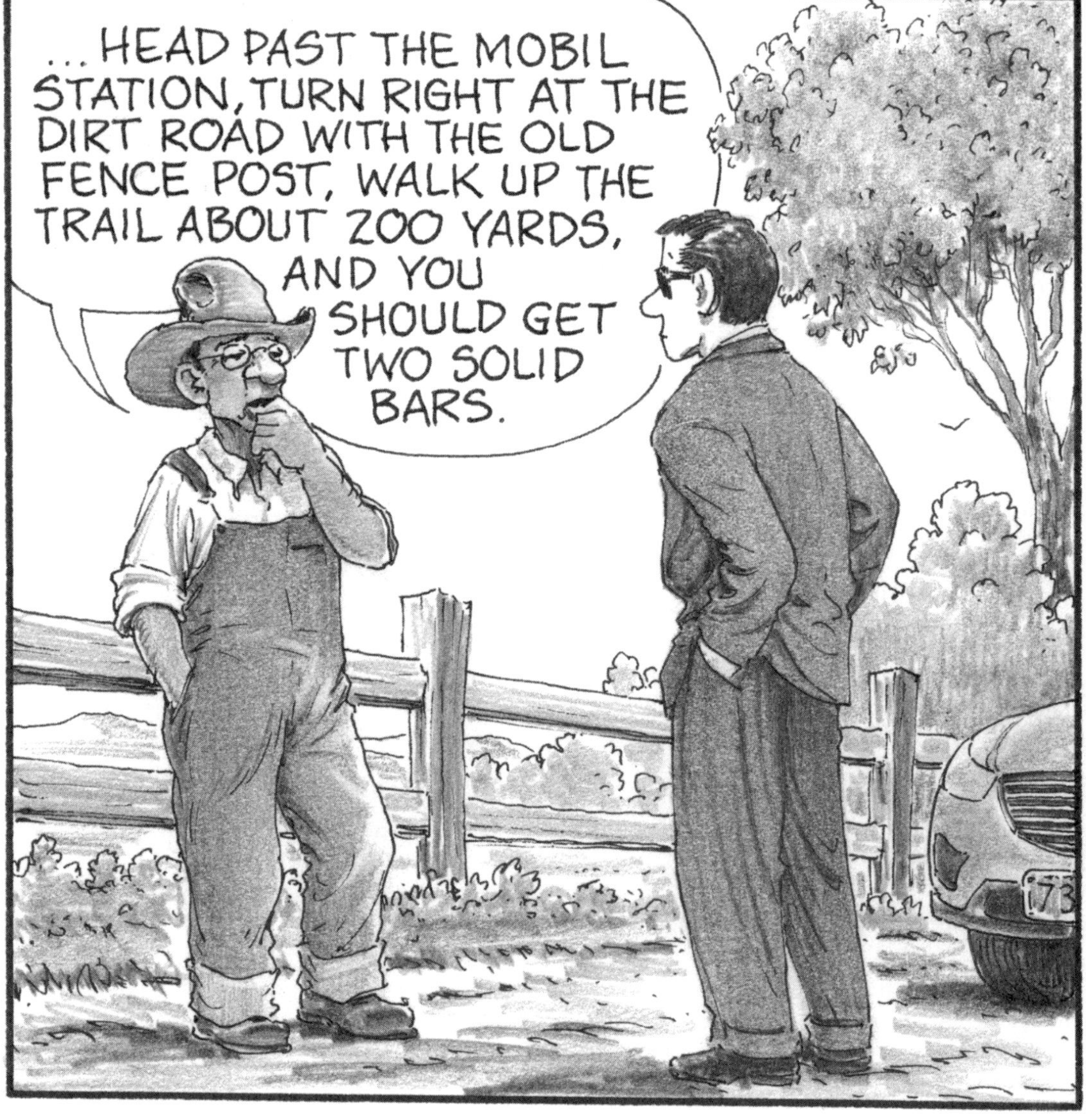
...HEAD PAST THE MOBIL STATION, TURN RIGHT AT THE DIRT ROAD WITH THE OLD FENCE POST, WALK UP THE TRAIL ABOUT 200 YARDS, AND YOU SHOULD GET TWO SOLID BARS.

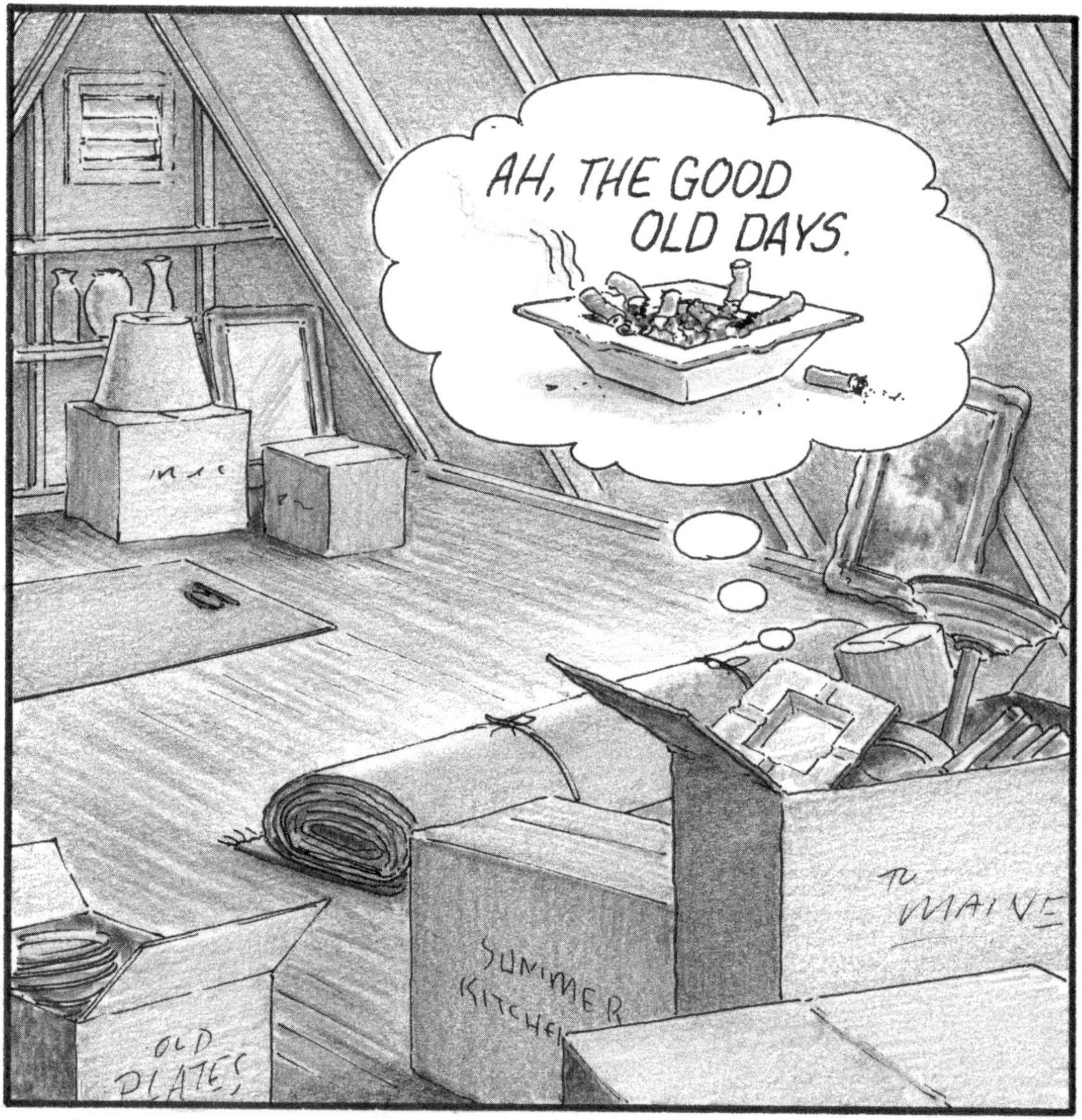
AH, THE GOOD OLD DAYS.
SUMMER KITCHEN
MAINE
OLD PLATES

VARIOUS ENTRANCES TO THE GATES OF HELL
CITING WIKIPEDIA AS A SOURCE.
QUESTIONABLE PLACEMENT OF SEMICOLON.
DUBIOUS USE OF "ENORMITY."

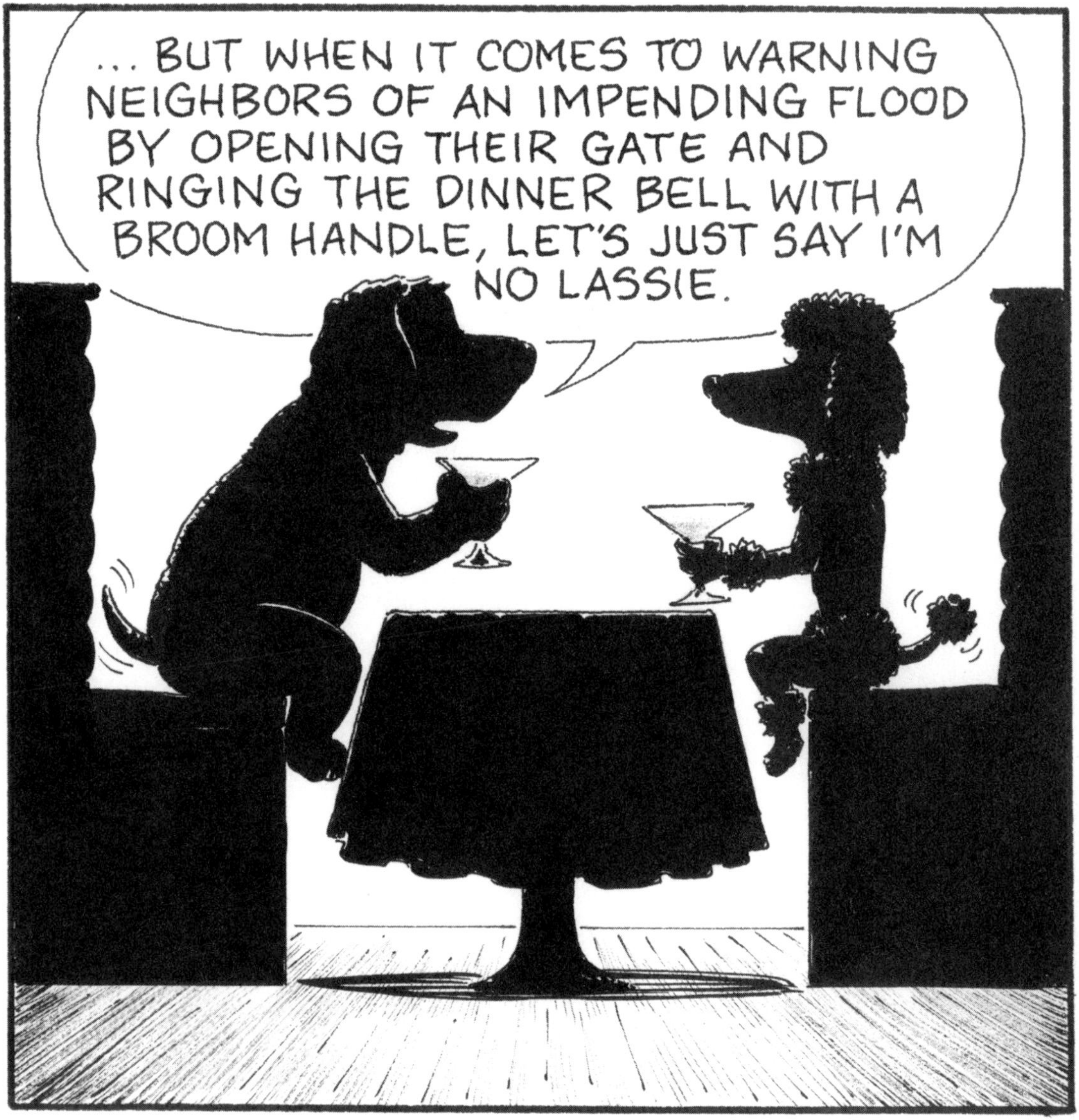
... BUT WHEN IT COMES TO WARNING NEIGHBORS OF AN IMPENDING FLOOD BY OPENING THEIR GATE AND RINGING THE DINNER BELL WITH A BROOM HANDLE, LET'S JUST SAY I'M NO LASSIE.

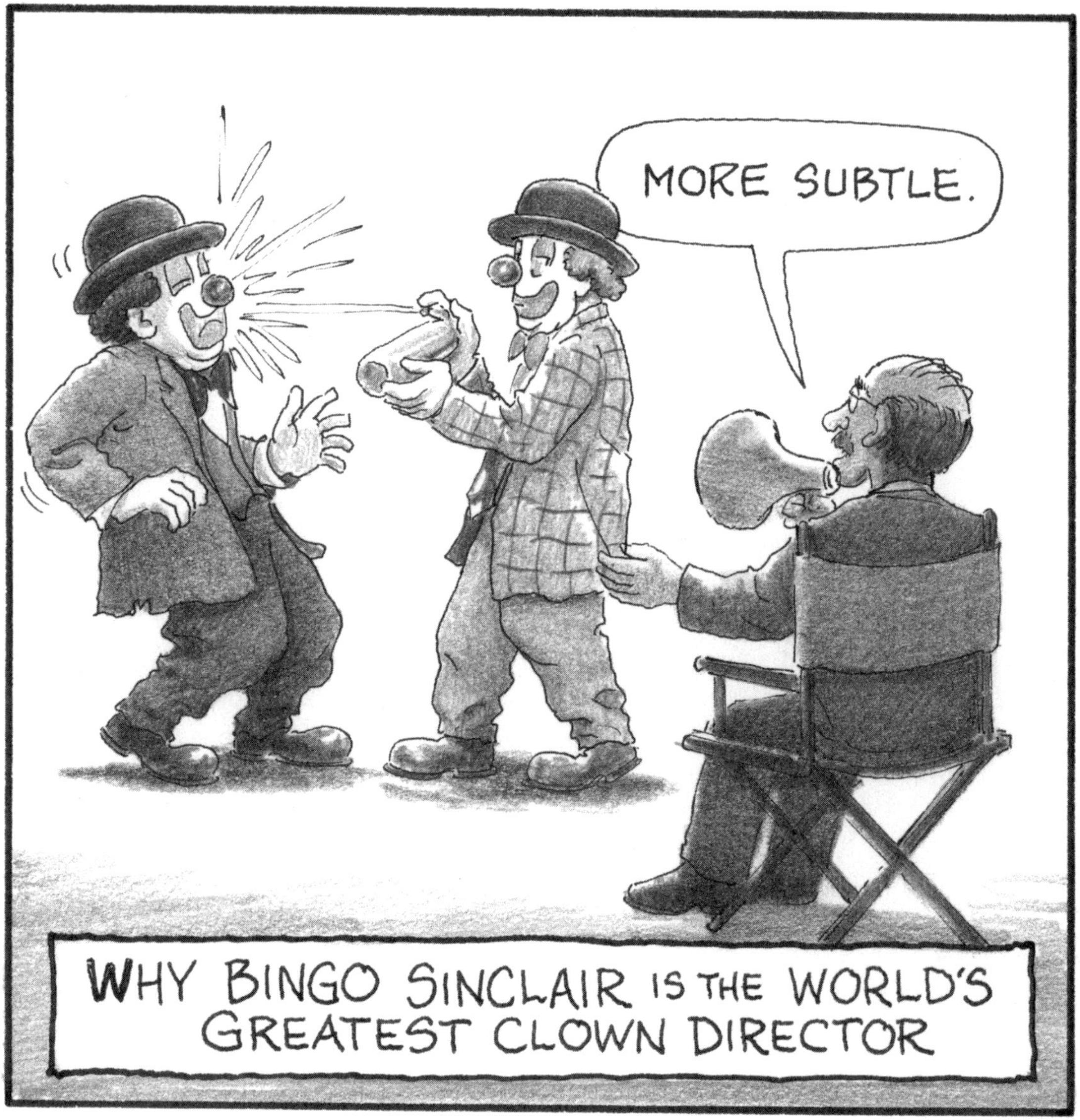
MORE SUBTLE.
WHY BINGO SINCLAIR IS THE WORLD'S GREATEST CLOWN DIRECTOR

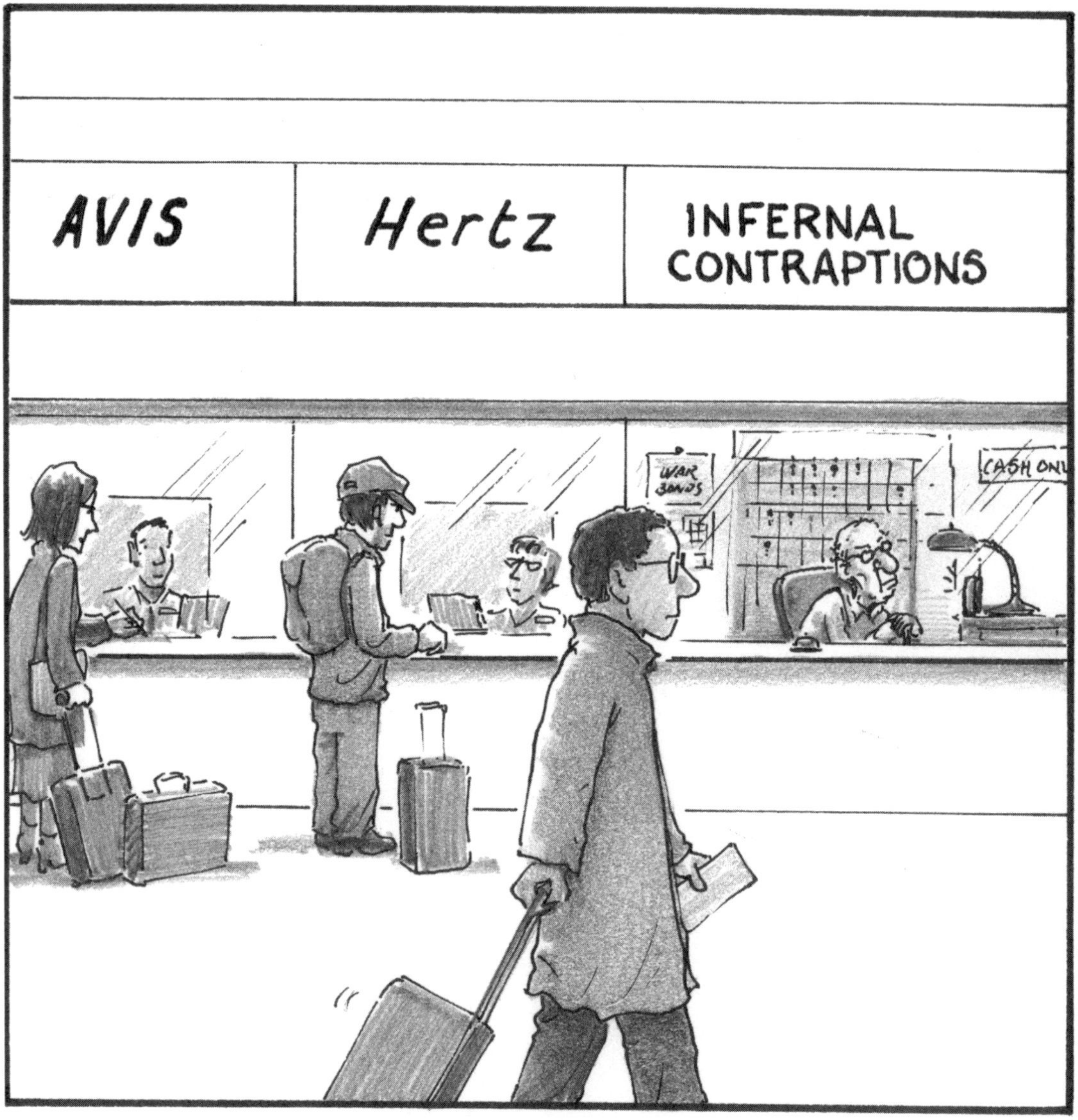
AVIS
Hertz
INFERNAL CONTRAPTIONS
WAR BONDS

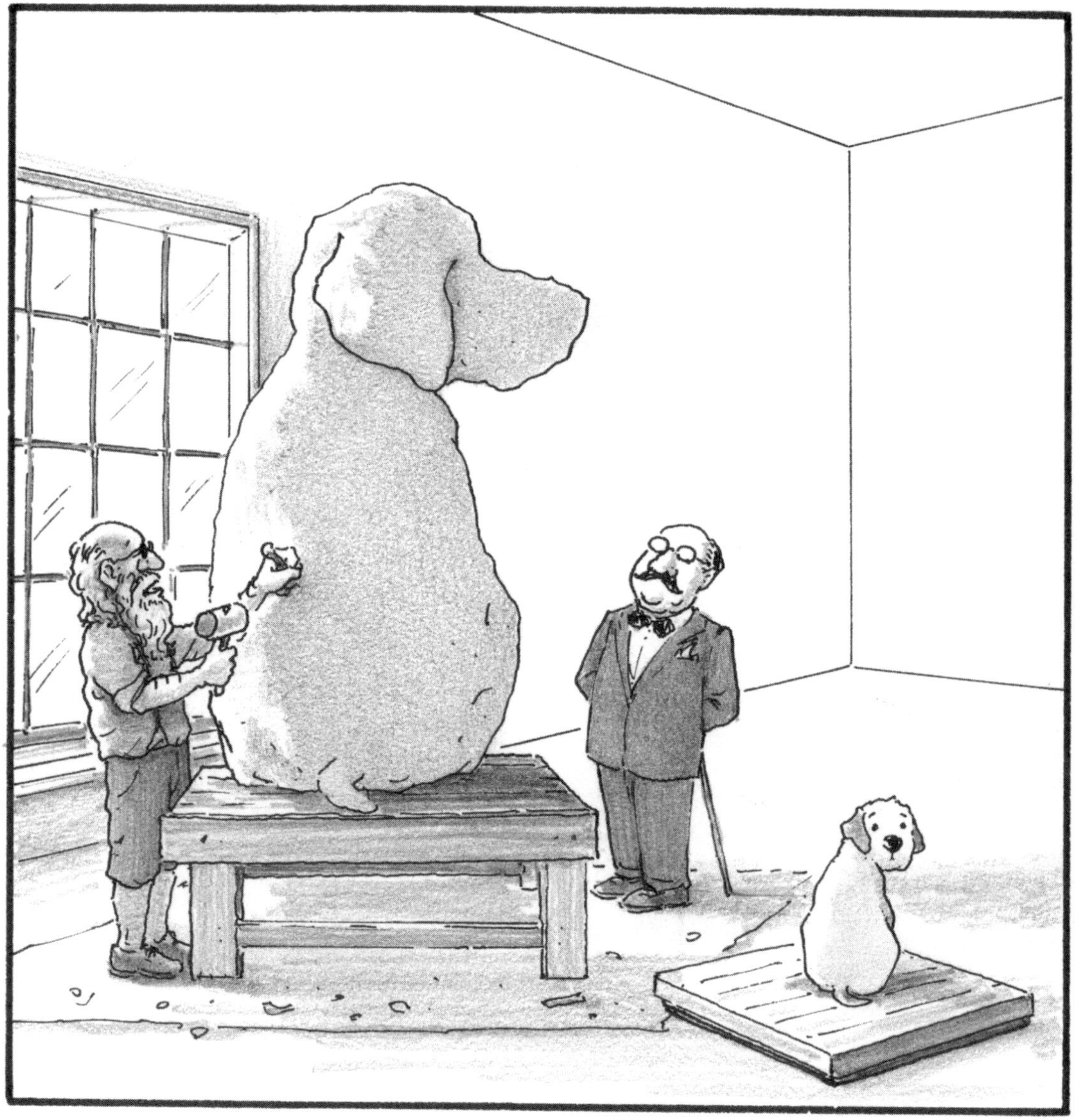

"SOMETIMES I FALL IN LOVE WITH MY MODEL."

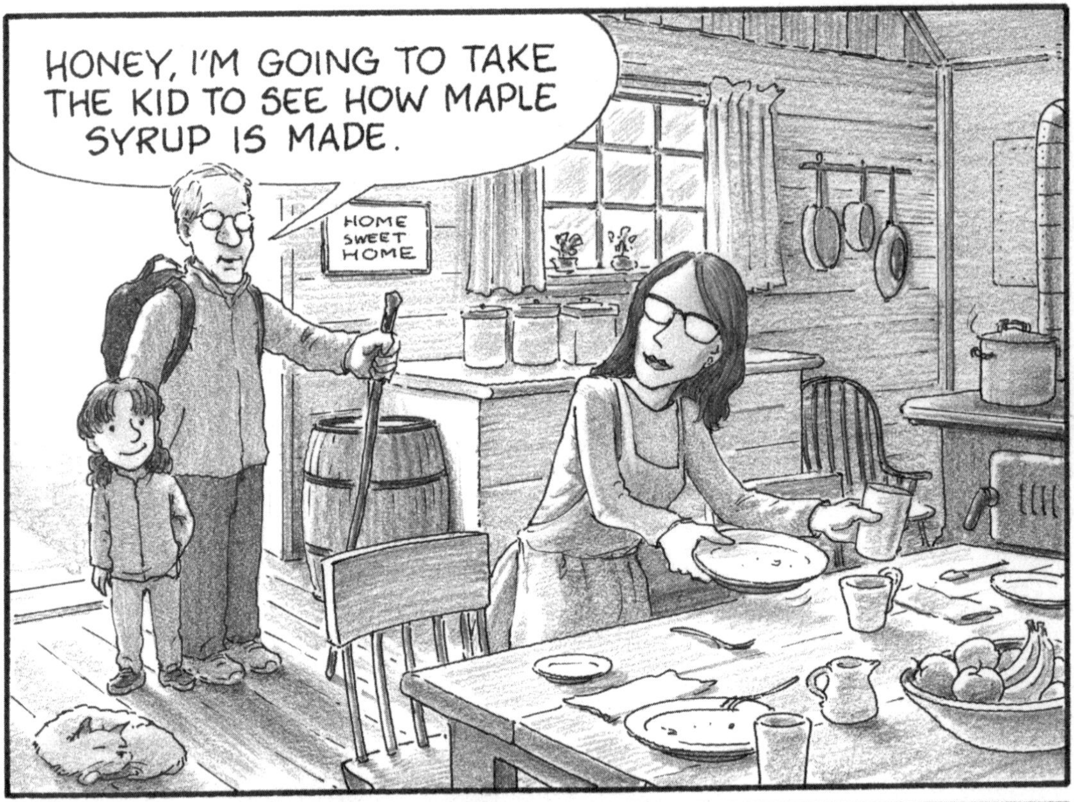
HONEY, I'M GOING TO TAKE THE KID TO SEE HOW MAPLE SYRUP IS MADE.
HOME SWEET HOME

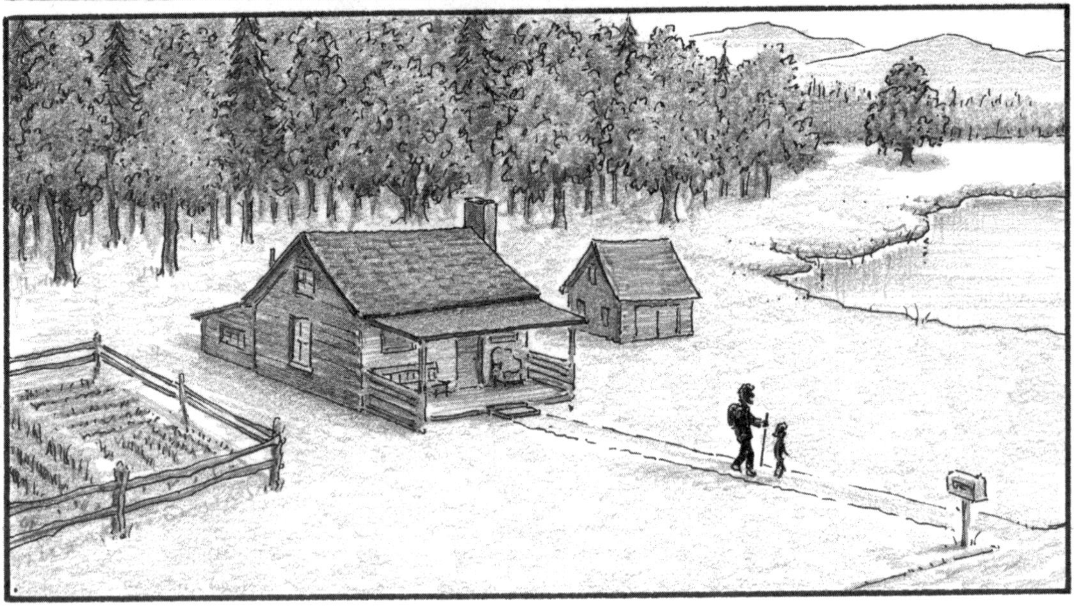

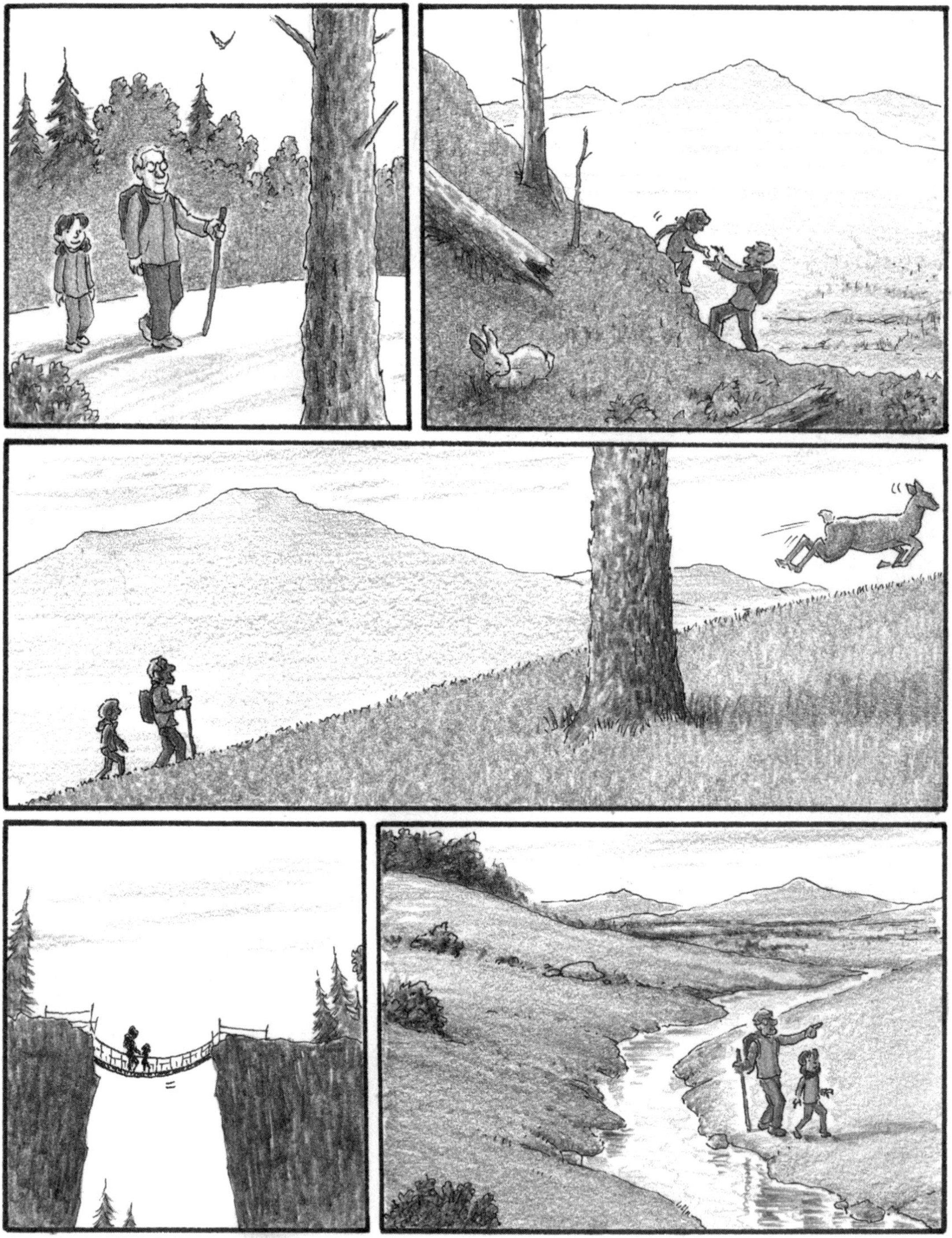

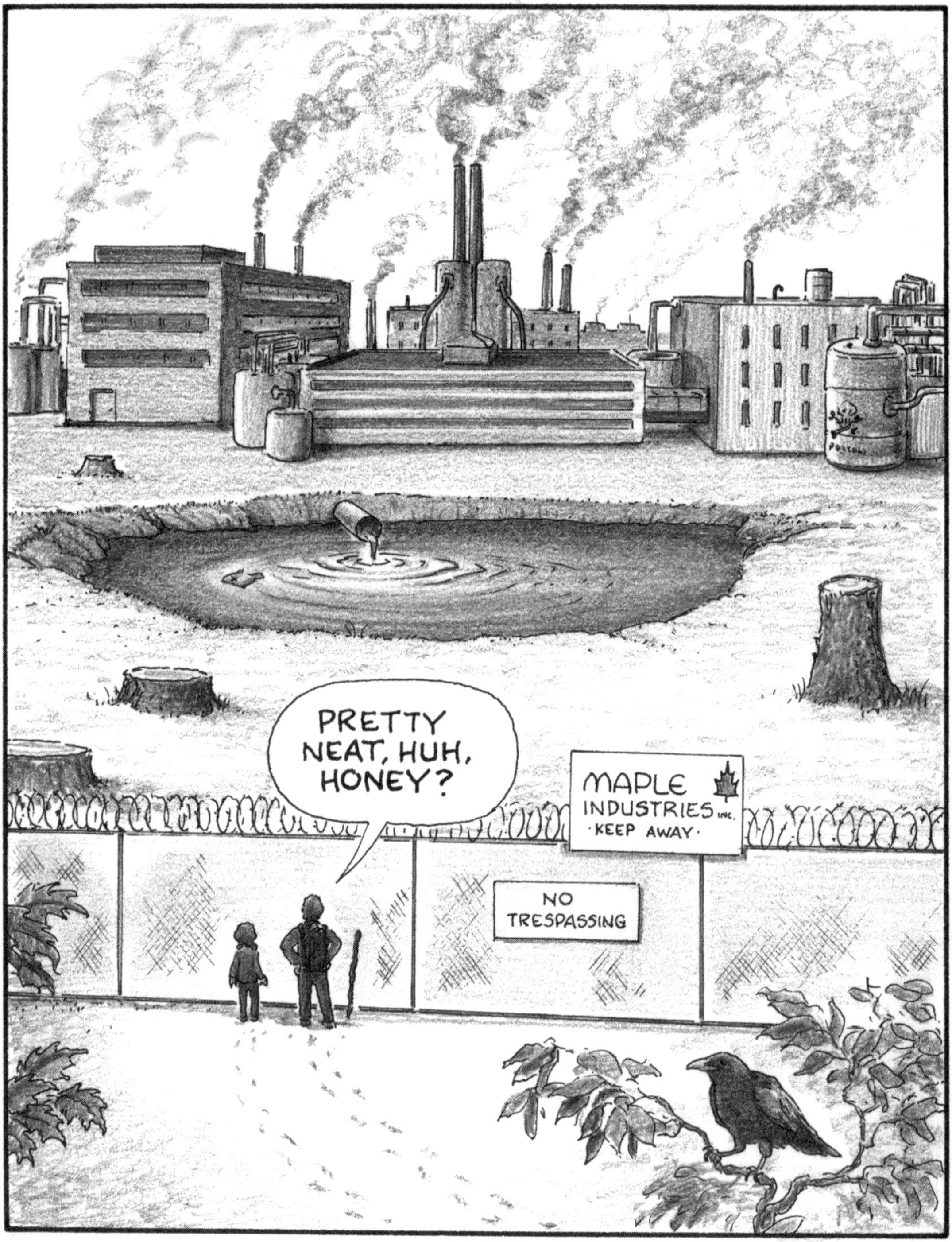
PRETTY NEAT, HUH, HONEY?
MAPLE INDUSTRIES INC.
·KEEP AWAY·
NO TRESPASSING

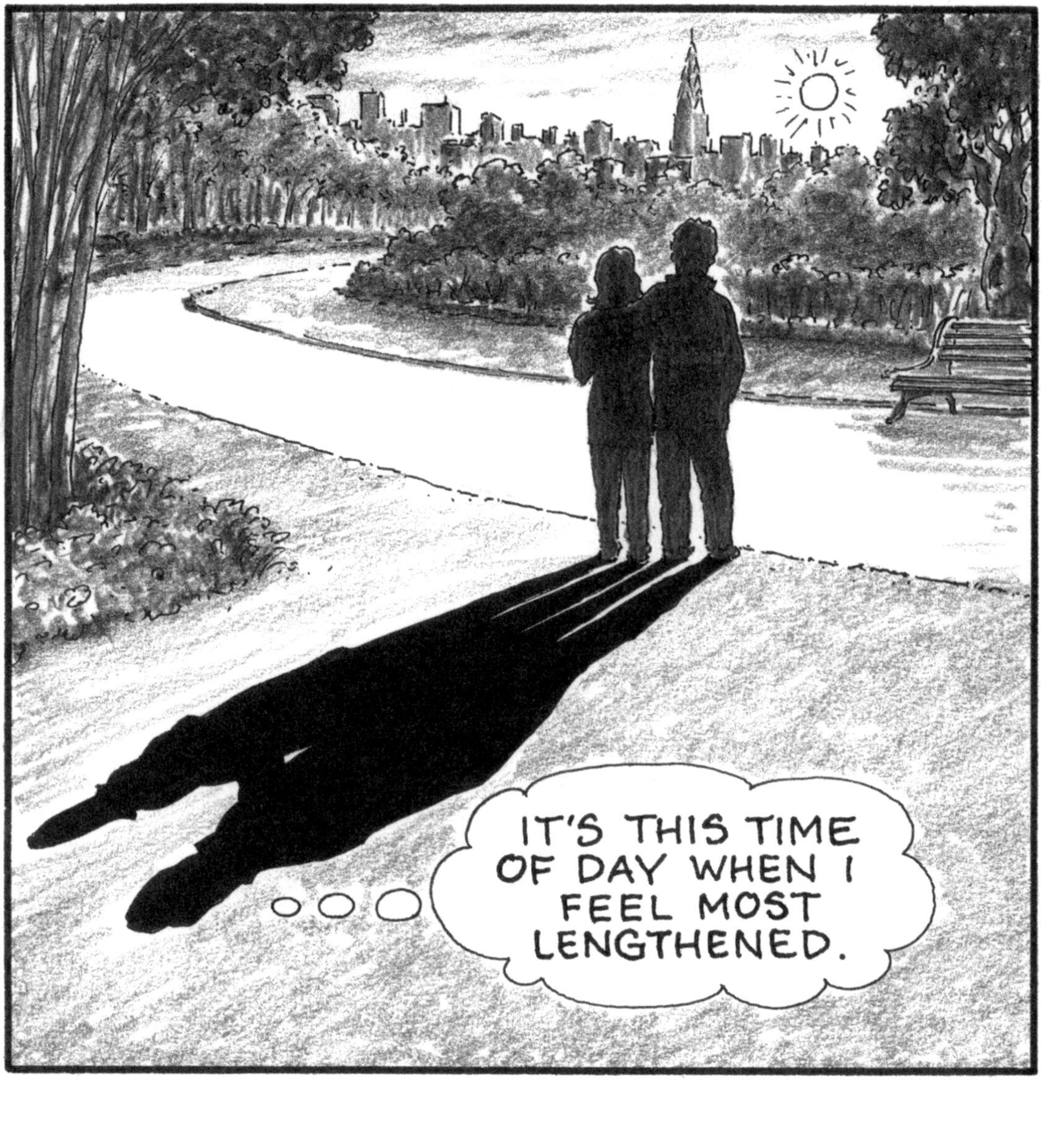
IT'S THIS TIME OF DAY WHEN I FEEL MOST LENGTHENED.

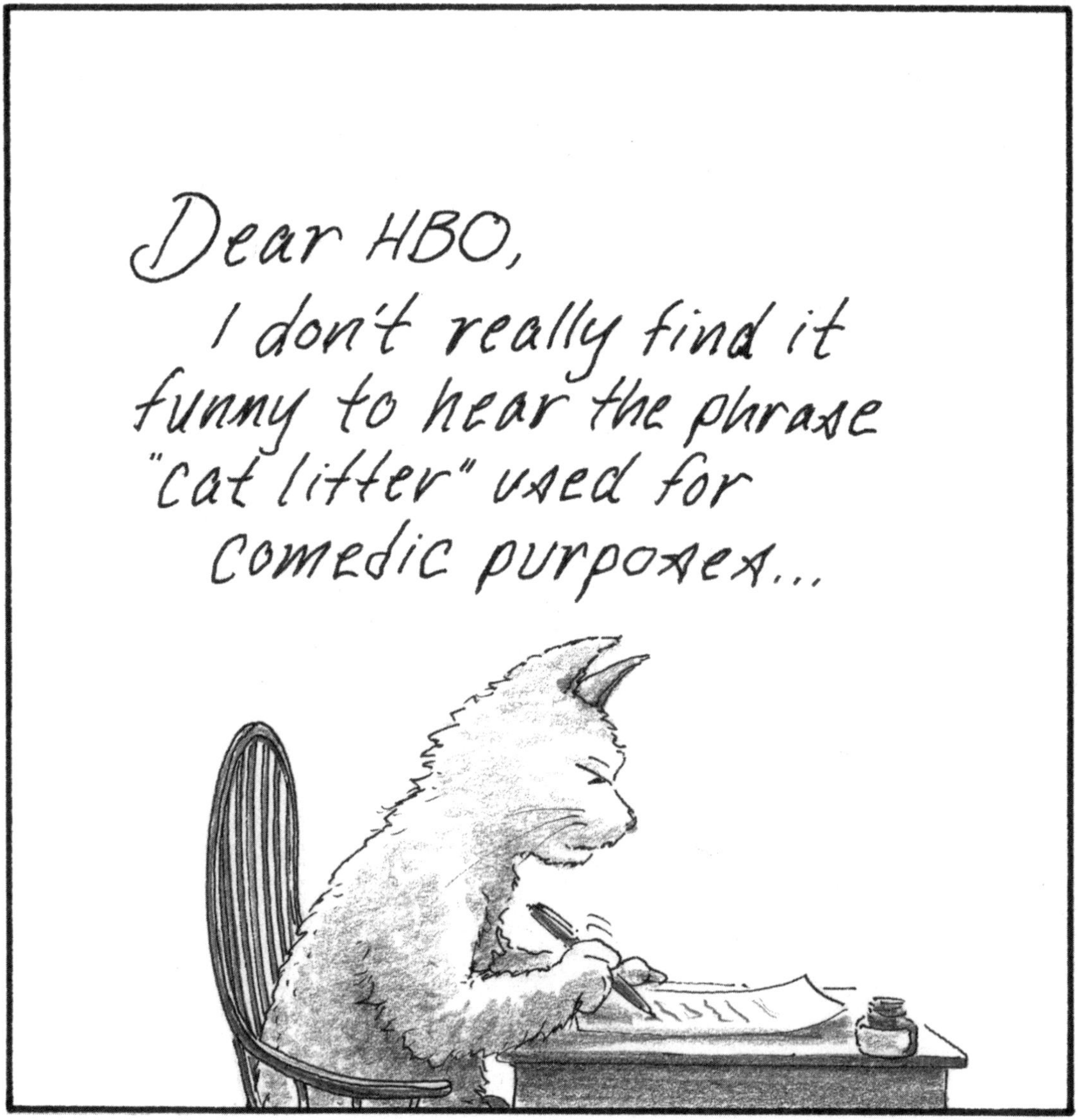
Dear HBO,
I don't really find it funny to hear the phrase "cat litter" used for comedic purposes...

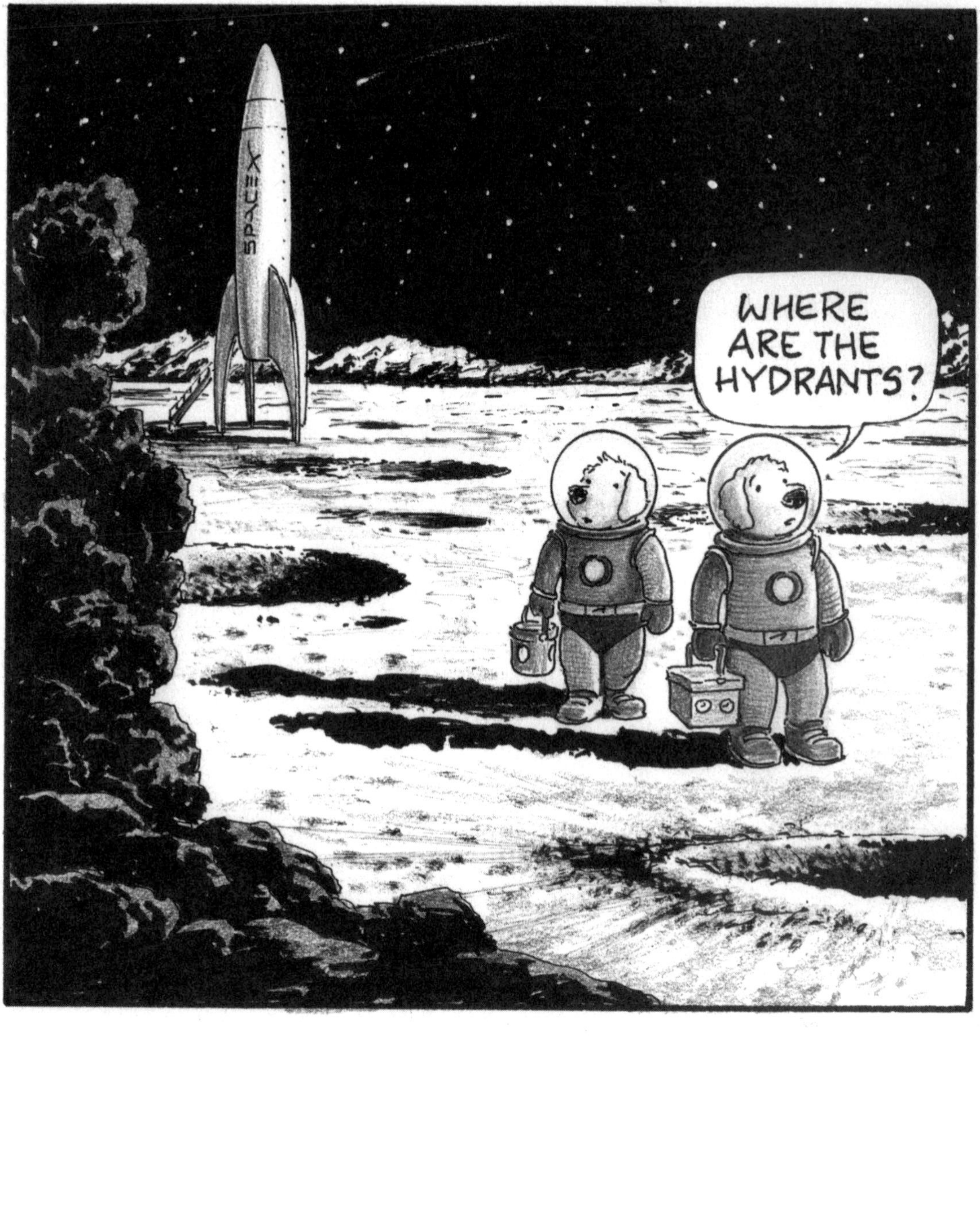
SPACEX
WHERE ARE THE HYDRANTS?

THERE ARE 74 CARTOONS IN THIS BOOK.
PLEASE ENTER YOUR RESPONSES BELOW.

☐ I GOT ALL THE CARTOONS.

☐ I GOT MOST OF THE CARTOONS.

☐ MY HEAD HURTS.

☐ WHAT AM I MISSING HERE?

☐ I'VE BEEN HAD.

HIT BUTTON TO (SEND)

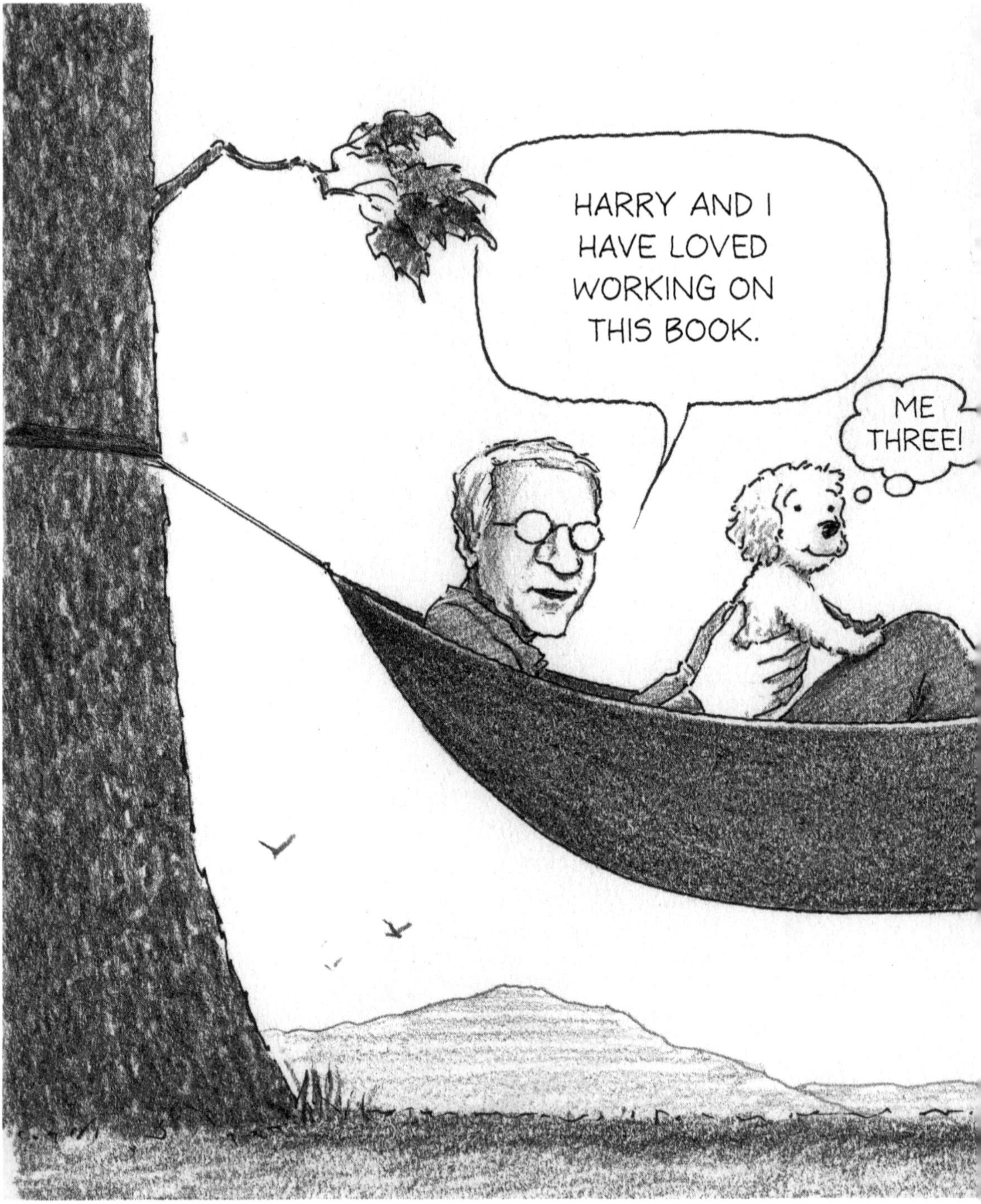
HARRY AND I HAVE LOVED WORKING ON THIS BOOK.
ME THREE!

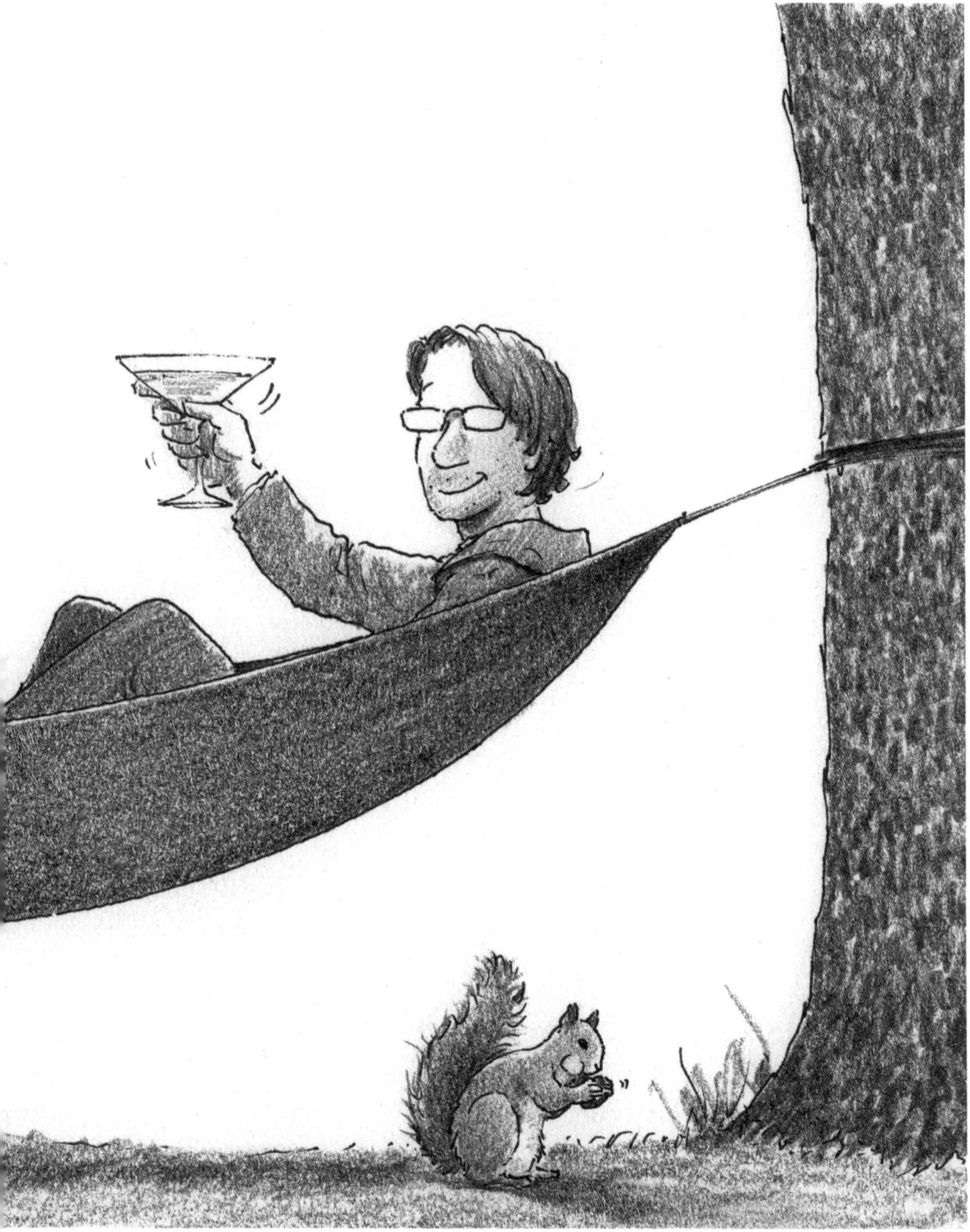

© DANNY CLINCH

© REBECCA RITCHEY

STEVE MARTIN IS ONE OF THE MOST WELL-KNOWN TALENTS IN ENTERTAINMENT. HIS WORK HAS EARNED HIM AN ACADEMY AWARD, FIVE GRAMMY AWARDS, AN EMMY, THE MARK TWAIN PRIZE, AND THE KENNEDY CENTER HONORS. AS AN AUTHOR, MARTIN'S WORK INCLUDES THE NOVEL *AN OBJECT OF BEAUTY*; THE PLAY *PICASSO AT THE LAPIN AGILE*; A COLLECTION OF COMIC PIECES, *PURE DRIVEL*; A CARTOON COLLECTION, *A WEALTH OF PIGEONS* WITH HARRY BLISS; A BESTSELLING NOVELLA, *SHOPGIRL*; AND HIS MEMOIR, *BORN STANDING UP.* MARTIN'S FILMS INCLUDE *THE JERK; PLANES, TRAINS AND AUTOMOBILES; ROXANNE; PARENTHOOD; L.A. STORY; FATHER OF THE BRIDE;* AND *BOWFINGER.*

HARRY BLISS IS AN INTERNATIONALLY SYNDICATED CARTOONIST AND COVER ARTIST FOR *THE NEW YORKER* MAGAZINE. HIS SYNDICATED COMIC *BLISS* APPEARS IN NEWSPAPERS INTERNATIONALLY. HE HAS WRITTEN AND ILLUSTRATED MORE THAN TWENTY BOOKS FOR CHILDREN AS WELL AS HIS CARTOON COLLECTION *A WEALTH OF PIGEONS* WITH STEVE MARTIN. HE IS THE FOUNDER OF THE CORNISH CCS RESIDENCY FELLOWSHIP FOR GRAPHIC NOVELISTS IN CORNISH, NEW HAMPSHIRE. VISIT HIS WEBSITE AT HARRYBLISS.COM.

CELADON

BOOKS

NEW YORK

FOUNDED IN 2017, CELADON BOOKS,

A DIVISION OF MACMILLAN PUBLISHERS,

PUBLISHES A HIGHLY CURATED LIST

OF TWENTY TO TWENTY-FIVE NEW TITLES A YEAR.

THE LIST OF BOTH FICTION AND NONFICTION IS ECLECTIC

AND FOCUSES ON PUBLISHING COMMERCIAL AND

LITERARY BOOKS AND DISCOVERING

AND NURTURING TALENT.

Steve/Peter Sellers...

IN 1980, my standup act was getting a bit of backlash, which is the natural arc of an act that has run its course and no doubt I'd been over exposed

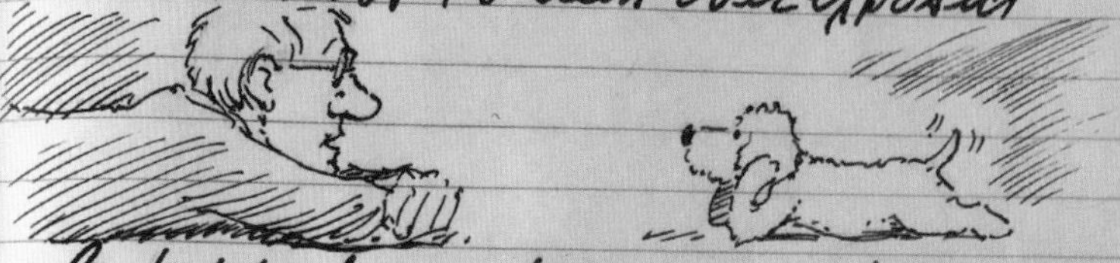

But I had something in my back pocket. 'The Jerk' was finished but unreleased.

I was in Hawaii doing promotion for the movie at an outdoor multi-film event. I walked from photo op to photo op, when Peter Sellers, who was promoting his film, stopped me and said,

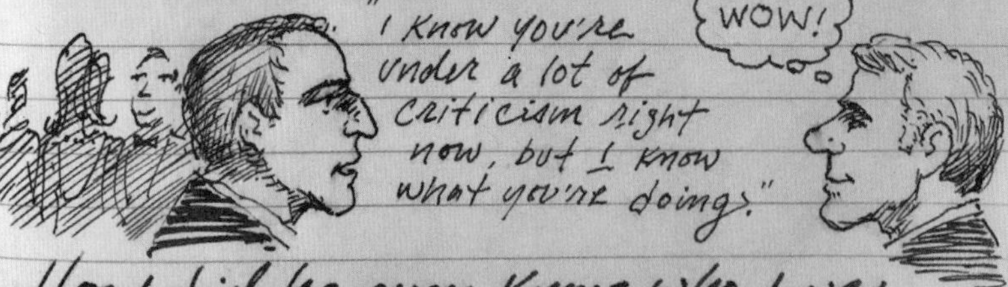
"I know you're under a lot of criticism right now, but I know what you're doing."
WOW!

How did he even know who I was, and how did he know I was under criticism?
Peter's comment was a generous moment from a master comedian to a newbie.

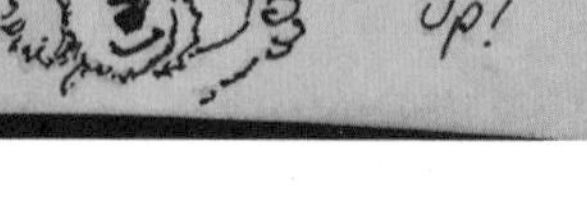
Thumbs up!